Moderns
&
Contemporaries

By the same author

Moderns
&
Contemporaries

Novelists, Poets, Critics

John Lucas

Professor of English and Drama
University of Loughborough

HARVESTER
PRESS
1970 — 1985
FIFTEEN
FORWARD-LOOKING
YEARS

THE HARVESTER PRESS • SUSSEX

BARNES & NOBLE BOOKS • NEW JERSEY

First published in Great Britain in 1985 by
THE HARVESTER PRESS LIMITED
Publisher: John Spiers
16 Ship Street, Brighton, Sussex
and in the USA by
BARNES & NOBLE BOOKS
81 Adams Drive, Totowa, New Jersey 07512

British Library Cataloguing in Publication Data
Lucas, John, 1937-
   Moderns and contemporaries: novelists, poets critics.
   1. English literature—19th century—History and criticism 2. English
   Literature—20th century—History and criticism
   I. Title
   820.9'008   PR451

   ISBN 0-7108-0927-1

Library of Congress Cataloging in Publication Data
Lucas, John, 1937-
   Moderns and contemporaries.
   1. English literature—20th century—History and criticism. 2.
American literature—20th century—History and criticism. 3.
Criticism—Great Britain. 4. Criticism—United States.   I. Title.
PR601.L8   1985   820'.9'0091   84-20349
ISBN 0-389-20530-3

Typeset in 11/12 point Garamond by Witwell Limited, Liverpool
Printed in Great Britain by
Whitstable Litho Ltd., Whitstable, Kent

For my colleagues and students at Loughborough
and in loving memory of
Kathleen Banks

Contents

Acknowledgements

The essay on Henry James first appeared in *The Air of Reality: New Essays on Henry James*, ed. John Goode, Methuen, 1972; the essay on Meredith in *Meredith Now*, ed. Ian Fletcher, Routledge and Kegan Paul, 1972; and the essay on Thomas Hardy and Donald Davie first appeared in *The Hardy Annual, No. 1*, ed. Norman Page, Macmillan, 1983.

The essays on Randall Jarrell, D.H. Lawrence, Roy Fuller, Peter Porter and recent British Poetry are reproduced by permission of the *Times Literary Supplement*. The essay on Sassoon is reproduced by permission of the *London Review of Books*. The essay on Edgall Rickword is reprinted by permission of the *Poetry Review*. The essay on F.R. Leavis first appeared in *Quarto*.

Special thanks go to Pamela Miller, for her expert typing and absolute efficiency.

Introduction

Moderns and Contemporaries is in some respects a companion volume to my previous collection of essays, *Romantic to Modern*, which The Harvester Press published in 1982. There are, however, rather more essays in this new book and they are mostly shorter. The reason for this is simple. They were originally written for a variety of literary newspapers, and such papers do not often allow you more than 4,000 words, at the most, in which to have your say. I do not object to this. On the contrary, the great advantage of having to keep to comparatively few words is that it helps to concentrate the mind. Still, there is brevity and brevity. Below a certain number of words you can do little more than make suggestions and tip likely winners. I very much enjoy being poetry reviewer for the *New Statesman*, but it never occurred to me to reprint any of those reviews. I hope I have done some sort of justice to the poets I there write about, but since I have to pack my comments into a few hundred words, it would be foolish to deny that the justice is often rough.

I cannot claim that way out with regard to the other journals for which I have regularly written. Nor would I want to. Some years ago it was widely agreed that serious literary criticism was more or less impossible in this country, because we lacked the journals to support it. This is no longer true. Since John Gross introduced the custom of named reviews to the *Times Literary Supplement*, the quality of reviewing in that journal seems to me to have increased very considerably. And when, as a result of industrial disputes, it was out of circulation for a year, two other journals began publication, both of which provided space for critics to write much as they pleased. *The London Review of Books*, brilliantly edited by Karl Miller, is now an established journal. Sadly, *Quarto* has disappeared. But during the year that Craig Raine edited it, *Quarto* was the ideal literary newspaper. It was tart, witty and combative. More important, its editor had an unerring sense of the news that would be likely to stay news.

I have been told that as a socialist I should not associate with such journals as those I have mentioned. But why not? Their editors never asked me to compromise or tone down my writing, nor does it seem to me to have been compromised by the contexts in which it appeared. There is something very silly about arguing on the one hand that establishment culture marginalises socialist thought and on the other that it is the duty of socialists to keep clear of the centre. If, as the newer socialist criticism has it, all writing is an act of intervention, you may as well hope for your intervention to be noticed by as many people and in as many places as possible.

This leads to a further point. Much contemporary socialist criticism is written in a deliberately encoded language. I say 'deliberately' because it is a commonplace of the left that all languages are encoded and that they therefore need to be deciphered before they can be fully understood. Put in its plainest terms, this means that race, gender and class are all likely to influence our choice of words. I agree, they do; and it is one of the proper achievements of socialist criticism to have shown that there is no such thing as an 'innocent' language. But it does not follow that you must therefore do your best to avoid 'ordinary' language because such language, in its presumed innocence but actual contamination, will infect your thoughts or those who read you. What happens to socialist critics who insist on using their own carefully encoded language is that they are understandable only to those who already know what they mean. In other words, their critical patois is available to those who have read what the writers themselves have read. As a result, the writer-critics cut themselves off from precisely those readers they should want to engage. The language of the new left seems to me another kind of self-imposed marginalisation; and the readiness with which its users reach for it surely argues a kind of bad faith. ('Nobody outside the charmed circle will understand us so we may as well talk to ourselves'.) I detest that kind of solipsism—hence the final essay in this book.

A last point. We all recognise that we are living through very bad times. I hope we may live beyond them, though I fear we may not. But if we are to survive, we need literature as much, if not more than, we have ever done. For as Camus remarked, the artist's

true vocation is 'to open the prisons and to give a voice to the
sorrows and joys of all. This is where art, against its enemies,
justifies itself, by proving that it is no one's enemy'. I recently had
heartwarming proof of Camus's thesis when I was discussing Clare
with some Workers' Educational Association students in
Bottesford, a rich spot in the Vale of Belvoir. We were studying his
great poem 'The Flitting', which is, among other things, an
extraordinarily passionate account of the sense of loss of
community and therefore of identity. One woman, middle-aged
and upper-class, suddenly said in tones of shocked wonderment,
'Why, it must be just like mining communities feel now'. Around
the table heads nodded. I know perfectly well that the enemies of
art are often its official custodians. But that was a great and
reassuring moment.

Part One

SOME AMERICANS

1

Henry James and *Washington Square*

I

Perhaps the first impression one takes from *Washington Square*[1] is of its unmistakable brilliance, for the novel has about it an entirely justified self-confidence and sureness both in style and the handling of events. James, you feel, is nowhere more certain of his powers than in *Washington Square*, and much of his poise must come from his strong sense of an audience. (The point I am making is not affected by the fact such a sense was largely misguided.) Take any sentence and you note its easy certainty of tone: you are made to feel that James is absolutely confident of his effects. For example: 'Marion Almond was a pretty little person of seventeen, with a very small figure and a very big sash, to the elegance of whose manners matrimony had nothing to add.' The tone of that sentence seems to me typical, even though, as I shall suggest, the unruffled search for the comic that it implies can come to seem strikingly at variance with the situations being treated.

The comic brilliance is, however, everywhere. It is there, for example, in the dialogue between Catherine and Arthur Townsend on the occasion of his bringing his cousin, Morris, to Washington Square:

'My cousin asked me to bring him, or I shouldn't have taken the liberty. He seemed to want very much to come; you know he's awfully sociable. I told him I wanted to ask you first, but he said Mrs Penniman had invited him. He isn't particular what he says when he wants to come somewhere. But Mrs Penniman seems to think it's all right.'

'We are very glad to see him', said Catherine. And she wished to talk more about him, but she hardly knew what to say. 'I never saw him before', she went on presently.

Arthur Townsend stared.

'Why, he told me he talked with you for over half an hour the other night.'

'I mean before the other night. That was the first time.'

'Oh, he has been away from New York—he has been all round the world. He doesn't know many people here, but he's very sociable, and he wants to know everyone.'

'Everyone?' said Catherine.

'Well, I mean all the good ones. All the pretty young ladies—like Mrs Penniman!' And Arthur Townsend gave a private laugh.

'My aunt likes him very much', said Catherine.

'Most people like him—he's so brilliant.'

'He's more like a foreigner', Catherine suggested.

'Well, I never knew a foreigner', said young Townsend, in a tone which seemed to indicate that his ignorance had been optional.

'Neither have I', Catherine confessed, with more humility. 'They say they are generally brilliant', she added, vaguely.

'Well, the people of this city are clever enough for me. I know some of them that think they are too clever for me; but they ain't.'

'I suppose you can't be too clever', said Catherine, still with humility.

'I don't know. I know some people that call my cousin too clever.'

(Ch. 5)

Much of *Washington Square* is conducted through dialogue, and James was justly proud of his achievement in this respect. For the comedy implicit in the exchange I have quoted is both satisfying in itself and fully relevant to the novel's concerns. It tells us so much: of Mrs Penniman's prompt readiness to create a romance for Catherine; of Catherine's involvement with Morris Townsend; of his past. And we learn a good deal more. For everything that is said is controlled by the social tone, so that *what* is said is inseparable from *how* it is said. The conversation that occurs between Arthur and Catherine is only possible within a definite social context, and it is in the way James makes the context palpable that so much of the brilliance of *Washington Square* lies. That is why, of course, there is not a great deal of point in comparing James's novel with *Eugénie Grandet*. For as the title of Balzac's novel implies, his focus is on the girl herself, whereas James is directing attention towards the social context that shapes his novel's events. To come to the crux of the matter by a slightly different route, one might say that *Washington Square* is best seen as a novel in the tradition that Jane

Austen's fiction inaugurates. Its drama depends on the range and subtlety of James's presentation of social relationships, with all that that implies of tone, habits of deference, poise, conscious civility and calculated decorum: all those elements, in short, in which certain lives are given definitive shape and to which they can become forfeit.

James's social world is, of course, America. More precisely, it is a certain area of New York city. For Ezra Pound at least, the unerring rightness of James's rendering of his milieu is not something that aliens can fully recognise. 'No one but an American', Pound says, 'can ever know, really know, how good he is at bottom, how good his "America" is.' And he goes on:

No Englishman can, and in less degree can any continental, or in fact anyone whose family was not living on, say, West 23rd Street in the old set-back two-storey-porched red brick vine-covered houses, etc. when Henry James was being a small boy on East 23rd Street; no one whose ancestors had not been presidents or professors or founders of Ha'vawd College or something of that sort, or had not heard of a time when people lived on 14th Street, or had known of someone living in Lexington or Newton 'Old Place' or somewhere of that sort in New England, or had heard of the New York that produced 'Fanny', New York the jocular and uncritical, or of people who danced with General Grant or something of that sort, would quite know *Washington Square* or *The Europeans* to be so autochthonous, so authentic to the conditions. They might believe the things to be 'real', but they would not know how closely they correspond to an external reality.[2]

Pound may be overstating the case, but he is surely right in wanting to insist on James's concern to render his milieu with the kind of accuracy and intensity that one associates with the presentation of *Highbury* and *Mansfield Park*.

The point needs some stressing, I think, because of the apparently widespread critical agreement that New York isn't of any great importance to the novel. When James was working on the book, he wrote to William Dean Howells:

I sympathize even less with your protest against the idea that it takes an old civilization to set a novelist in motion—a proposition that seems to me so true as to be a truism. It is on manners, customs, usages, habits, forms, upon all things matured and established, that a novelist lives—they are the very stuff his work is made of; and in saying that in the absence of those 'dreary and worn-out paraphernalia' which I enumerate as being wanting in American society, 'we have simply the whole of human life left', you beg (to my sense) the question. I should say we had just so much less of it as these same 'paraphernalia' represent, and I think they represent an enormous quantity of it.

Richard Poirier quotes this letter in his excellent book on James, but he does so only to argue that it supports his case that 'the public status of characters in *Washington Square* depends not at all on their social place or nationality, and is wholly a matter of their similarity to stock characters in stage melodrama and the fairy tale.'[3] My own feeling is that the novel itself everywhere contradicts Poirier's thesis, and that if characters do become like stock types in stage melodrama and fairy tale—and I agree that they do—it is because they see themselves called on to play parts created by their self-conscious awareness of what their society requires of them. This applies just as much to Dr Sloper as it does to Morris Townsend, as I shall try to establish. It is for this reason that I find F.W. Dupee's remarks on the novel so odd:

> It is not essential to *Washington Square* that its scene is America. The Old New York setting is lovely but insubstantial, an atmosphere and no more; and so familiar seems the fable of the girl jilted by her fortune-hunting suitor that we are surprised to learn from James's notebooks that he was following quite closely an actual incident related to him by Fanny Kemble.[4]

Dupee is without doubt quite right to note the familiarity of James's theme. It is indeed an old one. But *Washington Square* differs very importantly from the numerous sentimental novels where the theme had been thoroughly at home. For James's novel is a perfect blending of his 'gaping habit' before life—his rendering of events without interference—and what can be regarded as his crucial desire to make the ordinary interesting. And here it is worth noting the reasons he gives, in an essay of 1876, for disliking the Goncourts:

> They inevitably went into 'realism', but realism for them has been altogether a matter of taste—a studio question, as it were. They also

find the disagreeable particularly characteristic, and there is something odd in seeing these elegant erudites bring their highly complex and artificial method—the fruit of culture, and leisure, and luxury—to bear upon the crudities and maladies of life, and pick out choice morsels of available misery upon their gold pen-points.[5]

It is not impossible to imagine those words being applied to James's own later fiction. It would, of course, be unfair—but not outrageous. But it *would* be outrageous to apply them to *Washington Square*. For what *Washington Square* reveals, among other things, is James's relentless and detailed study of very ordinary goings-on in a particular society. The life he draws on is unspectacular, mundane; as mundane, shall we say, as the life that Crabbe treats in *Procrastination*, or which Jane Austen studies in *Persuasion*. In all three cases it is the fineness of analysis, the subtlety of enquiry, that creates great art. Speaking of Stendhal, James noted that he felt 'as soon as he began to observe, that character, manners and civilisation are explained by circumstances, and that in the way of observing and collecting circumstances there was a great work to be done'. *Washington Square* is best seen, I think, as a study of circumstances that will sufficiently explain why its people are what they are and why they behave as they do. There is nothing artificial in James's method. On the contrary, it has about it the feel of inevitable rightness that springs from the certainty with which he can place everyone in the environment that so takes his attention and which, if it doesn't amount to the manners, customs, usages, habits and forms that he found in the European novel, is certainly the next best thing. His care over the rendering of context explains, I think, why he could so surely speak of Hawthorne as pure, simple and unsophisticated,[7] and why he could rightly characterise *The Marble Faun* as incurring the penalty 'of seeming factitious and unauthoritative, which is always the result of an artist's attempt to project himself into an atmosphere in which he has not a transmitted and inherited property'.

To go back to the dialogue from which I have already quoted, it is worth noting how carefully Morris is socially placed by what James has his characters say. When Arthur explains that Morris had asked him to bring him, and when he explains that Mrs Penniman has given the idea her blessing, we are bound to notice

the social offence that Morris is giving and the way in which he is
playing the part of interloper, pretending to a social position that
he doesn't in fact have. Arthur's words reveal that Morris has got
to Washington Square either by lying or by accepting the socially
irresponsible methods of Mrs Penniman, and we never lose sight of
Morris's social wrongness. That he plays a part only makes more
apparent the fact that he is acting out the requirements that
society places upon him. His name makes very clear how we are to
take him. He does not belong to the Square, the then-fashionable
centre of New York, but to the town's end, where indeed Dr
Sloper has to go when he wants to see Townsend's sister, Mrs
Montgomery. Morris is the inevitable product of the society
which tries to exclude him and in which he tries to be included. He
is not a male equivalent of Becky Sharpe, but certainly all that he is
and does depends on the society with which he has to deal. So that
D.W. Jefferson's remark that Morris Townsend is 'obviously
shallow and rootless from the outset; neither he nor our
knowledge of him undergoes any development' manages to be at
once wrong (since Morris, as we shall see, does develop), irrelevant
(since we aren't meant to see him as a mysterious figure) and
absurd (since it reveals that Jefferson hasn't at all understood the
novel's concern with circumstance).[8] It is, however, true that
Morris is out of place in Washington Square. His brilliance may
not be that of the foreigner, but it is certainly not native, natural,
to New York society. The unnaturalness is made apparent in
James's beautifully deft rendering of Morris's indifference to the
codes of behaviour that mark the society into which he has
intruded. Take, for example, his proposal to Catherine that she
shall meet him in the Square, since he can't come to the house
where he has been insulted:

> She hesitated awhile; then at last—'You must come to the house',
> she said; 'I am not afraid of that.'
> 'I would rather it were in the Square', the young man urged. 'You
> know how empty it is, often. No one will see us.'
> 'I don't care who sees us. But leave me now.'
> He left her resignedly; he had got what he wanted ... Her father
> said nothing ... Mrs Penniman also was silent; Morris Townsend had
> told her that her niece preferred, unromantically, an interview in a
> chintz-covered parlour to a sentimental tryst beside a fountain

sheeted with dead leaves, and she was lost in wonderment at the oddity—almost the perversity—of the choice.

(Ch. 9)

The irony that attends Mrs Penniman's pondering the perversity of Catherine's choice is, admittedly, a simple one, but it does help to pinpoint the impropriety of Morris's suggestion—'You know how empty it is, often. No one will see us.' To understand from where James took his sense of rendering the socially indecorous, one would have to go back to something like Jane Austen's study of the relationship between Jane Fairfax and Frank Churchill. And to say this is to suggest that *Washington Square* is very much a novel in an established mode, not so much because of its subject but because of its treatment of that subject. Indeed,it might even seem to come close to a pastiche of Jane Austen. But what saves it from that is James's aloof distaste for the society he presents. There is a cool, detached and scalpel-sharp dissection of society at work in this novel, a kind of ironic ruthlessness that compares favourably with James's rendering of English society in, say, *The Portrait of a Lady*, which is unintentionally much nearer to pastiche in its treatment of English society. Finely though James writes about Lord Warburton, for example, one is aware that he is dealing in an atmosphere 'in which he has not a transmitted and inherited property'. But there can be no temptation to apply his criticism of Hawthorne to *Washington Square*.

To pick almost at random. How brilliantly he shows Morris's abandoning of 'manner' when he is in Mrs Penniman's company, since with her the young man does not need to keep up his act. And how Morris's coarseness comes out in conversation with her. (And by coarseness I don't mean merely social ineptitude). There is the occasion when he meets Mrs Penniman just before Catherine's trip to Europe. Mrs Penniman tells him they must walk where they will not be observed:

Morris was not in high good-humour, and his response to this speech was not particularly gallant. 'I don't flatter myself we shall be much observed anywhere.' Then he turned recklessly towards the centre of town. 'I hope you have come to tell me that he has knocked under', he went on.

'I am afraid I am not altogether a harbinger of good; and yet, too, I

am to a certain extent a messenger of peace. I have been thinking a
great deal, Mr Townsend', said Mrs Penniman.
  'You think too much.'
  'I suppose I do; but I can't help it, my mind is so terribly active.
When I give myself I pay the penalty in my headaches, my famous
headaches—a perfect circlet of pain! But I carry it as a queen carries her
crown. Would you believe that I have one now? I wouldn't, however,
have missed our rendezvous for anything. I have something very
important to tell you.'
  'Well, let's have it', said Morris.

(Ch. 21)

It is part of the more obvious comedy of the novel that while Mrs
Penniman acts at her finest with Morris, he doesn't act with her at
all. Really, he hardly needs to: Mrs Penniman's notion of romance
so fully takes in anything that is opposed to social decorum that
she has no room to observe or understand the implications of
Morris's behaviour:

> Mrs Penniman's real hope was that the girl would make a secret
> marriage, at which she should officiate as bride's woman or duenna.
> She had a vision of this ceremony being performed in some
> subterranean chapel; subterranean chapels in New York were not
> frequent, but Mrs Penniman's imagination was not chilled by trifles;
> and of the guilty couple—she liked to think of poor Catherine and her
> suitor as the guilty couple—being shuffled away in a fast-whirling
> vehicle to some obscure lodging in the suburbs, where she would pay
> them (in a thick veil) clandestine visits; where they would endure a
> period of romantic privation; and when ultimately, after she should
> have been their earthly providence, their intercessor, their advocate,
> and their medium of communication with the world, they would be
> reconciled to her brother in an artistic tableau, in which she herself
> should be somehow the central figure.

(Ch. 15)

The absurdities hinted at in Mrs Penniman's name—the
pennilessness that causes her to batten on to the Sloper household,
and the simpering interest in men which makes her a prime cause
of Catherine's miserable love-affair—are fully present in this
passage. Always her behaviour springs directly from her desire to
act out a chosen role, which—further irony—Dr Sloper, in his
kindness at taking her in, has made more possible. Mrs Penniman

is a very stupid woman, comically stupid, but also dangerously stupid. The comedy surrounding her depends to a large extent on the neatness with which James catches her nuances of speech—the phrases and habits of expression that she borrows from cheap novels and plays. She takes an interest in the 'sentimental shadows' of what she sees as Catherine's 'drama'; she wishes the 'plot to thicken'; she advises Catherine to act—'in your situation the great thing is to act'. She tells her niece that 'if you succumb to the dread of your father's wrath ... I don't know what will become of us'; and when Catherine tells her not to make any more appointments with Morris, 'Mrs Penniman rose with considerable majesty. "My poor child, are you jealous of me?" she asked.' Her danger lies precisely in her stupidity, the romantic notions which close her mind to the nature of Morris's act.

It is, of course, Dr Sloper who sees through Morris:

> 'He is not what I call a gentleman; he has not the soul of one. He is extremely insinuating; but it is a vulgar nature. I saw through it in a minute. He is altogether too familiar—I hate familiarity. He is a plausible coxcomb.'
> 'Ah, well', said Mrs Almond, 'if you make up your mind so easily, it's a great advantage.'
> 'I don't make up my mind easily. What I tell you is the result of thirty years of observation; and in order to be able to form that judgement in a single evening, I have had to spend a lifetime in study.'
> 'Very possibly you are right. But the thing is for Catherine to see it.'
> 'I will present her with a pair of spectacles!' said the Doctor.
>
> (Ch. 7)

Sloper speaks with authority here, but this kind of authority is a judgement on him as much as on Morris. For Sloper has spent thirty years taking care to become a gentleman. He has moved up town to Washington Square and he has used his intelligence to get himself a rich wife. Sloper is something of a fortune-hunter himself. Which is why, as Richard Poirier points out, he is perfectly positioned to understand Morris's type.

James draws attention to the Doctor's fear of vulgarity: 'He had a dread of vulgarity, and even a theory that it was increasing in the society around him.' But he also lets us realise that there is a considerable streak of vulgarity in the Doctor. In the ways in which James fillets out this vulgarity we can see something of that aloof and disenchanted gaze which he turns onto the 'best' society of *Washington Square*. Sloper's vulgarity lies essentially in the rigid mask of irony which he identifies with urbanity and which he clamps onto himself, assuming it to be proper for his position. Like Morris, Sloper plays a part in society, and it is one that causes him to become his own victim, as in the crucial conversation with Morris at Mrs Almond's. The conversation takes place partly because of Sloper's uneasy suspicion that he might 'appear ridiculous to this young man, whose private perception of incongruities he suspected of being keen'. Morris tells the Doctor that he has only his good right arm by which to earn work. The Doctor's irony—his social front—comes into play:

'You are too modest', said the Doctor. 'In addition to your good right arm you have your subtle brain. I know nothing of you but what I see; but I see by your physiognomy that you are extremely intelligent.'

'Ah', Townsend murmured, 'I don't know what to answer you when you say that. You advise me, then, not to despair?'

And he looked at his interlocutor as if the question might have a double meaning. The Doctor caught the look and weighed it a moment before he replied. 'I should be very sorry to admit that a robust and well-disposed of young man need ever despair. If he doesn't succeed in one thing, he can try another. Only, I should add, he should choose his line with discretion.'

'Ah, yes, with discretion', Morris Townsend repeated, sympathetically. 'Well, I have been indiscreet, formerly; but I think I have got over it. I am very steady now.' And he stood for a moment, looking down at his remarkably neat shoes. Then at last, 'Were you kindly intending to propose something for my advantage?' he inquired, looking up and smiling.

(Ch. 9)

Sloper is caught out and his irony made to look very vulnerable at this moment. It is his own fault; he has shown his vulgarity in wanting to outwit Morris. In playing the other man's game he has lost. (One might note in passing that it is very like Osmond's conversation with Rosier in *Portrait*, where Osmond's very marked distaste for being vulgar in fact commits him to vulgarity.)

For Sloper, as for Osmond, fear of vulgarity is fear of losing social poise, which in turn means fear of losing the ironic possibilities of any moment. This is very finely caught in a scene between the Doctor and Catherine, just before they go to Europe. Catherine tells him that:

> '... if I don't obey you, I ought not to live with you—to enjoy your kindness and protection.'
> This striking argument gave the Doctor a sudden sense of having underestimated his daughter; it seemed even more than worthy of a young woman who had revealed the quality of unaggressive obstinacy. But it displeased him—displeased him deeply, and he signified as much. 'That idea is in very bad taste', he said. 'Did you get it from Mr Townsend?'
> 'Oh no; it's my own', said Catherine, eagerly.
> 'Keep it to yourself, then', her father answered, more than ever determined she should go to Europe.
>
> (Ch. 22)

It is very subtly done, the way James modulates the Doctor's awareness of the possibility of loss into a matter of taste. Of course, taste is involved, for if Catherine leaves him, his social reputation is bound to suffer. Taking her to Europe is therefore his way of educating her into good taste—making her see how socially impossible marriage with Townsend would be. More than that, the trip is to make her see how much her father needs her. For what we are allowed to recognise behind his words about taste is his very real feeling for Catherine, although it is a feeling constantly at the mercy of his irony; that is, his better self is inhibited by the social mask. That is why James can bring off the master-stroke of the Doctor's effort to break through to unironic communication with his daughter in the lonely Alpine village. As Poirier has pointed out, this is a melodramatic scene in which there is no hint of parody, but I think it not enough merely to remark that Sloper's intensities at this moment seem to arise from a 'compelling emotional necessity'. They do, of course, but it is possible to be more precise than Poirier wants to be and to say why the scene is so right, why it rings so true. The reason for the Doctor's confession—for that is what it amounts to—is surely that at last he feels sufficiently remote from that social context which seemed to require of him a permanence of ironic posture, to dare to tell Catherine more of the truth than he has ever before been able to show her:

The Doctor looked up and down the valley, swinging his stick; then
he said to her, in the same low tone,
'I am very angry.'
She wondered what he meant—whether he wished to frighten her.
If he did, the place was well chosen: this hard, melancholy dell,
abandoned by the summer light, made her feel her loneliness. She
looked around her, and her heart grew cold; for a moment her fear was
great. But she could think of nothing to say, save to murmur, gently, 'I
am sorry.'
'You try my patience', her father went on, 'and you ought to know
what I am. I am not a very good man. Though I am very smooth
externally, at bottom I am very passionate; and I assure you I can be
very hard.'
She could not think why he told her these things. Had he brought
her there on purpose, and was it part of a plan? What was the plan?
Catherine asked herself. Was it to startle her suddenly into a
retraction—to take an advantage of her by dread? Dread of what? The
place was ugly and lonely, but the place could do her no harm. There
was a kind of still intensity about her father which made him
dangerous, but Catherine hardly went so far as to say that it might be
part of his plan to fasten his hand—the neat, fine, supple hand of a
distinguished physician—in her throat. Nevertheless, she receded a
step. 'I am sure you can be anything you please', she said; and it was her
simple belief.
'I am very angry', he replied, more sharply.
'Why has it taken you so suddenly?'
'It has not taken me suddenly. I have been raging inwardly for the
last six months. But just now this seemed a good place to flare out. It's
so quiet, and we are alone.'

                                                        (Ch. 24)

It is without doubt a very remarkable scene, remarkable above all
for the fact that because Catherine and the Doctor are removed
from any social context—'we are alone'—he can drag out truths
about himself and his feelings for his daughter which she cannot
possibly understand. There is really terrible irony in his remark
'you ought to know what I am'. For Catherine has no chance of
knowing what he is, as her reply makes him realise: '"I am sure you
can be anything you please." "I am very angry", he replied, more
sharply'—angry because he has to face the bleak certainty that she
can never understand him. He has been only too successful in
meeting the requirements of his social position, has become finally

trapped by Catherine's unshakeable belief in him as the supreme ironist. She cannot know that the mask is not the actuality. The acts which society demands of people are beyond her comprehension. Being the only truthful person in the novel she cannot see that Morris is playing a part, and she cannot see that her father is playing a part also. Whereas because the two men are very conscious of the roles they act out, they understand each other perfectly well.

II

But at this point we need to take deeper soundings of James's art and of the subtleties that allow him to perceive and exploit the differences between how Sloper customarily presents himself and how, at the one moment I have analysed, he is revealed. In his first essay on Balzac, James remarked that:

> If, instead of committing to paper impossible imaginary tales, he could have stood for a while in some other relation to the society about him than that of a scribbler, it would have been a very great gain. The general defect of his manner ... is the absence of fresh air, of the trace of disinterested observation[10]

Disinterested observation is one of the most obvious and satisfying features of *Washington Square*, and it connects with a habit of mind that is familiar enough, the Jamesian insistence that the novelist should be an invisible narrator of his own tales. Nor is this simply a personal preference. The fact is that James believes that the deepest kind of realism can be attained only by the novelist's refusal to intercede, to let plot dictate to probabilities, or to let moral approval or disapproval cloud his sense of telling it like it is. He makes the point succinctly in his review of Froude's *Short Studies on Great Subjects*:

> In history it is impossible to view individuals singly, and this point constitutes the chief greatness of the study. We are compelled to look at them in connexion with their antecedents, their ancestors, their contemporaries, their circumstances. To judge them morally we are obliged to push our enquiry through a concatenation of causes and effects in which, from their delicate nature, enquiry very soon becomes

impracticable, and thus we are reduced to talking sentiment. Nothing is more surprising than the alertness with which writers like Mr Froude are ready to pronounce upon the moral character of historical persons, and their readiness to make vague moral epithets stand in lieu of real psychological facts.[11]

These sentences can be linked to the remark about Stendhal which I have already quoted. Taken together they provide a sure indication of James's unwillingness to use vague moral epithets of any of the characters of *Washington Square*. Nor is this to suggest that his art may be seen in terms that he used to criticise Gautier's poetry, of an atmosphere 'unweighted with a moral presence ... unstirred by the breath of reflection'.[12] The point is rather that James's way of presenting character in terms of circumstance forbids us the easily satisfying kinds of judgement which a lesser artist would offer. In *Washington Square* the concatenation of causes and effects by which individuality becomes asserted is far too complex to allow us fairly to make such statements as that the novel is about 'a bad case of parental despotism', even though at least one critic has seen the novel in those terms. To judge Sloper as a despot is merely to become trapped in Mrs Penniman's view of him, and to have to feel that there may be justice in her concealing Morris's letters to Catherine inside her own. And though it is with Sloper that a simplistic view is most damaging, it inhibits an understanding of all the characters. I want to touch on some of the ways in which James's 'disinterested observation' allows him to focus on the damage which is done to Catherine while forbidding us the satisfaction of swift judgement on those who do the damage.

Mrs Penniman is a good example. She is silly, vapid, romantic, quite incapable of understanding the damage she is doing to Catherine. Yet how much conspires to give her the kind of influence by which she creates harm! The Doctor's kindness in giving her a home, Catherine's susceptibility, Morris Townsend's willingness to take advantage of her, Sloper's own deliberate overacting of the role to which he knows she has assigned him and which strengthens her sense of doing right—all contribute to this end. The comedy of observation sets before us these complications and their results. Without them, Mrs Penniman would be helpless:

She was romantic; she was sentimental; she had a passion for little secrets and mysteries—a very innocent passion, for her secrets had hitherto always been as unpractical as addled eggs. She was not absolutely veracious; but this defect was of no great consequence, for she had never had anything to conceal.

(Ch. 2)

Marvellous, the way the balanced phrases and sentences show at once Mrs Penniman's potential for harm and her actual ineffectiveness. As the paragraph continues, the sinuous process of the syntax begins to entwine her with her brother and alert us to Mrs Penniman's future role:

her brother, who was very shrewd, understood her turn of mind. 'When Catherine is about seventeen', he said to himself, 'Lavinia will try to persuade her that some young man with a moustache is in love with her. It will be quite untrue; no young man, with a moustache or without, will ever be in love with Catherine. But Lavinia will take it up and talk about it ... Catherine won't see it, and won't believe it, fortunately for her peace of mind; poor Catherine isn't romantic.'

But the problem is, after all, one that eludes the Doctor's shrewdness. He doesn't bargain for a young man who actually presents himself as a lover. He may understand his sister's character, but his quite unable to prevent the consequences of her operations when those are helped by a turn of events he can't control.

It would be boring—and unnecessary—to work through the novel in this way; and my purpose in drawing attention to the paragraph quoted above is only to provide an indication of the subleties of James's mind as it works to unravel something as inevitable as the happenings in *Washington Square,* which don't allow for a simple moral response on our part.

However, I do want to continue to point out the way in which the inevitabilities come about, dictated as they are by the opportunities which individuals create out of their need to take their place in a social context. What Morris and Dr Sloper do is inextricably bound up with what they are—the social outsider trying to get in and the social celebrity anxious not to lose his poise, his tone. Only because of the selfishness that these acts involve can

Mrs Penniman be so powerful—and she is very powerful. When Morris continues to see Catherine after the Doctor has made clear his disapproval of the young man, we are told:

> Mrs Penniman delighted of all things in a drama, and she flattered herself that a drama would now be enacted. Combining as she did the zeal of the prompter with the impatience of the spectator, she had long since done her utmost to pull up the curtain. She, too, expected to figure in the performance—to be the confidante, the Chorus, to speak the epilogue. It may even be said that there were times when she lost sight altogether of the modest heroine of the play in the contemplation of certain great scenes which would naturally occur between the hero and herself.
>
> (Ch. 10)

I have already mentioned that in *Washington Square* people are forced to play their parts in assuming social roles, and this passage makes it obvious that the imagery of the theatre, of the drama, is functional to the novel's purpose; people are always being caught out in gestures, and their being so enables that subtle investigation of the gap between the act and the actuality which James manages so finely. Mrs Penniman indeed is caught out time and again: in the oyster saloon, for example; but also, of course, in the drama that takes place in her mind, for that is the most obvious example in the novel of the gap between the act and the actuality.

But if the gap is great for us, for Mrs Penniman it doesn't really exist, and the confusions of her mind show themselves in the comic manner of James's disinterested observer—the narrator—through which her behaviour is recorded:

After Dr Sloper has turned Townsend down, we are told:

> Mrs Penniman took too much satisfaction in the sentimental shadows of this little drama to have, for the moment, any great interest in dissipating them. She wished the plot to thicken, and the advice she gave her niece tended, in her own imagination, to produce this result. It was rather incoherent counsel, and from one day to another it contradicted itself; but it was pervaded by an earnest desire that Catherine should do something striking. 'You must act, my dear; in your situation the great thing is to act,' said Mrs Penniman, who found her niece altogether beneath her opportunities.
>
> (Ch. 15)

The act she requires is, of course, one that Catherine isn't capable of, divided as she is between Morris and her father; but it is very important in the novel that acting and choice do not go together. For if we take the play on the word 'act' as we are meant to, we can see that for the other involved characters 'acting' is a way of avoiding choice; they aim to escape from their dilemmas by the assumption of a role which will free them from painful decisions or from facing the truth.

And it is here, therefore, that the triumph of disinterested observation shows itself most forcefully. The comic manner shows us how unmistakably at odds with actuality the acts are. There is, for example, the moment when, after Morris's desertion of Catherine, the girl attempts to keep the disaster to herself:

> her innocent arts were of little avail before a person of the rare perspicacity of Mrs Penniman. This lady easily saw that she was agitated, and if there was any agitation going forward, Mrs Penniman was not a person to forfeit her natural share in it.
>
> (Ch. 30)

There the manner becomes consciously inadequate to deal with the shattering nature of Catherine's loss, and it is so because of the inadequacy of Mrs Penniman herself. Chapter 30 is, in fact, a good example of the triumph of James's method. It features what might be called a showdown between Mrs Penniman and Catherine, except that given the individuals, a showdown is not really possible. Instead, Mrs Penniman is caught out in a series of ridiculously inadequate gestures:

> 'My plans have not changed!' said Catherine, with a little laugh.
> 'Ah, but Mr Townsend's have', her aunt answered, very gently.
> 'What do you mean?'
> There was an impervious brevity in the tone of this enquiry, against which Mrs Penniman felt bound to protest ... 'Ah well', she said 'if he hasn't told you! ...' and she turned away.
> Catherine watched her a moment in silence; then she hurried after her, stopping her before she reached the door. 'Told me what? What do you mean? What are you hinting at and threatening me with?'
> 'Isn't it broken off?' asked Mrs Penniman.
> 'My engagement? Not in the least!'
> 'I beg your pardon in that case. I have spoken too soon!'

'Too soon? Soon or late', Catherine broke out, 'you speak foolishly and cruelly.'

When the girl finally tells her aunt 'Why can't you leave me alone? I was afraid you would spoil everything; for you *do* spoil everything you touch!', we are told that Mrs Penniman 'was scared and bewildered'; and she tells Catherine 'Do you scold me for talking to him? I'm sure we never talked of anything but you.'

At the end of the chapter, Mrs Penniman's stupidity again comes out as she gives away—without realising that she is involving herself—that she and Townsend had been in the plot together:

Catherine . . . spoke at last as if she had not heard or understood her. 'It has been a regular plan, then. He has broken it off deliberately; he has given me up.'
'For the present, dear Catherine; he has put it off, only.'
'He has left me alone', Catherine went on.
'Haven't you *me*' asked Mrs Penniman with some solemnity.

As I have said, the comic manner won't let us see Mrs Penniman as morally evil. She is shown as too 'bewildered' for that, too caught out between act and actuality; and we know indeed that although she prods Townsend on towards the series of actions which combine with others to create the disaster, she doesn't really understand the full force of what she is doing. So, for example, when Morris takes seriously her plan of a quick marriage—the drama of which appeals to her—we are told 'She was a little frightened, but she went on with considerable boldness'. That is the most that can be urged against Mrs Penniman: she is sometimes a little frightened.

But the comic manner in Chapter 30 allows of something more considerable than just an understanding of Mrs Penniman's inadequacy. For there is also the awfulness of Catherine's isolation, the terrible feeling of desolate loneliness that results from her giving up her father for Morris, who for that reason gives her up, without the hope of Mrs Penniman to turn to as reasonable friend. When Mrs Penniman asks 'Haven't you *me*' the comedy moves away from the absurdity of her remark to the pathos of Catherine's final loneliness. But to see how that is brought about, we need to look at Morris for a moment and *his* inadequacy, *his* act.

I have said that this act is forced on him by the social context in which he finds himself, and that the Doctor sees through it to a correct judgement of him. But Morris is in the happy situation of being a reasonably good actor before a very appreciative audience: for neither Mrs Penniman nor Catherine sees through the act, since for different reasons neither has any cause to suspect it. Still, we can see Morris time and again being caught out. James's gaping habit allows him to reveal to us what is hidden from many of the characters. This is neatly shown when Catherine tells Morris that her father had said the young man was interested in her money:

> 'He told me to tell you . . . that if I marry without his consent, I shall not inherit a penny of his fortune. He made a great point of this. He seemed to think—he seemed to think—'
> Morris flushed, as any young man of spirit might have flushed at an imputation of baseness. 'What did he seem to think?'
> 'That it would make a difference.'
> 'It *will* make a difference—in many things . . . But it will make none in my affection.'
> 'We shall not want the money', said Catherine; 'for you know I have a good deal myself.'
> 'Yes, my dear girl, I know you have something. And he can't touch that.'
> 'He would never', said Catherine. 'My mother left it to me.'
> Morris was silent awhile. 'He was very positive about this was he?' he asked at last. 'He thought such a message would annoy me terribly and make me throw off the mask, eh?'
> 'I don't know what he thought', said Catherine sadly.
> 'Please tell him that I care for his message as much as for that!' And Morris snapped his fingers sonorously.

(Ch. 20)

Though Catherine doesn't notice Morris's slip in saying that the message was intended to 'make me throw off the mask, eh?', we do. Morris is not really a *very* good actor: the finger-snapping is so obvious a gesture. Equally obvious is his notion of the scene that Catherine and her father might play out in Europe, a scene in which the Doctor would be won over to his future son-in-law:

> over there, among beautiful scenes and noble monuments, perhaps the old gentleman would be softened . . . He might be touched by her gentleness, her patience, her willingness to make any sacrifice but *that*

one; and if she should appeal to him some day, in some celebrated
spot—in Italy, say, in the evening; in Venice, in a gondola, by
moonlight—if she should be a little clever about it, and touch the right
chord, perhaps he would fold her in his arms, and tell her that he
forgave her.

(Ch. 23)

   When Catherine realises that Morris has left her, we are told
that 'it seemed to her that a mask had suddenly fallen from his
face'. I do not need to underline the implications of that phrase;
but I do want to examine for a moment the presentation of
Morris's dramatic inadequacy, by means of which the mask is seen
to fall. Their last scene together takes place in Chapter 29. (It is
worth drawing attention, by the way, to the manner in which
James hurries the crisis up; the feeling of relentless exposure to the
events as they pile up is quite extraordinary, I think, and helps to
show how he creates the awareness for the reader of Catherine's
very sudden fall into misery.) In that chapter Morris tries to retain
a grip on events that are rapidly passing beyond his control. Indeed
he's already guessed that they would. Like Mrs Penniman he has
become a little frightened at the prospect of what he has done to
Catherine; and he tries to get her aunt to prepare the girl for their
separation. He is, indeed, the coward that he has already been
shown to be by his allowing Catherine to be the one to break the
news of their proposed engagement to her father. In what he says
we can sense the fright he feels at having discovered the
unpredictability of his captive audience—Catherine—and his
inability to deal with her response to his act. (Something of the
same trick is worked in the scene between Owen Gereth and Fleda
Vetch in Chapter 16 of *The Spoils of Poynton*, where Owen
discovers to his amazement that Fleda is in love with him.)

   'Prepare her—try and ease me off.'
   Mrs Penniman stopped, looking at him very solemnly.
   'My poor Morris, do you know how much she loves you?'
   'No, I don't. I don't want to know. I have always tried to keep from
knowing. It would be too painful.'
   'She will suffer much', said Mrs Penniman.
   'You must console her. If you are as good a friend to me as you
pretend to be, you will manage it.'

(Ch. 28)

The cowardice is particularly present in his last meeting with Catherine. Here his act breaks down completely, and he is revealed as pathetically inadequate. Catherine tries to get him to promise to come and see her the following day:

> 'If I am prevented from coming tomorrow, you will say I have deceived you', he said.
> 'How can you be prevented? You can come if you will.'
> 'I am a busy man— I am not a dangler!' cried Morris, sternly. His voice was so hard and unnatural that, with a helpless look at him she turned away; and then he quickly laid his hand on the door knob. He felt as if he were absolutely running away from her. But in an instant she was close to him again, and murmuring in a tone none the less penetrating for being low, 'Morris, you are going to leave me.'
> 'Yes, for a little while.'
> 'For how long?'
> 'Till you are reasonable again.'
> 'I shall never be reasonable, in that way.' And she tried to keep him longer; it was almost a struggle. 'Think of what I have done!' she broke out. 'Morris, I have given up everything.'
> 'You shall have everything back.'
> 'You wouldn't say that if you didn't mean something. What is it?—what has happened?—what have I done?—what has changed you?'
> 'I will write to you—that is better', Morris stammered.
> 'Ah, you won't come back!' she cried, bursting into tears.
> 'Dear Catherine', he said, 'don't believe that. I promise you that you shall see me again.' And he managed to get away, and to close the door behind him.
>
> (Ch. 29)

This very moving scene is the more remarkable in that we become aware that for the first time Morris has something like genuine feeling for Catherine; his inadequacy stems in fact from that feeling. The reason is that he has suddenly found that entanglement with her doesn't mean that he can comfortably 'know' who she is, and that even Catherine is a far more complex person than he had bothered to think her. What makes his act so inadequate is that he can't cope with this knowledge. He has depended on his own idea of Catherine, but more on his act, and when he sees its effect he is incapable of improvising successfully. His gestures are caught, and his act becomes—even to himself—disgraceful. Both he and Mrs Penniman have brought Catherine to life, and they don't realise the complications of this until it is too late.

For all his cleverness Dr Sloper is also inadequate. He too is caught out in his gestures; for he also acts out his role, and it creates complications over which he has no control. Sloper, as we have seen, comes to realise that he needs his daughter, and he dares to approach telling her of his love for her. That one should have to put the matter in such a way suggests, of course, his inadequacy; but it's an inadequacy of which Sloper himself becomes aware as he acts out his role of deserted father. I have in mind the scene between Catherine and himself in which she tells him that she hasn't given Morris up. Just how he acts his part comes out in what he says to her in reply to her remark 'But we can wait a long time':

> 'Of course, you can wait till I die, if you like.'
> Catherine gave a cry of natural horror.
> 'Your engagement will have one delightful effect upon you; it will make you extremely impatient for that event.'
>
> (Ch. 18)

What one is meant to notice here is, I think, the vulgarity of the Doctor's act, of which at one moment, indeed, he himself becomes aware. Catherine says to him, ' "If I don't marry before your death, I will not after." ... "Do you mean that for an impertinence?" he enquired; and enquiry of which, as he made it, he quite perceived the grossness.'

As with Mrs Penniman and Morris, so with Sloper. All three are caught out because of Catherine's ability to surprise them with an unexpected (but to us, entirely natural) response. Faced with this , the Doctor cannot improvise, and he has therefore to fall back on the vulgarity of pathos. This is pointed up by the deliberate overwriting at the end of the chaper, which emphasises the self-consciously melodramatic note in the Doctor's performance, and catches him out in his cliché posturing:

> He went to the door and opened it for her to go out. The movement gave her a terrible sense of his turning her off. 'It will be only once, for the present', she added, lingering a moment.
> 'Exactly as you choose', he repeated, standing there with his hand

on the door. 'I have told you what I think. If you see him, you will be an ungrateful, cruel child; you will have given your old father the greatest pain of his life.'

This was more than the poor girl could bear; her tears overflowed, and she moved towards her grimly consistent parent with a pitiful cry. Her hands were raised in supplication, but he sternly evaded this appeal.

But when, just before they go to Europe, he repeats his act of calculated pathos, we realise that it has a kind of necessity for him. It is the only way he can bring himself to hint at his true feelings for her. Because he cannot entirely free himself from the grip of irony, he is forced to turn pathos into bathos. Only outside all social context, as I have pointed out, dare he drop irony, drop the act. As it is, in that pre-Europe scene, Catherine says that she must tell Townsend she is going:

> Her father fixed his cold eyes upon her. 'If you mean that you had better ask his leave, all that remains to me is to hope he will give it.'
> The girl was sharply touched by the pathetic ring of the words; it was the most calculated, the most dramatic little speech the Doctor had ever uttered.
>
> (Ch. 22)

Of course, the fact that the Doctor doesn't grow nearer his daughter during their European tour leads to their ultimate estrangement and to the resumption of that ironic pose which entails, for example, the supremely vicious moment when he raises his hat to her after she has finally lost Morris. A moment such as that is both dramatically right and extremely shocking. Right, because it is exactly how he would behave; shocking, because it crystallises the damage he has done to himself and to her, and indicates the vast gulf that now separates them. No talk about tyranny or despotism will do justice to the complexities that James has unravelled in his study of the father-daughter relationship.

I come back to an earlier point. *Washington Square* resists simple moral attitudes and judgements. Not even the terrible stagnation of Catherine at the end of the book—one notices how often the word 'rigid' is used of her in the last pages, as though she has become arrested at a certain point forever—not even this allows us to bandy about terms like 'evil' in describing Morris or

Mrs Penniman or the Doctor. Not, anyway, unless we are prepared to see their inadequacies as evil. And this is really the nub of the matter. For the brilliance of James's novel depends on the way in which its comic surface is played off against the tragic events, so that nothing strident is allowed to substitute for its unruffled and sure study of circumstance, of context, of concatenation of cause and effect. It is the ordinariness which is so extraordinary about *Washington Square*.

Notes

1. Henry James, *Washington Square*, currently available in three editions (London: Heinemann Educ. 1970, Penguin 1970; Oxford: Oxford University Press 1982).
2. *Literary Essays of Ezra Pound*, ed. T.S. Eliot (London, 1954), p. 302.
3. R. Poirier, *The Comic Sense of Henry James* (London, 1967), pp. 165-7.
4. F.W. Dupee, *Henry James* (London, 1951), p. 63.
5. *Literary Reviews and Essays*, ed. A. Mordell (New York, 1957), pp. 158-9.
6. *Ibid.*, p. 153.
7. James, *Hawthorne* (New York, 1966), pp. 142, 155.
8. D.W. Jefferson, *Henry James and the Modern Reader* (London 1964), p. 106.
9. Poirier, *op. cit.* p. 172.
10. *French Poets and Novelists* (New York, 1964), p. 70.
11. *Literary Reviews*, p. 273.
12. *Ibid.*, p. 96.

2
The Poetry of Edwin Arlington Robinson

When Edwin Arlington Robinson died in 1935, his loss was mourned not only by America's writers but by statesmen and citizens whom one would not readily accuse of an interest in literature. Robinson was a famous man. Now, some thirty years later, the fame has shrunk, and it is my guess that the works are very little read. Certainly it is a matter of some difficulty to find a copy of his collected works. Not that Robinson has been neglected by literary historians or wiped from the record of American poetry. Far from it; his position has never been more secure. But that is just the trouble. Talking recently with some American undergraduates about modern American poetry, I asked them why it was that Robinson was so little read nowadays. 'Well, you see', one of them explained, 'we know just about where he stands'. The implication was that once you had got your author firmly placed, any need to read his works had more or less disappeared. It was an unnerving instance of what can happen to the ideal of discrimination, and even more of what literary history frequently comes to mean to students of literature. It seems to me worth the effort, therefore, to try to unsettle some of the suavely held convictions about Robinson, not so much in the interest of quarrelling with his standing as to suggest that, whatever that may be, he is a poet whose best work deserves to be kept alive.

But where does Robinson stand? Not very high, to be sure. He comes a long way below Frost, for example, though some way above Jeffers, and it is easy enough to put him in his place. A gesture in the direction of 'Luke Havergal', mention of 'The Man Against the Sky', a word of judicious praise for 'Eros Turannos', and that is more or less that. If more is said, it likely enough consists of making out a table of faults. And since these are obvious, there is no great problem about setting them down. Robinson wrote too much; he fashioned too many long narrative poems out of too little material; his plays are uniformly dull; at times he falls into a ponderous prosiness of style, especially in his later years; his regard for the trivial is often trivial. But I think that the faults can be cheerfully admitted because they do not harm the virtues. When we have done with listing all Robinson's vices and pointing to the pages can be skipped, there still remains a sizeable body of work that anyone who cares about poetry should want to read and re-read. There is also, I have found, work that you prepare to skip and then forget to. For Robinson has the ability to write the plainest of plain tales in which his fascination with the quotidian of life becomes so remarkable that you find yourself either compelled to share it or to speculate on the manner of mind that could retain such open-eyed awe before the trivial.

This awe is an essential part of his vision. It is how he chooses to see and record his America. As is well known, Robinson's America is small-town New England, and he is the most distinguished product of a generation of writers that was rediscovering a need to voice a consciousness of being American. Now that this need has been written into the literary histories it seems obvious enough, but at the time itself it came as a revolutionary impulse. For the story of American poetry at the end of the nineteenth century is largely one of gentle, drab imitative work versus new and for the most part unrecognised efforts to cope with the American experience. The imitators looked East for their models; they hoped for nothing more than to come in a discreet second-best to Europe's literature, and predictably enough their work was highly praised. As late as 1915, for example, Fred Pattee, in *A History of American Literature Since 1870*, was full of kind words for Celia Thaxter, Richard Hovey, Richard Watson Gilder and Emma Lazarus, among others, while completely ignoring Robinson, and this though much of Robinson's best work had by then been published. True, Pattee thought Emily Dickinson's poems should have been buried with her—'to compare her eccentric fragments with Blake's elfin wildness is ridiculous'. But this merely provides further proof of how representative he is of what American critics wanted from their poets.

Yet the odd and, in a way, heartening thing is, that several of the poets Pattee so admired had an inkling that their deferential attitude to the old world wouldn't really do. One of them, Emma Lazarus, spoke out on behalf of a native American poetic:

> How long, and yet how long
> Our leaders will we hail from over seas,
> Masters and kings from feudal monarchies,
>   And mock their ancient song
> With echoes weak of foreign melodies?

But as that stanza makes very clear, she herself had to sing in decidedly weak echoes of foreign melodies. Although she has the good sense to realise that:

> The echo faints and fails;
> It suiteth not, upon this western plain,
> Our voice or spirit

Her own voice never emerges from the borrowed language of nineteenth-century English poetry. Before 1890 the only alternative to this appeared to lie in the verse of journalists like Ben King, Eugene Field and James Whitcomb Riley, whose work amounts to the home-spun wisdom of old codgers tricked out in the various dialects of the middle west. *The Leaves of Grass*, it seems, was not an example to be followed.

The first, hesitant steps in breaking away from this appalling inheritance of native hayseed and imported pre-Raphaelitism were taken in the verse of William Vaughan Moody and Trumbull Stickney. (I leave out of account Stephen Crane who, though certainly a remarkable talent, was too isolated and exceptional a case to be of any use to his contemporaries.) Here at last was an attempt to write serious verse that could cut free of tepid imitation. Stickney and Moody were Harvard poets, and a certain academicism shows in their verse; they are a little too eager to impose their sense of a classical philosophy on American observations; they dislike much of what they have to record but trust to a well-trained mind and a tasteful stoicism to see them through the worst. Neither is a considerable poet, though Stickney might have become one had he lived, and Moody has some commendable passages. (I take it that one of his better poems, 'Ode in Time of Hesitation', is a starting point for Lowell's 'For the Union Dead'.)

But more important than their poetic achievements was the climate for poetry that Moody and Stickney did so much to create during their Harvard years. They edited the Harvard *Monthly*, which under them won an enviable reputation as a magazine of high literary standards, and they set about looking for young contemporaries who could help them achieve the renaissance of American poetry. Curiously, however, they overlooked Robinson. Robinson entered Harvard in 1891, and he soon began publishing verse in the *Advocate*. But he never made the pages of the *Monthly*. Why this should be is difficult to say, for he was by far the most gifted of the Harvard poets, and by rights he ought to have been exactly the poet Moody and Stickney were looking for. But his personal situation may account for much. In his study of the *American 1890s*, Larzer Ziff points out that Robinson 'was somewhat older than the average freshman, he was not a regular student, he came with academic deficiencies, and he had no social connections.'[1] These are bulky obstacles, and they may be enough to explain why Robinson was not taken up by the reigning literary clique. They may also help to explain a self-conscious literariness that hangs about some of his work. A poem such as 'Many are Called' has something of the auto-didact about it, and others seem to exist more as proof that the academic deficiencies have been made good than because Robinson has anything important to say.

Yet although Robinson achieved no literary fame at Harvard—and indeed after two years he was forced to leave and return to his impoverished family in Gardiner, Maine—the atmosphere he encountered during his university years obviously encouraged him in his determination to succeed as an American poet. That determination was strong enough to carry him through years of poverty, hardship and neglect. It created in him an unswerving loyalty to his craft and a fierce pride in his vocation. One result of this was that when Theodore Roosevelt interceded to get him finally settled in a decent job, Robinson chose to regard Roosevelt's action as that of a patron which required him to honour his part by writing poems on national affairs (they are nearly all poor), and by showing himself capable of steady work at his art. He therefore made it a duty to publish volumes at regular intervals for the rest of his life. But Robinson's early experiences left their scar on him. He held himself aloof from public displays of friendship or admiration. I have been told that when, in 1934, he was to go to New York from his home in Boston to receive a literary award, he deliberately evaded the party of well-wishers that Merrill Moore had organised at Boston station to cheer him on his way. Very probably it is his own sufferings that are reflected in his life-long interest in those defeated yet unyielding figures who people so many of his poems.

In 1896 Robinson published at his own expense a volume of poems called *The Torrent and the Night Before*. The following year he paid a vanity publisher to bring out *The Children of the Night*, which duplicated work from the earlier volume and added seventeen new poems. Neither volume brought him the slightest attention, and indeed this only began with *Captain Craig and Other Poems* in 1902. For though Moody and Stickney might be encouraging new poetry at Harvard, the public at large was still looking for poetry which would prove its worth by looking nearly as good as English verse. And so, in the same year that Robinson published *The Children of the Night*, John Bannister Tabb brought out to considerable applause his third volume of poems called, simply enough, *Lyrics*. Here is an entirely representative poem from that collection, 'My Secret':

> 'Tis not what I am fain to hide,
>   That doth in deepest darkness dwell,
> But what my tongue hath often tried,
>   Alas, in vain, to tell.

Tabb throughout his life was a well-received poet, and he continued to enjoy a reputation at least until the publication in 1926 of Robert Shafer's two-volume anthology of *American Literature*. Shafer called Tabb a true poet who 'deserves to be read and remembered' (Pattee, by the way, had said that Tabb's lyrics possessed 'beauty and finish and often distinction'). *Lyrics* had a generous press. But this poem met with silence:

> Whenever Richard Cory went down town,
> We people on the pavement looked at him;
> He was a gentleman from sole to crown,
> Clean favored, and imperially slim.
>
> And he was always quietly arrayed,
> And he was always human when he talked;

> But still he fluttered pulses when he said,
> 'Good morning', and he glittered when he walked.
>
> And he was rich—yes, richer than a king—
> And admirably schooled in every grace:
> In fine, we thought that he was everything
> To make us wish that we were in his place.
>
> So on we worked, and waited for the light,
> And went without the meat, and cursed the bread;
> And Richard Cory, one calm summer night,
> Went home and put a bullet through his head.

Well, it isn't a perfect poem, but it is certainly a remarkable one and especially if you think of it beside 'My Secret'. It has the plain-jane manner that Robinson loves to affect and as a result of which he gains for himself just the right amount of freedom to let otherwise unremarkable phrases stand out. Taken in context, the phrase 'imperially slim', for example, has an almost sensuous, supple, and therefore slightly mocking grace about it. 'Richard Cory' is wry, grim, laconic: it is a typical Robinsonian perception of the bleak comedy of the human condition, and this perception features in much of his best—and worst—work. In addition, the poem has that first-rate anecdotal quality which Robinson shares with Hardy.

Hardy, in fact, was a congenial poet, and Robinson shares some of the Englishman's least impressive and most imitable tactics and attitudes; he too has his poems about life's little ironies, and remarkably predictable they are More importantly, however, he also shares with Hardy the ability to tell a story in verse in such a way as to let the smallest and most insignificant detail take on meaning and value. (Even the calm' summer night in 'Richard Cory' isn't quite the irrelevant detail it may at first seem, though the point it is making is admittedly an obvious one.) But another English poet was still more congenial. In his first volume, Robinson published a sonnet on George Crabbe, and it shows just how exactly he had taken Crabbe's measure. Crabbe has been forgotten by later poets, Robinson says, and yet his real value is desperately needed and cannot be dismissed (a claim Pound was to make some twenty years later). Crabbe's

> hard, human pulse is throbbing still
> With the sure strength that fearless truth endows

and we should never forget or deny Crabbe's enviable possession of 'plain excellence and stubborn skill'. The praise not only memorably catches Crabbe's especial distinction, it points to Robinson's very similar strengths. For Crabbe's 'plain excellence' is of course that of the unadorned style. Moreover, the phrase has a sly wit to it, it hints at the unarguable fact of that excellence, and this laconic turn of expression is also common to both men.

In the last analysis, Crabbe's human pulse is the harder. Robinson, like Moody and Stickney, was more apt to be under the sway of the eternal sadness of things. (Though unlike them he wasn't trying to demonstrate this as a cultivated stance, so that his sadness—whether wry, grim or resigned—is more authentic than theirs.) But for all their differences, Robinson shares with Crabbe the ability to write memorably and truthfully about certain very ordinary people. Robinson's people belong to Tilbury, that small New England town clearly modelled on Gardiner; he brings his open-eyed awe to bear on them so intently that he becomes their special poet. He is the first and still the best poet-historian of this essential part of America, just as Sarah Orne Jewett is its first prose historian. (Her collection of stories, *The Country of the Pointed Firs*, about the Maine fishing village, Dunnet Landing, appeared in 1898.) Because he is the first to write about them, the people he puts into his work are for the first time given an identity in literature. Adam naming the animals, perhaps. Yet the formulation won't really do, because Robinson's eye isn't as innocent as all that; for though his reverence for the quotidian of life suggests something of the sheer wonder of being human at this time and in this place, he tends to focus on moments of sadness, of deprivation and loss. This can be seen here, in 'Reuben Bright', an entirely typical and honourable performance:

> Because he was a butcher and thereby
> Did earn an honest living (and did right),
> I would not have you think that Reuben Bright
> Was any more a brute than you or I;
> For when they told him that his wife must die,

He stared at them, and shook with grief and fright,
And made the women cry to see him cry.

And after she was dead, and he had paid
The Singers and the sexton and the rest,
He packed a lot of things that she had made
Most mournfully away in an old chest
Of hers, and put some chopped-up cedar boughs
In with them, and tore down the slaughter-house.

And ... and ... and. A story, Forster said, tells you what happened next; it amounts to saying 'and then'. A plot tells you *why* something happened next. 'Reuben Bright' is a story which has the hint of a plot running through it. The poet doesn't try to interpret the events, he merely sets down how one thing followed on from another, and his tone is seemingly neutral and detached. But inside the tiny anecdote we are allowed to guess at the connection of events and to feel how Reuben Bright's behaviour has been affected almost to madness by his wife's death. He may well appear a 'brute' (even his name feels as though it should contract to the word), yet Robinson tells us a great deal about the butcher's crude tenderness of regard in the detail of the 'chopped-up cedar boughs'. To get away with that a poet must be able to speak without a hint of condescension, and he must also care so passionately for our having the exact facts of the case that he will be prepared to risk the near-bathetic enjambement on 'an old chest/Of hers'. Who cares whose chest it is? Robinson, of course, just as he cares that his audience shouldn't snigger at Reuben Bright. Why else that inscrutable tone of the opening lines, which is hardly chosen to put an audience at its ease? What it does is to guard against any possibility that Reuben Bright, the small-town epitome of the Protestant ethic, could be dismissed as humanly uninteresting or trivially corrupt. The tone feels at first merely prim, but the more you study it, the slyer it becomes and the more difficult to pin down. It guarantees precisely the grudged interest in its subject that a more defenceless tone might lose. Not that I am wanting to put Robinson forward as defendant of the Protestant ethic; he is more properly described as its sardonic satirist (as in 'Cassandra'), and after all, it was he who wrote that wicked sonnet on 'New England':

Passion is here a soilure of the wits,

> We're told, and Love a cross for them to bear;
> Joy shivers in the corner where she knits
> And Conscience always has the easy chair,
> Cheerful as when she tortured into fits
> The first cat that was ever killed by Care.

But Robinson is also determined that there shall be no snobbish dismissal of the people he wants to record in his poetry. 'Miniver Cheevy' is a fair example of his ability to identify and discomfort the enemy.

It is when you are alerted to Robinson's generous fair-mindedness, the intelligent humility that characterises his attitude to the people he writes about, that you become conscious of just where he is a better poet than Frost. Even Randall Jarrell, Frost's most eloquent admirer, was forced to acknowledge the lack of generosity, the hard vanity and complacency that mar so much of Frost's writing. Robinson has none of these faults. Indeed if it were not for his wit, he would be a peculiarly self-effacing poet. The reason is not hard to find. It lies in the fact that he is so absorbed in the lives he records that his art goes into rendering his characters with all the love, skill and justice he can muster. What Rilke said about works of art applies exactly to Robinson's way with the inhabitants of Tilbury Town. 'Works of art', Rilke wrote to his young friend Kappus, 'are of an infinite loneliness and with nothing so little to be reached as with criticism. Only love can grasp and hold and be just towards them.' Substitute 'people' for 'works of art' and you have Robinson's attitude to perfection. Poem after poem testifies to his loving concern to be just to his characters, and through all of them runs the hesitant conviction that people are of an infinite loneliness, since they can never communicate the ultimate truth that the poet is called upon to utter—that life is marked by the defeat of hopes through the agencies of death, of time, or of what he vaguely calls 'Destiny'. When Robinson is riding the idea of destiny too hard, his poems tend to sink towards a lugubrious sadness; but others, like 'Calvery's' and 'Clavering', have the note of resigned, impersonal wisdom that we find in Hardy's 'An Ancient to Ancients' and 'During Wind and Rain'. And such a poem as 'For a Dead Lady' survives its worst prosiness to become an unforgettable statement about the ravages of time in the great, apparently plain but in fact singing, humming manner of Turberville or Gascoigne. Here is the last stanza:

> The beauty, shattered by the laws
> That have creation in their keeping,
> No longer trembles at applause,
> Or over children that are sleeping;
> And we who delve in beauty's lore
> Know all that we have known before
> Of what inexorable cause
> Makes Time so vicious in his reaping.

Many of Robinson's poems succeed in this way. Turn to any of his volumes and you will find that it is so. Above all, there is 'Mr Flood's Party'. But what can a critic hope to say about this poem? That it is one of the most beautifully considerate, tender poems about loneliness ever written; that it combines wit and pathos in a way that makes it intensely sympathetic and yet scrupulously intelligent towards its subject? As for its tone—Conrad Aiken once remarked that Robinson's characteristic tone hovered somewhere between the ironic and the elegiac, and this is perhaps as near as we can come to catching the tone of 'Mr Flood's Party'. The poem is about a lonely, ageing drunkard, a disreputable outcast from his community, more comic than pitiful, a man who has kept his dissolute wits about him. But though Robinson doesn't waste any pity on Mr Flood, sympathy is powerfully present by virtue of the attentiveness, the plain excellence that sets down his story:

> Old Eben Flood, climbing alone one night
> Over the hill between the town below
> And the forsaken upland hermitage
> That held as much as he should ever know
> On earth again of home, paused warily.

It is the withheld word that does the trick: not wearily, but 'warily'. This old man has too much native wit to be the object of sentimental pity. For Robinson to draw our attention to this fact is proof enough of the comic regard in which he holds Mr Flood, but it surely emerges in the very way the story opens. How can you resist a poem that starts as this one does? It is so compelling, so much in the manner of the born story-teller. As the poem continues, the tale becomes more comic, more outrageously strange, more humanly fascinating. Robinson is so completely in command that he can switch the changes in the third stanza from the near-mocking grandiloquence of the opening lines to the closing lines, which shame our smiles:

> Alone, as if enduring to the end
> A valiant armor of scarred hopes outworn,
> He stood there in the middle of the road
> Like Roland's ghost winding a silent horn.
> Below him, in the town among the trees,
> Where friends of other days had honoured him,
> A phantom salutation of the dead
> Rang thinly till old Eben's eyes were dim.

Yet the closing lines clearly need the bracing effect of the mock-heroic that plays about the first half-stanza if they are not to stray into mere pathos. And consider how much Robinson risks, and brings off, in the fourth stanza:

> Then, as a mother lays her sleeping child
> Down tenderly, fearing it may awake,
> He set the jug down slowly at his feet
> With trembling care, knowing that most things break;
> And only when assured that on firm earth
> It stood, as the uncertain lives of men
> Assuredly did not, he paced away,
> And with his hand extended paused again:

The control of language in that stanza is as perfect as anyone could wish for. The simile of the tipsy old man setting his jug down, like a mother, with 'trembling care', is so audacious and yet so obviously written out of regard for him and not for cleverness' sake, that it doesn't seem the least bit ingenious or self-regarding. Moreover, the laconic phrase, 'knowing that most things break', strikes me as exactly the sort of triumph that Robinson's style can bring him: it quite miraculously holds the balance between the poet's resistance to bathos and his need to honour that slightly indulgent but sure knowledge that Mr Flood carries with him. So it is with the rest of the poem. But here I have simply to quote:

'Well, Mr Flood, we have not met like this
In a long time; and many a change has come
To both of us, I fear, since last it was
We had a drop together. Welcome home!'
Convivially returning with himself,
Again he raised the jug up to the light;
And with an acquiescent quaver said:
'Well, Mr Flood, if you insist, I might'.

'Only a very little, Mr Flood—
For auld lang syne. No more, sir; that will do.'
So, for the time, apparently it did,
And Eben evidently thought so too;
For soon amid the silver loneliness
Of night he lifted up his voice and sang,
Secure, with only two moons listening,
Until the whole harmonious landscape rang—

'For auld lang syne'. The weary throat gave out,
The last words wavered; and the song being done,
He raised again the jug regretfully
And shook his head, and was again alone.
There was not much that was ahead of him,
And there was nothing in the town below—
Where strangers would have shut the many doors
That many friends had opened long ago.

There is really nothing to say about that, except how wonderful it
is. You can note the great line 'There was not much that was ahead
of him', the wit that is unwaveringly attentive towards Eben's
caution ('Secure, with only two moons listening'), the comic
'Convivially returning with himself'; and so on. But ticking off the
points that make 'Mr Flood's Party' a masterpiece comes to feel a
very trivial exercise. What perhaps is worth saying is that it is
precisely because Robinson finds such scenes worth recording that
he is so invaluable a poet. For the subject of 'Mr Flood's Party'
hardly seems to warrant a poem at all and certainly not the major
poem that Robinson fashions. Yet it is just because of his shrewd,
sad, but comically receptive open-eyed awe that Robinson *can* find
the right way of recording his ordinary citizens. This is his
distinctive role as poet: he is spokesman for the inarticulate, for
those who, whatever the reason, have been forced into

incommunicable loneliness. So he becomes the historian of people as Masters, with his slick cynicism, and Sandburg, all squashily sentimental, could not hope to be. 'Mr Flood's Party' belongs not with them but with the Frost of 'Home Burial' and 'Death of the Hired Man', which is not to deny that Frost is the greater poet. It is, however, to say that Robinson deserves to be set beside the great poets of the language.

Figures like Mr Flood recur throughout Robinson's poetry, even when he is not writing about Tilbury Town. Not all of them are comic, but they have in common the fact that invariably they are old men who have known repeated disappointments and defeats and yet have sufficient resilience to journey on to the defeat of whatever hopes are left to them. They include the Dutchman, the Wandering Jew and Rembrandt. All of them possess the Jew's 'old, unyielding eyes', and they are therefore far too tough to surrender to their gnawing self-doubts. It is, of course, utterly characteristic of Robinson that he should have written a monologue for the Rembrandt of the late self-portraits. Clearly he recognised those great remorseless studies for what they are: indomitable self-scrutinies that triumph by their willingness to face and acknowledge the worst. Robinson's Rembrandt is perhaps rather less fiercely courageous than his real-life counterpart; and for that reason the poem does not provide the great kick at misery that Rembrandt's self-portraits do. But it does testify to Robinson's ceaseless curiosity about human nature, his wanting to track down the way a man thinks and suffers and lives in his mind.

There are occasions when this brings him face to face with a blank wall. The monologue given to Ben Jonson, in which Jonson is made to tell of his acquaintance with Shakespeare, ends in disappointment because there is nothing Robinson can have Jonson say that we don't already know; and Robinson is clearly not the poet to invent when he is dealing with the actual. With Rembrandt he has the paintings to help him; but with Shakespeare there is really nothing, once he has decided not to see Prospero as an autobiographical figure, or *Measure for Measure* as written in time of personal distress. Accordingly, Robinson's best monologue and narrative poems are the ones which are entirely works of invention. Though many are too slight and respectful to the mundane, a few stand out as among the supreme achievements

of their kind. Of all the narrative poems, 'Isaac and Archibald' is
the surest triumph.

It has its faults, of course, and they are very representative ones.
There are, for example, moments when diction and cadence
imitate Tennyson imitating Wordsworth:

>   and the world
> Was wide, and there was gladness everywhere.

Some lines are blatantly stuffed out to fill up the pentameter:

> At the end of an hour's walking after that
> The cottage of old Archibald appeared.
> Little and white and high on a smooth round hill
> It stood.

Once or twice the poem falls into unfocused Miltonics, as when the
narrator tells of going down to Archibald's cellar:

>   down we went
> Out of the fiery sunshine to the gloom,
> Grateful and half sepulchral

Yet the flaws stand for amazingly little compared with what the
poem achieves. In outline, at least, it is simplicity itself. A man
recalls a summer day of his childhood when he had gone with an old
man, Isaac, to see the man's equally aged friend, Archibald. As they
walk along, Isaac tells the boy he is worried Archibald will not have
cut his field of oats, and this is the pretext for him to add that he is
certain Archibald will shortly die. 'The twilight warning of
experience' has made him aware, he says, that 'Archibald is going'.
But when they arrive at Archibald's cottage they find the field of
oats newly cut and a spruce Archibald extending them a ready
welcome. Isaac goes for a walk and instructs Archibald to stay 'and
rest your back and tell the boy/A story'. Archibald does so, and he
also tells the boy that he fears Isaac will shortly die. 'I have seen it
come/These eight years', he says. Isaac returns, and the two old men
play cards while the boy day-dreams and keeps score for them. And
that is all.

But no account of this tale can hope to do justice to its beauty

and integrity of manner. It tells of loneliness and the defeat of
hopes; but it is also full of humorous warmth. And it is considerably
less simple than appears. For it isn't only that Isaac and Archibald
upset each other's point of view and in so doing comically illustrate
the difficulties of truthful communication (are they lying or
mistaken?); behind their words is the fear of death that neither can
quite bring himself to voice. Yet the old men are not defenceless
objects of pity. Like Mr Flood, they still have their wits about
them. As the boy observes, when he is striding along in the fatiguing
heat with Isaac:

> First I was half inclined
> To caution him that he was growing old
> But something that was not compassion soon
> Made plain the folly of all subterfuge.

The old men are also partly comic creations. This is not just a
matter of their anxious solicitude for what each insists is the other's
failing health. It is more, because the poem is everywhere soaked in
the affectionate comedy of observation. As here, early on:

> The sun
> Was hot, and I was ready to sweat blood;
> But Isaac, for aught I could make of him,
> Was cool to his hat-band. So I said then
> Something about the scorching days we have
> In August without knowing it sometimes;
> But Isaac said the day was like a dream,
> And praised the Lord, and talked about the breeze.

Isaac praises the Lord a good deal, and especially when he is
drinking Archibald's cider:

> 'I never twist a spigot nowadays',
> He said, and raised the glass up to the light,
> 'But I thank God for orchards'.

Archibald is also fond of his own cider, which he declares to be
newly tapped and 'an honor to the fruit'. Under a barrel

Glimmered a late-spilled proof that Archibald
Had spoken from unfeigned experience.

But neither Isaac nor Archibald is a figure of fun. The comedy of
this poem is in no sense reductive. On the contrary, its observations
and memories let us in on the affectionate regard with which the
narrator holds the old men. Take this, for example:

There was a fluted antique water-glass
Close by, and in it, prisoned, or at rest,
There was a cricket, of the brown soft sort,
That feeds on darkness. Isaac turned him out,
And touched him with his thumb to make him jump,
And then composedly pulled out the plug
With such a practised hand that scarce a drop
Did even touch his fingers.

That tells us a great deal about Isaac, just as we are told much of
value about Archibald when his

                                                          dry voice
Cried thinly, with unpatronizing triumph
'I've got you, Isaac, high, low, jack, and the game!'

The poem is full of these loving observations, and if that were all
there was to it 'Isaac and Archibald' would still be a considerable
achievement. But there is so much else. In the first place, we are
bound to notice the elegiac air that hangs over it, and which
supplies us with the clear hint that the narrator is drawn to his
memories because he has found his life very different from the
innocent and hopeful day-dreams in which he indulged while Isaac
and Archibald were playing cards:

                                        Now and then my fancy caught
A flying glimpse of a good life beyond—
Something of ships and sunlight, streets and singing,
Troy falling and the ages coming back,
And ages coming forward: Archibald
And Isaac were good fellows in old clothes,
And Agamemnon was a friend of mine:
Ulysses coming home again to shoot

With bows and feathered arrows made another,
And all was as it should be. I was young.

Going with this hint of defeated hopes is the suggestion that he has
come to a saddening recognition of the limits of friendship. In his
childhood dreams he was the friend of Agamemnon and Ulysses,
but now, years later, he is led to recall the two old friends who had
been unable to communicate their fears of death to each other. He
also, of course, realises that life isn't art or literature.

But what more than anything stands out from the memories of
that far-off day is the fact of loneliness. Isaac tells the boy that he
cannot expect to understand 'the singular idea of loneliness'. It is a
paradoxical effort at communication, and both Isaac and
Archibald talk to the boy in the hope of making him understand
their own predicaments. Thus Archibald tells him to remember
what he has said about 'the light behind the stars'. Yet he knows
the boy cannot understand his words and what they imply:

>   'But there, there,
> I'm going it again, as Isaac says,
> And I'll stop now before you go to sleep—
> Only be sure that you growl cautiously,
> And always where the shadow may not reach you.'
> Never shall I forget, long as I live,
> The quaint thin crack in Archibald's voice,
> The lonely twinkle in his little eyes,
> Or the way it made me feel to be with him.

Beyond all else, the old men want to be remembered. Archibald says
to the boy, 'Remember that: remember that I said it.' But the actual
words are not really what he's talking about; for, facing the ultimate
loneliness of death, the old man wants somehow to be assured that
his identity will survive in another person's acceptance of him. And
the same holds true for Isaac. He says:

>   'Look at me, my boy,
> And when the time shall come for you to see
> That I must follow after him, try then
> To think of me, to bring me back again,
> Just as I was today. Think of the place
> Where we are sitting now, and think of me—

> Think of old Isaac as you knew him then,
> When you set out with him in August once
> To see old Archibald.'—The words come back
> Almost as Isaac must have uttered them.

'*Almost* as Isaac *must* have uttered them.' The narrator of this poem is too truthful not to accept that much that Isaac and Archibald hoped would be saved in fact had to die with them.

But it would be wrong to give the impression that the poem settles merely for the sadness of incommunicable isolation. While acknowledging that this must be so, it also pays tribute to the power of human regard that in some measure, at least, triumphs over the loneliness in which each person must be trapped. For the narrator honours and celebrates Isaac and Archibald simply by the vitality of memories that clamber from years of neglect in order to testify to the enduring warmth of affection he has for the old men, and the memories savour the cadences of remembered speech so that the old men return almost like Hardy's ghosts. Besides, the poem doesn't end on a dying fall but with a last hint of a companionship that almost throughout had seemed beyond reach:

> I knew them and I may have laughed at them;
> But there's a laughing that has honor in it,
> And I have no regrets for light words now.
> Rather I think sometimes they may have made
> Their sport of me;—but they would not do that,
> They were too old for that. They were old men,
> And I may laugh at them because I knew them.

These last lines are beautifully just; they bring the poem to a close by accepting the inscrutability of human behaviour at the same time as matching it with the kind of knowledge derived from a source that implies communication. They suggest a good deal about Robinson's characteristic method. For if, like his admired Crabbe, Robinson is the poet of plain realities, he is also like Crabbe the poet of surprises, and these are likely to show themselves in the precise ways he responds to the mysteriousness of people, no matter how ordinary they may seem. This is the hallmark of an unfailing curiosity, and it makes Robinson one of the necessary poets.

Note

1. Larzer Ziff, *The American 1890s: Life and Times of a Lost Generation* (Lincoln, Nebraska: University of Nebraska Press 1930).

3

The Poetry of Theodore Roethke

Anyone seriously interested in Theodore Roethke must be struck by the very odd state of his reputation. Considering the number of poets and critics who are prepared to call him a great writer, it is surprising, to say the least, to find the contempt or indifference which he gets from others. For some he is a genius, for others a charlatan. (They don't put it quite that way, but it's what they mean.) Carolyn Kizer, for example, has said that 'my opinion, which is shared by many, is that Roethke has made the most significant contribution to poetic language since Yeats and Joyce'. She also compares him to St Augustine. But reading between the lines of M.L. Rosenthal's *The New Poets*, it becomes clear that Rosenthal sees Roethke as a severely limited practitioner and part poseur.[1] If we want futher evidence of this wild variance in estimating Roethke's work, we can point to the fact that there are now several books on him, and yet that Steven Stephanchev's *American Poetry Since 1945* makes no mention of him at all. Even the fact that Stepanchev's study is an arrant piece of book-making reveals a good deal, because he obviously knows whose stock is riding high. He has sections on projective verse, on Ginsberg, on that dreariest of poets, Charles Olson, and an obligatory piece on Lowell. But he apparently feels no obligation to do anything about Roethke. Indeed, it is probably more accurate to say that he clearly feels an obligtion to do nothing about him.

One very good reason for this neglect or downgrading of Roethke is the New York literary stockmarket. Roethke has been dead five years now, and he simply doesn't belong with what is new on the scene. As example of what *is* new we could take *A Controversy of Poets*, an anthology compiled by two New York poets, Paris Leary and Robert Kelly. This collection, which first appeared in 1965, is mostly limited to younger poets, but the editors note that they have included any poet 'whose work has come into special prominence since 1950'. When one considers that *Praise to the End* was published in 1951, *The Waking*, 1953, won the Pulitzer Prize, and *Words for the Wind*, 1958, won seven major awards, including the Bollingen Prize, it is reasonable to suppose that Leary and Kelly might find room for Roethke. But not only is he absent, it is next to impossible to find a single poem that owes anything to him. Roethke has been expunged. (So, I may add, have Berryman, Simpson and Dugan, while Robert Lowell is represented by three poems. But Olson gets eighteen pages.) Of course, it is easy to quibble about exclusions from anthologies, and if it seems particularly easy with *A Controversy of Poets*, I recognise that the editors had a programme to map out in including, say, Robin Blaser and excluding Robert Bly. But leaving out Roethke is rather more questionable, especially in view of the dross they print. Besides, among other absentees are Carolyn Kizer, William Stafford, Richard Hugo, David Wagoner and Richard Hanson, who have in common the fact that they make up the anthology *Five Poets of the Pacific Northwest*, edited by Robin Skelton and dedicated to Roethke.[2]

What Stephanchev's study and Leary's and Kelly's anthology testify to is a new regionalism, or perhaps counter-regionalism. They are part of New York's response to the fact that many of the best poets in America do not live there and say that they are happier away from it. The new regionalism has nothing to do with the old southern stand of the twenties and thirties; it merely demonstrates many poets' indifference to becoming part of the New York literary scene (as James Dickey said in an interview in *Shenandoah*). This has led to an almost comic provincialism among New York writers. A recent article by Stephen Koch unwittingly demonstrates this much. The situation must have become fairly desperate when we can be offered John Ashbery as an important poet and told that Kenneth Koch is 'perhaps the most polished wit writing in English'. (We are given this example of the polished wit: 'We laughed at the hollyhocks together/and then I sprayed them with lye. /Forgive me. I simply do not know what I am doing.') It would be too simple to say that Stepanchev, Leary and Kelly are getting even with Roethke for not living in New York, but without doubt their attitude to him contains a sizeable element of pique. For Roethke was, of course, the poet of Seattle, and during his stay there—from 1948 until his death in 1963—he seems to have been in large part responsible for making it so lively a centre for poetry. The north-west had its own canonized poet—Roethke was made 'Poet in Residence' at the University of Washington in 1962. In 1959 Carolyn Kizer founded *Poetry Northwest*, and Skelton's anthology followed in 1964. If there is any excuse for the studied indifference of Stepanchev, Leary and Kelly towards Roethke, it is to be found in the way Roethke's friends in and around Seattle tended to praise him to the point of adulation, while insisting on their shared—almost secret —friendship. In general his admirers seem to see him as both 'Ted' and Mage. The cult perhaps needed deflating.

But there is another reason for the wild swings in Roethke's reputation, and this has less to do with what others thought of him than with what he took himself to be, although the views clearly fortified each other. 'Being not doing, is my first joy' he remarks in one of his poems, and one of the things he found it necessary to be was 'a poet'. However sympathetically we study Roethke's writing, it is impossible to avoid the feeling that some of it springs from an effort of will. Certainly his determination to be a 'philosophical' poet often rings false. Besides that, there is his insistence that a poet is to be identified by his separateness. In his own case, as is well known, this was the recurrent and humiliating mental illnesses that he never managed to shake off. He came to see these as intimately connected with his gifts. In one poem he asked:

> What's madness but nobility of soul
> At odds with circumstances?

In 'Heard in a Violent Ward', a lovely and even gay lyric, he linked himself to Smart, Blake and Clare. He also composed tirades under the pseudonym of Winterest Rothberg as a way of releasing the poison. Here he anathematised those poets he perhaps saw as a threat to his own status. Reading, say, 'A Tirade Turning', one is inevitably reminded of the atmosphere that surrounded the poetry and career of Dylan Thomas, a poet for whom Roethke felt much sympathy. There is the same mixture of the genuine and fake, the same hysterical shouting, the same blurring of lines between being a poet and acting the part. Yet the act must have seemed convincing at the time, at least if Louise Bogan's 'Several Voices Out of A Cloud' can be used as evidence (surely written with both Roethke and Thomas in mind):

> Come, drunks and drug-takers; come, perverts unnerved!
> Receive the laurel, given though late, on merit; to whom and
>   wherever deserved.
> Parochial punks, trimmers, nice people, joiners true-blue,
> Get the hell out of the way of the laurel. It is deathless
>   and it isn't for you.

What made Roethke act as he did had much to do with his involvement in American academic life, which he attacked in one of the Rothberg pieces called 'Last Class'. This staggering piece of invective rages against 'Hysteria College', with its mindless students and emotionally dead teachers. It is very like René Char's poem to Rimbaud, although it lacks Char's controlling wit: "Tu as eu raison d'abandonner le boulevard des parasseux, les estaminets des pisselyres, pour l'enfer des bêtes." (I should point out that Roethke seems to have admired Char and may even have owed some of his aphoristic qualities to the Frenchman.) I do not wish to argue that for Roethke the University of Washington was 'l'estaminet des pisselyres', but on the other hand it is true that a university provides at once a tame audience and a certain weight of indifference to poetry. Stephen Spender tells an anecdote about Roethke which catches his attitude to the academic world in which he found himself. Roethke was going to read his own poems:

> He was introduced by the chairman of the English department at a midwestern university, who was, perhaps, a bit overelaborate (through nervousness, I suspect) in his introduction. After a few minutes of hearing his virtues analyzed, Roethke, who was strategically seated well behind the chairman, spread out his arms in an enormous shrug, twisted his head, fidgeted in his chair, heaved enormous sighs, and pulled lamentable faces. It was a gigantic act of dissociation from what was being said about him.

It is unpleasant, of course, and without doubt the act was to some degree self-conscious. But one can also sense a degree of genuineness. The pity is that Roethke became so bound up in his role-playing that it extended beyond the bounds of his public image to his actual writing. Time and again he writes prose that makes you wince for its overblown insistence on his powers. Nor does the poetry escape. For example, the notorious Yeatsian stance of the later poems remains a problem in spite of all the defences that have been made of it. I do not think that Roethke steals more than he borrows, and I cannot see in the work a monarchical invasion of Yeats' rights—let alone those of Stevens' or Eliot's. This is not to deny that Roethke has his successes; but we can hardly avoid recognising that he frequently puts on the Yeatsian singing-robes in order to insist on his own stature. Nor do I think we have accounted for his borrowings when we have called them 'deliberate', as some of his more abject admirers do. Indeed, my guess is that this mistaken defence has been in large part responsible for the dismissal of Roethke in some quarters. The plain fact is that however deliberate the borrowings were, the question of their propriety has still to be settled.

Roethke knew this himself. In 'How to Write like Someone Else' he defended his policy of imitation and borrowing on the grounds that it could help him to discover his own identity. Equally important, though he doesn't say so, it helped him discover who he wasn't. As his first volume, *Open House* reveals, that included Allen Tate, Stanley Kunitz, Emily Dickinson, Elinor Wylie, Leonie Adams and Auden. The echoes of Auden are the most damaging. They nearly all occur in the fifth section. 'Lull', dated November 1939, is a good example:

> The winds of hatred blow
> Cold, cold across the flesh
> And chill the anxious heart;
> Intricate phobias grow
> From each malignant wish
> To spoil collective life.
> Now each man stands apart.

No, he is not Auden, nor was meant to be. Nor is he Emily Dickinson ('Open House'), Allen Tate ('Feud'), Stanley Kunitz ('Prayer') or Wylie ('No Bird'). But he does find help from Leonie Adams, on whom he leans heavily in 'Slow Season' and 'The Coming of the Cold'. This latter poem has close affinities with

Adams' 'Country Summer'. Roethke first:

> The late peach yields a subtle musk,
> The arbor is alive with fume
> More heady than a field at dusk
> When clover scents diminished wind.
> The walker's foot has scarcely room
> Upon the orchard path, for skinned
> And battered fruit has choked the grass.

And Adams:

> Now the rich cherry, whose sleek wood
> And top with silver petals traced
> Like a strict box its gems encased,
> Has split from out that cunning lid,
> All in an innocent green round,
> Those melting rubies which it hid.

But though Roethke is working Adams' vein, he differs from her in two important ways. First, his decision about rhyme is more interesting than hers; it keeps the poem moving forward as well as allowing for greater amplitude of statement. Second, his rhythms have an energy that hers lack (admittedly, in her company they look perhaps more powerful than they are), and they are helped by the vitality the lines pick up from the number of stressed verbs. Even so derivative a poem as 'The Coming of the Cold' undoubtedly is, shows a directness of response, a quality of participation as opposed to mere observation, that marks Roethke's individuality. *Open House* is a conventional volume, but Roethke's own voice begins to emerge in one or two poems. It is there, though not entirely successfully, in 'The Heron', where too many adjectives hold back the powerful perception of violence in the emphatic end-stopped lines:

> He jerks a frog across his bony lip,
> Then points his heavy bill above the wood.
> The wide wings flap but once to lift him up.
> A single ripple starts from where he stood.

What is recognisably Roethkean about the poem is its ultrasensitive thin-skinned response to the external world (To make an obvious point, his use of the present tense is an important tactic in focussing the directness of response.)

But Roethke's voice is also recognisable in a rather different way. The title poem ends with the confession that:

> Rage warps my clearest cry
> To witless agony

The last stanza of 'Feud' runs:

> You meditate upon the nerves,
> Inflame with hate. This ancient feud
> Is seldom won. The spirit starves
> Until the dead have been subdued.

Taking the two statements together, we can say that Roethke is sensing the need to try and cope with a destructive force inside himself that he connects with his past. The idea is more fully developed in probably the finest poem of *Open House*, 'Premonition', which I quote in entirety:

> Walking this field I remember
> Days of another summer.
> Oh that was long ago! I kept
> Close to the heels of my father,
> Matching his strides with half-steps
> Until we came to a river.
> He dipped his hand in the shallow:
> Water ran over and under
> Hair on a narrow wrist bone;
> His image kept following after,—
> Flashed with the sun in the ripple.
> But when he stood up, that face
> Was lost in a maze of water.

It is a poem about death, of course. More particularly, it is about the fear of dissolution, which the poet connects with his father and which exists for him as a present threat. Without doubt, this fear haunted Roethke all his life. It recurs again and again in his work and is responsible for much of his finest poetry. One way of trying to cope with it was by burrowing back into those days of another summer, to see if he could drag out into the open the roots of the dark terror that fastened onto his mind. Hence, his next volume, *The Lost Son*.[3]

There are those for whom the poems of *The Lost Son* represent Roethke's finest work. I am not entirely happy with this judgement, but I have no wish to underestimate the enormous power and originality of the volume; and any attempt to write about recent American poetry without taking it into account is an act of lunacy. *The Lost Son* is divided into four sections, and Roethke's genius emerges only in the first and last. But all four have their parts to play in building up an image of the lost son. The first is about the stages of life up to adolescence, which becomes the subject of the second section. The third section tries to build on the insights and discoveries of the first in recognising the cyclic course of life—water to water; and the fourth, armed with this recognition, explores the ways in which the poet is linked to the past and may through knowledge escape its tyranny. (The volume's title suggests not only that the past is unrepeatable but that it is gladly abandoned.)

It is in the first section that we meet the new Roethke. In only one poem, 'Moss-Gathering' is there an undue dependence on another voice, and Roethke's poem is uneasy in its debt to Lawrence's 'Snake'. But the rest is triumph. Since this is perhaps commonly enough acknowledged, it may be as well to point to something not so frequently noticed, that the poems of the section form their own sequence, from the moment of birth through sentience to some knowledge of the self as a separate being. The first poem, 'Cuttings', is about the earliest organic stirrings, the 'one nub of growth' that in the next poem, 'Cuttings, (*later*)' becomes the moment of breaking into life:

> I can hear, underground, that sucking and sobbing,
> In my veins, in my bones I feel it,—
> The small waters seeping upward,
> The tight grains parting at last.
> When sprouts break out,
> Slippery as fish,
> I quail, lean to beginnings, sheath-wet.

As we all know, Roethke grew up surrounded by greenhouses, and the poems of the first section of *The Lost Son* concern the poet's identification with the processes of nature as a way of delving into his own growth. The identification goes beyond the level of literary metaphor; it is sustained by a deep and valid awareness of growth, of becoming, in which all living things participate. (Which is why his use of the present tense in these poems is so vital to his effort to discover and render the process of growth.) 'Root Cellar' and 'Forcing House' are about the fearful fascination of developing awareness. There is a powerful recognition here that growth brings with it horror as well as delight. But I do not feel that this is presented in a moral or metaphysical way; original sin does not seem to me very important in these poems, no matter what critics have said. 'Weed Puller', for example, is a wonderful poem about the nascent self-consciousness of sexuality, and works through astonishing tactile rhythms and language. Roethke's involvement is physical/psychological; it is, if you like, Lawrence and Blake without the metaphysic of either. The poem is full of distaste and compulsive fascination; and it makes its appeal so directly that commentary is beside the point:

> Under the concrete benches,
> Hacking at black hairy roots,—
> Those lewd monkey-tails hanging from drainholes,—
> Digging into soft rubble underneath,
> Webs and weeds,
> Grubs and snails and sharp sticks,
> Or yanking tough fern-shapes,
> Coiled green and thick, like dripping smilax,
> Tugging all day at perverse life:
> The indignity of it!—
> With everything blooming above me,
> Lilies, pale-pink cyclamen, roses,
> Whole fields lovely and inviolate,—
> Me down in that fetor of weeds,
> Crawling on all fours,
> Alive, in a slippery grave.

It is no surprise that the next poem, 'Orchids', should be about pubescent sex—it is a little like 'Snap-Dragons', though more oblique in its method, belonging to an earlier phase of growth.

After 'Orchids', however, the sequence comes to a halt. Individual poems are fine, but they have no integral relation to the process of growth that the earlier ones chart, and we return to that only in 'Child on Top of a Greenhouse', a recreation of a momentary perception of new isolation, with 'The half-grown chrysanthemums staring up like accusers' and 'everyone, everyone pointing up and shouting'.

I have spoken about these poems as though we can tear out their meanings, and this is the necessary evil of criticism. But it is worth emphasising that the poems of the first section of *The Lost Son* resist any abstraction of 'theme'; they are neither fables, allegories, nor metaphors, and only in and through their texture is their meaning discoverable. For the poems are not so much about growth as involvements in it. The same can hardly be said of the poems in the second section. They are very obviously 'about' something: the ennui and melancholia of adolescence, the pretentious sadness of youth and the 'pricklings of sixteen-year-old lust'. The poems are also, in a very limited and limiting sense, aware of the social-political world; and in this they correspond to the Audenesque poems of *Open House*. More than one critic has noted Roethke's lack of interest in anything beyond himself, and it is true that the world of men engages him very little. But it needs to be said that he made a wise decision in deciding to abandon the effort to look outward, even if that produces an inevitable monotony in his work. For his efforts to engage with the social world are at best pallid and derivative, at worst disastrous. The second section of *The Lost Son* shows that all too clearly.

The third section is even less rewarding than the second. The poems here are simply declarative or explanatory goings-over of what had been so finely rendered in the first section. 'River Incident', for example, tells us that when the poet went wading in river water, he became aware that he

> had been there before,
> In that cold, granitic slime,
> In the dark in the rolling water.

'The Cycle' is a flat retelling of the processes of life, and the poems of this section have a hand-me-down diction, especially in the use they make of Freudian and Jungian symbolism (as though Roethke

feared that the poems of the first section would prove too opaque).
'Night Crow' shows what is wrong:

> When I saw that clumsy crow
> Flap up from a wasted tree,
> A shape in the mind rose up:
> Over the gulfs of dream
> Flew a tremendous bird
> Further and further away
> Into the moonless black,
> Deep in the brain, far back.

This has none of the perceptiveness of 'The Premonition'; the
crow and the wasted tree are manufactured images, the rhythms
and diction not really authentic. I make this point because I want
to suggest that Roethke is never at his happiest when his reading
shows through. At different points in his career he owes far too
much to Jung and Tillich. But this is something to pick up later.
First, I have to speak of a masterpiece.

The fourth section opens with the long title-poem, which is
quite unlike anything that has gone before. It is a poem built of
extremely disturbing material—presumably a severe mental crisis
and the need to trace this to its root. It is worth examining this
poem in some detail, because its difficulties repay close attention,
and also because it holds the clue to what I regard as a real
weakness in Roethke's poetry as a whole. 'The Lost Son' uses very
varied means—fragmented memories, nursery-rhymes, scraps of
nonsense verse—as ways of tunnelling back into the cause of the
illness, so that there can be a rebuilding towards health. For the
need to move forward is a constant theme with Roethke, from
first to last: 'many arrivals make us live', he says in a late poem, and
that includes self-arrivals. But the first section of 'The Lost Son' is
all regression. Its title is 'The Flight' and it is about the poet's
desire to find a way out of his present self-alienation:

> Tell me:
> Which is the way I take;
> Out of what door do I go,
> Where and to whom?
> Dark hollows said, lee to the wind,

The moon said, back of an eel,
The salt said, look by the sea,
Your tears are not enough praise,
You will find no comfort here,
In the kingdom of bang and blab.
Running lightly over spongy ground,
Past the pasture of flat stones,
The three elms,
The sheep strewn on a field,
Over a rickety bridge,
Toward the quick-water, wrinkling and rippling.
Hunting along the river,
Down among the rubbish, the bug-riddled foliage,
By the muddy pond-edge, by the bog-holes,
By the shrunken lake, hunting, in the heat of summer.

They are difficult lines but not impenetrable ones. Indeed, they begin to clear as soon as we recognise that 'The Lost Son' starts from a crisis of identity that has been forced on the poet by a sense of unbearable isolation. The first line of the poem, 'At Woodlawn I heard the dead cry', suggests that the poet is unable to shake off that fear of his father's dominance of which he had spoken in 'Feud'. A little later we come upon:

> Sat alone in an empty house
> Watching shadows crawl

and we realise the potency of the cry is such that he has not found it possible to live with his own isolation. The advice he receives from the moon, dark hollows and so on, is to trace his way back to the original dark of the womb and to give praise for the life-process by getting beyond mere 'tears' of self-pity. (The moon and back of the eel are obvious symbols of mother and father.) But it would be a mistake to feel that the lines need to be rigidly interpreted. Of course, they are not meaningless, but if we reach too irritably after fact we shall miss their power of presentation, the heightened quality of vision that comes through in the details of the three elms, the sheep strewn on the field and the barely controlled terror of 'spongy' and 'rickety', or the build-up to the desperate, near-hysterical rhythms of the lines about hunting.

The short second section, 'The Pit', discovers the point from which growth starts. Roethke here dives straight through the argumentative or sophisticatedly referential qualities of language to come as nakedly at his subject as he knows how:

> Where do the roots go?
>   Look down under the leaves.
> Who put the moss there?
>   These stones have been here too long.
> Who stunned the dirt into noise?
>   Ask the mole, he knows.
> I feel the slime of a wet nest.
>   Beware Mother Mildew.
> Nibble again, fish nerves.

And having got back to the moment of inception, the poet begins to travel forward. Section three, 'The Gibber', is about the fearful awareness of isolation that comes with the poet's dawning sexuality:

> Dogs of the groin
> Barked and howled.
> The sun was against me,
> The moon would not have me.

The boy feels hostility to his father (the sun) but cannot return to the incestuous satisfaction of the womb. And from fear of his father grows a sense of guilt that is present in the onanistic preoccupations of this lyric:

> What gliding shape
> Beckoned through halls,
> Stood poised on the stair,
> Fell dreamily down?
> From the mouths of jugs
> Perched on many shelves,
> I saw substance flowing
> That cold morning.
> Like a slither of eels
> That watery cheek
> As my own tongue kissed my cheeks awake.

But the lyric is a way of putting things, but not very satisfactorily; and following immediately from its sentimental evocation of the adolescent's dream-woman is a grosser evaluation of such sexuality:

> I have married my hands to perpetual agitation
> I run, I run, to the whistle of money.
>   Money, money, money
>   Water, water, water

Up to this point 'The Lost Son' is magnificent. It is difficult, certainly, but not unjustifiably so, and Roethke has a sure control over his material. At great pain, I would think, he has managed to create a meaningful poem of terrific honesty and intelligent self-exploration. But the section ends with the weakest lines in the poem. Roethke himself spoke of these lines as '"rant" almost in the manner of the Elizabethans'. If this is so, he must have had very minor Elizabethans in mind, for the lines are not only literary, they are extremely inept:

> These sweeps of light undo me.
> Look, look, the ditch is running white!
> I've more veins than a tree.
> Kiss me, ashes, I'm falling through a dark swirl.

The interesting question is, why should these lines be so bad? In terms of the movement of the section, disgust at sex has here reached a point where the poet breaks down completely. He does not manage to cope with his sense of guilt at discovered sexuality, instead it overwhelms him. But this is not dwelt on: the 'rant' is so perfunctory and weakly written that it suggests Roethke couldn't bear to acknowledge the reason for the breakdown, or even that it had occurred. We have, then, to look to the fourth section to see what develops from this breakdown. For up to this point the poet has been trying to break through to the acceptance of his sexuality which will allow him to shake off the dread of his father's ghost. But when we turn to the fourth section, 'The Return', we find that the problem of acceptance has been shelved. True, the section is about the attainment of a new calm and sanity, but this comes about not because of a breakthrough but from a turning away. In fact, at this point the poem ceases to move forward and turns back on itself, no matter how the structure and general intention suggest the opposite. The serenity of this section springs from the poet's retreat from his problems back to childhood. The setting is the greenhouse where the young boy has spent the night and to which his father comes in the morning light; and if there is acceptance of the father, it is because the poet has slipped back to an innocence that predates whatever guilt starts up with the cry of the dead:

> A fine haze moved off the leaves;
> Frost melted on the far panes;
> The rose, the chrysanthemum turned toward the light.
> Even the hushed forms, the bent yellowy weeds
> Moved in a slow up-sway.

The title of this section is unintendedly suggestive, I think. Roethke clearly means 'The Return' to suggest a return to sanity, to identity; but it *feels* as though what has happened is a return to that womb from which he had insisted on the need to escape.

I am certain that Roethke knew, no matter how obscurely, what was happening to this poem. In the fifth and final section, 'It Was Beginning Winter', he tries to disguise its reversal of direction by offering new—and unjustified—grounds for the breakthrough he has claimed in the fourth section. The clue is contained in such lines as:

> Was it light?
> Was it light within?
> Was it light within light?

The echoes of Eliot are not accidental. In this section Roethke tacitly suggests that the youth's new mental health is due to an accession of spiritual grace. But if this is so, the first three sections become pointless, since they have been concerned with a psychological process. For the poet to make his earthly father suddenly melt into a heavenly one is plainly cheating. Roethke destroys the integrity of his own poem, I think, because in spite of recognising the need to move forward, he cannot finally come to terms with his own sexuality. It is impossible to know why this should be, but I suggest that it is closely connected with that terror of dissolution that came regularly to him, as so many of his poems reveal. The fear of breaking away from his parents into adult freedom—which would include the freedom to give himself to another person—involved too great a threat to selfhood. In a fine lyric, 'My Papa's Waltz', he writes of the guilt, terror and love he felt for his father, and his sense of how he depended, (in more than one sense) on him: 'But I hung on like death'. The use of the cliché is exactly judged.

Now he says:

> A lively understandable spirit
> Once entertained you.
> It will come again.
> Be still.
> Wait.

The echoes of 'Ash-Wednesday' take on even more point if we remember the cry at the end of Eliot's poem:

> Suffer me not to be separated.

In the poems that make up the remainder of the volume there is a fundamental evasiveness. 'The Long Alley' and 'A Field of Light' have fine moments, but they lack a genuine coherence, and in reading them you have a persistent feeling that they come to something without knowing why—the something being, of course, a new calmness of spirit. I also think that Roethke begins to use the technical innovations of 'The Lost Son' as a way of blinding himself, and perhaps the reader, to his own evasions. There is a sense that vast battles are being fought and won; but in the end little seems actually to have taken place.

This charge must extend to his next volume. The poems of *Praise to the End* at first sight seem disturbingly honest in their apparent willingness to pursue the truth. Indeed they do pursue it up to a point—which is always the same one, of onanistic guilt, connected with father fear. Then come the familiar hiatus and the assertion of new maturity. For this reason, I find the quasi-therapeutic nature of these confessional poems pretentious in a quite literal sense. They offer much more than they achieve. They are also extremely repetitive in structure and linguistic means, both of themselves and of the poems of the final section of *The Lost Son*, and although they customarily receive high praise, they seem to me near failures as works of art. For one thing, they rely far too heavily on Jung and Freud. (Carolyn Kizer's statement that when Roethke wrote these poems he had read neither strikes me as incredible.) For another, they are a bit like cyphers. Once you have puzzled out their meanings there seems little else to do with them. I am not much tempted to re-read the volume.

Most of the language of *Praise to the End* is impenetrably private. A former pupil of Roethke's has said that the line 'a black scow bumping over rocks' represents the unborn child's impression of its mother's heartbeats. I do not see how we can be expected to guess this. In addition, there are many reminiscences of Dylan Thomas; a typical instance is:

> Later I did and danced in the simple wood

Nor is this just a matter of diction. Dylan Thomas is very important to Roethke's volume, in terms of subject—the opening section of 'The Shape of the Fire' presumably owes something to 'If My Head Hurt a Hair's Foot'—and as a more general influence. Much of Thomas's work struggles with the pain of adult sexuality and the irrecoverable joys of childhood, and this is precisely the territory of *Praise to the End*. But as in 'The Lost Son', Roethke never manages to break through, and although he does intermittently understand this, I think—particularly in the title-poem—it is hardly satisfactory, because it undermines his intention. For the poems of *Praise to the End* form a sequence, much in the manner of the previous volume. Nearly all of them drive back to the earliest memories and sensations, but they move progressively nearer to maturity, or towards that moment which forms for Roethke the barrier to maturity. It would be tedious to examine the poems in detail, but it is fair to state their individual concerns. The first poem, 'Where Knock Is Open Wide', (the title is from Smart's *Song of David*) is about childhood and the attempt to return to the sexual innocence of childhood:

> I'll be a bite. You be a wink.
> Sing the snake to sleep.

The next poem moves towards pubescent sexual awakening:

> Who's ready for pink and frisk?
> My hoe eats like a goat.

This theme becomes more urgent in 'Bring the Day', with its sense of childhood's radiance fading into the light of common day:

> Hardly any old angels are around me any more.

The youth's senses are now alert to the rank fertility of nature; as he puts it, 'the herrings are awake' (cf. Thomas's 'All the herrings smelling in the sea'). From there we move obviously enough to the theme of 'Give Way, Ye Gates':

> Believe me, knot of gristle, I bleed like a tree;
> I dream of nothing but boards;
> I could love a duck.

But in face of the desire for sexual fulfilment the poem acknowledges the intrusion of fears about the taint of sex:

> I hear the clap of an old wind.

In the next poem, 'Sensibility! Oh La!' we find that the breakthrough has not occurred.

> My sweetheart still in her cave

he laments, echoing the *Visions of the Daughters of Albion*, which he will use again later. The reason given for this failure is, as we might expect, his inability to break away from his parents.

> 'There's a ghost loose in the long grass'

he says, with obvious reference to his father, and 'The moon abides'. And the first part of *Praise to the End* closes with 'O Lull Me, Lull Me', in which the poet confesses:

> I'm still waiting for a foot.

The second part opens with 'Praise to the End' itself, whose title comes from *The Prelude*. This part of the volume is meant, I think, to carry the poet through to a new wholeness (otherwise, why the division of parts and the reference back to Wordsworth's 'thanks to the means which Nature designed to employ'?). But it does not. The title poem is passionately aware of the father's dominance in its feeling of guilt at onanistic sex:

> Father, forgive my hands.

And although the final section claims that the poet is 'awake all over', this is bound to seem an empty assertion. If there is a new sense of identity with nature it does not go with any psychological growth; it has merely happened:

> I believe! I believe!
> In the sparrow, happy on gravel;
> In the winter-wasp, pulsing its wings in the sunlight.

But the lines suggest more insistence than real belief, and indeed the tone of these poems frequently contradicts the ostensible meaning. In the next poem, 'Unfold! Unfold!' the poet announces a rejection of his regressive tendencies:

> I can't crawl back through these veins,
> I ache for another choice.

Yet this must be set against a passage which speaks with great relief of a return to infancy:

> I was pure as a worm on a leaf; I cherished the mold's children.
> Beetles sweetened my breath.
> I slept like an insect.

The relief also shows, though for a rather different reason, in the next poem 'I Cry Love! Love!', its title taken from the *Vision of the Daughters of Albion*. This strives to 'proclaim a condition of joy', but there is little in the poem itself to justify it, and what there is springs from a deferment of experience rather than an engagement with it:

> Feet run over the simple stones,
> There's time enough.
> Behold, in the lout's eye,
> Love.

time enough is what brings relief.

The sequence concludes with a poem that was first published in *The Waking*, 'O, Thou Opening, Thou', which ends:

> Going is knowing.
> I see; I seek;
> I'm near

(For the very complex history of the ordering of the sequence see the note at the end of this essay.)[1] The assertion sounds uncomfortably familiar, but this time it turns out to be true; for in *The Waking* the breakthrough actually occurs. Its possibility may be seen in a poem called 'The Visitant'. This poem is in three short parts. In the first of these the poet identifies himself with nature:

> Dearest tree, I said, may I rest here?
> A ripple made a soft reply.

In the second part his visitant, a girl, comes towards him:

> she came
> The wind in her hair,
> The moon beginning.

In part three we find that the experience she offers has been refused. That is certainly familiar enough, but what is new is the sense of real desolation that follows on the poet's recognition that he can't escape back to being pure as a worm; he is now clearly aware that loneliness stems from his refusal to journey towards another person:

> Where's she now, I kept saying,
> Where's she now, the mountain's downy girl?

> But the bright day had no answer.
> A wind stirred in a web of appleworms;
> The tree, the close willow, swayed.

It is a great relief to come on this poem after reading through *Praise to the End*, not only because it abandons the tricksiness of that volume, but because you feel that Roethke has stumbled on clear statement in discovering the true nature of his problem. By facing it, he learns to cope with it, to break through to the outside world. *The Waking* is aptly titled. It contains, moreover, two of his most beautiful poems, 'Elegy for Jane' and 'An Old Lady's Winter Words'. Both of these poems face up to the anguish of life, and yet both are celebrations beyond anything he had managed in *Praise to the End*. Roethke lets the lady speak her own winter words, and I take it this is an important tactic for him; he abandons the constrictions of selfhood in an act of sympathetic understanding. By getting inside the skin of an old lady who is on the edge of death, he explores the worst that he can know: knowing is going. 'Elegy for Jane' is a love poem. It celebrates the girl's power to wake the ends of life for the poet, and although it has slightly arch moments—Roethke is not used to addressing people—it is a wonderful success because of the vitality of its celebration. It does not declare or cry belief. That declares itself in the redeeming accuracy of eye and ear, the given awareness of 'the moss wound with the last light', and of 'the bleached valleys under the rose'. Stephen Spender has said that to read Roethke's poems is to wonder a good deal about him, and although I am in no position to know how closely woven Roethke's life and art were, it is impossible not to feel that all his poems testify to his own condition. 'Elegy for Jane' represents a decisive moment of development. Certainly you would not expect to find the poem occurring in any of the earlier volumes. Nor would you expect to find 'Four for Sir John Davies'.

This poem focuses on sexual love, and it enquires into the possible consequences of involvement with another person. In 'Elegy for Jane' the poet can keep a certain distance from his subject because the girl is dead, and because, as he himself says, he is 'Neither father nor lover'. But 'Four for Sir John Davies' is about himself, and for this reason is less unquestioning in its celebration of the way love wakes the individual to full life and creates harmony between the microcosm and macrocosm. I say this, recognising that the poem is customarily seen as one of unhesitating celebration. I do not believe it is, because reading his work I cannot think that Roethke ever managed to stamp out the fear of involvement which he saw that love demanded. Temporarily, yes, and he has his poems of praise; but they do not define his position any more surely than poems of disgust. 'Four for Sir John Davies' is a better poem if we admit its hesitancies and doubts; significantly, its worst section is one of insistent celebration. Also significantly, the poem is full of questioning. In his admirable essay on Roethke, John Wain has said that these questions all expect the answer Yes. I am not so sure. For instance, the second poem, 'The Partner' begins:

> Between such animal and human heat
> I find myself perplexed. What is desire?
> The impulse to make someone else complete?
> That woman would set sodden straw on fire.
> Was I the servant of a sovereign wish,
> Or ladle rattling in an empty dish?

It ends:

> Things loll and loiter. Who condones the lost?
> This joy outleaps the dog. Who cares? Who cares?
> I gave her kisses back, and woke a ghost.
> O what lewd music crept into our ears!
> The body and the soul know how to play
> In that dark world where gods have lost their way.

The questions of the first stanza are not so much answered as set aside by the power of sexual appeal—'That woman would set sodden straw on fire.' And if it is said that that is the answer, the fact remains that the concluding lines are decidedly ambiguous. The image of the ladle is, after all, one of distaste, and even being the servant of a sovereign wish may not be so fine as it sounds. There is an uncomfortable if distant echo of Shakespeare's Sonnet 57, and a decidedly close echo of Yeats' mocking celebration of the

> serving man, who could divine
> That most respected lady's every wish.

If both questions of the last two lines of that stanza expect the answer yes, I would not think that they showed Roethke's easy acceptance of love. The other stanza quoted is equally hesitant.

The ghost that's woken by his kiss is surely his father, which is hardly reassuring, and the lewd music that accompanies the man and woman's play in the dark world could be either the frank happiness of sexual love, or the Comus-like rout that breeds disgust. The stanza seems to me fine just because it manages to include both possibilities. It would be less honest if it didn't.

The third poem, 'The Wraith', is more positive. It is also less honest. Roethke suggests that the climax of physical love creates a new dimension of life, but the language is far from convincing.

> We rose towards the moon and saw no more

is surely disastrously close to comic cliché; at the very best, it falls a long way short of the aphoristic finality of 'they read no more that day'. And far from the insight into new life feeling authentic, it is very certainly borrowed:

> When glory failed, we danced upon a pin.
> The valley rocked beneath the granite hill;
> Our souls looked forth, and the great day stood still.

The quotation from Donne gives the game away. The apparent confidence of the lines is not Roethke's at all.

The fourth poem, 'The Vigil', uses sexual puns to point the poet's uncertainties, although it ends with what I suppose is meant for triumphant affirmation:

> The world is for the living. Who are they?
> We dared the dark to reach the white and warm.
> She was the wind when wind was in my way;
> Alive at noon, I perished in her form.
> Who rise from flesh to spirit know the fall:
> The word outleaps the world, and light it all.

I take the first line to mean that the living (lovers?) create their own world, or animate an otherwise dead universe. But there is no certainty that the poet has accomplished this act of creation; 'perishing', with its pun on the little death, may mean that the poet has died out of his old limited self into new life (alive at noon), or that he has destroyed his identity through involvement with his

Beatrice (Roethke compares himself and the woman to Dante and Beatrice). Knowledge of the fall may come from transcending it or from descent into it. (In a later poem Roethke speaks of falling back from love into the world of men.) The last line seems to me merely a rhetorical gesture, an attempt to blot out the complications the poem has concerned itself with: the flesh is made word and banishes the dark world in which gods have lost their way. But the previous stanza has ended with the confession that:

> We danced to shining; mocked before the black
> And shapeless night that made no answer back.

I have wanted to correct what I think is a common misunderstanding about 'Four for Sir John Davies' because to see the poem aright makes it a finer achievement and also explains the love poems of Roethke's next volume. In 1953 the poet married Beatrice O'Connell, and as Carolyn Kizer has said, there followed a five-year honeymoon, resulting in the wonderful love poems of *Words for the Wind*. In these poems of praise, the cadence 'taken from a man named Yeats' shows itself most unmistakably and, I would say, justifiably. Because although the debt can become burdensome, as Roethke's borrowings so often do, I don't find his own voice inhibited; at least, not often, though there are occasions when the cadence is too derivative, as in 'The Pure Fury':

> Dream of a woman and a dream of death.

This is pointless, a mere habit of mind that also shows itself in the semi-quotation from Webster in 'I Knew a Woman'. But we can admit the occasional failure and still accept the fact that Yeats allows Roethke to find his own voice. It may be against all the rules, but it works, finely in 'The Dream', but most in 'Words for the Wind'. It would be quite wrong to think of this poem as merely a lyric celebration of love. It is that, but it is much more besides. As with 'Elegy for Jane' it declares belief through the amazing resourcefulness of technique and vision that give authority to its assertion that all who embrace, believe. It establishes the harmony of correspondences that 'Four for Sir John Davies' had queried:

> The sun declares the earth;
> The stones leap in the stream

It is so astonishingly alive in its responsiveness that you readily forgive the few moments of strain (they are mostly lapses of language). Certainly, if you have read steadily forward through Roethke's work it is extremely moving to come on the measured gratitude of the final lines:

> [I] see and suffer myself
> In another being, at last.

Yet, it did not last. As 'Four for Sir John Davies' suggests, Roethke could not always avoid the possibility that love involved self-destruction, that the lover was merely the ladle rattling in an empty dish. In a poem called 'The Beast' the poet refuses the chance to see and suffer himself in another being. The poem ends in the same isolation that he had confessed to in 'The Visitant':

> The long lush grass lay still;
> And I wept there, alone.

Why? The answer, I think, is to be found in a powerful poem, 'The Sensualists'. This is about disgust at sexual involvement and the fearful recognition that a living woman cannot be Dante's Beatrice, that a dream of woman is better than the real thing. ('The Sensualists' has striking affinities with Robert Graves' 'Succubus'.)

> there beside
> The gin and cigarettes,
> A woman stood, pure as a bride,
> Affrighted from her wits,
> And breathing hard, as that man rode
> Between those lovely tits.

For some inexplicable reason Denis Donoghue calls this a great love poem. He must have some very odd ideas about love. 'The Sensualists' is, however, an honest poem because it is a look at the worst, and I wish to contrast it with 'The Pure Fury', since it was this latter poem that Roethke called 'a sign of spiritual health, a willingness to take a look—if not Hardy's 'full look'—at the worst.'

'The Pure Fury' is an attempt to explain the attitude of 'The Sensualists'; it argues a philosophical position about the need for isolation in terms of being and nonbeing. I find it a fundamentally dishonest poem:

> How terrible the need for solitude:
> That appetite for life so ravenous
> A man's a beast prowling in his own house,
> A beast with fangs, and out for his own blood
> Until he finds the thing he almost was
> When the pure fury first raged in his head
> And trees came closer with a denser shade.

This third stanza is badly confused. It is difficult to see how a need for solitude can be an appetite for life (cliché that it is), and it is tempting to read 'That appetite for life's so ravenous', which would oppose sex and solitude. But it is probably more correct to say that Roethke is trying to persuade himself that solitude is life; the way out is the way back. The thing he almost was is, I take it, an achieved human being who has been destroyed by the fury of sexual involvement which has blotted out the light. In the next and last stanza he asks:

> When will that creature give me back my breath?

and hopes to look at 'a brighter sun'. The idea is nonsense.

This breakdown in meaning happens because, as always, Roethke finds it difficult to acknowledge that the real problem for him is his fear of sexual involvement. As Malkoff has shown, the second stanza of 'The Pure Fury' is derived from Tillich. It seems to me fatally dependent on him. In *The Courage to Be*, Tillich wrote:

> Nonbeing is one of the most difficult and most discussed concepts. Parmenides tried to remove it as a concept. But to do so he had to sacrifice life ... Plato used the concept of nonbeing because without it the contrast of existence with the pure essences is beyond understanding. It is implied in Aristotle's distinction between matter and form ... Jacob Boehme ... made the classical statement that all things are rooted in a Yes and a No.

Roethke wrote:

> The pure admire the pure and live alone.
> I love a woman with an empty face.
> Parmenides put Nothingness in place;
> She tries to think, and it flies loose again.
> How slow the changes of a golden mean:
> Great Boehme rooted all in Yes and No;
> At times my darling squeaks in pure Plato.

It is a bad imitation of a famous stanza of 'Among School Children'; and it doesn't really make sense. Malkoff suggests that Roethke is saying he sees his darling not only as body (presumably her empty face is meant to suggest that her body thinks, but the phrase is weak), but also as spirit 'capable of the Platonic "squeak" of undying essences'. I do not see why essences are supposed to squeak and the image, grotesque as it is, makes sense only if we suppose the woman is a kind of vampire-bat who threatens his existence. But hardly because of thought, as he pretends—the fear of nothingness flying loose when she thinks—but because of her body. Even with Tillich's sentences to guide us, we cannot really understand the stanza, and without them it is impenetrable. Roethke has confused his poem by trying to argue a metaphysical case in terms of being and nonbeing. What he does not admit to is what 'The Sensualists' reveals: that a psychological problem is at the root of his difficulties in accepting involvement with another person (though at the beginning of the last stanza he does admit that dream of a woman is a dream of death).

It is important we grasp this because I think that much of Roethke's failure as a poet lies in his misunderstanding or misinterpretation of his difficulties. He is neither a metaphysical nor a philosophical poet, although these roles have been claimed for him by Peter Levi and others. When he tries to construct a metaphysical argument from his psychological problems he becomes not only bad, but repetitive—many of his poems are an attempt to systematise or 'fix' mood. This point bears particularly on his posthumous volume, *The Far Field*. Here, moods are captured and held fast in a way that makes for a great deal of bad verse. Only two sections need concern us, the first and last. With the exception of two touching and graceful poems, 'Wish for a

Young Wife' and 'The Happy Three', the love poems of the second section are dull, and although the third section, 'Mixed Sequence', has its successes, they do not seem to me many or considerable.

The opening section, 'North American Sequence' is about death. The poems try to find a mode of accepting the dissolution of identity, the inevitable future extinction of self. There is one fine poem, 'Meditation at Oyster River', and the other poems in the sequence try to recapture its success by repeating its mood of calm resignation. The result is that they seem to be written to formula. As usual where Roethke is trying to convince himself, these poems are dressed in borrowed robes. Here, for example, is the last section of 'The Far Field':

> The lost self changes,
> Turning towards the sea,
> A sea-shape turning around—
> An old man with his feet before the fire,
> In robes of green, in garments of adieu.
> A man faced with his own immensity
> Wakes all the waves, all their loose wandering fire.
> The murmur of the absolute, the why
> Of being born fails on his naked ears.
> His spirit moves like monumental wind
> That gentles on a sunny blue plateau.
> He is the end of things, the final man.
>
> All finite things reveal infinitude:
> The mountain with its singular bright shade
> Like the blue shine on freshly frozen snow,
> The after-light upon ice-burdened pines;
> Odor of basswood on a mountain-slope,
> A scent beloved of bees;
> Silence of water above a sunken tree:
> The pure serene of memory in one man,—
> A ripple widening from a single stone
> Winding around the waters of the world.

I confess to finding this almost totally fake. Partly it is because of the blatant echoes of Stevens and Eliot, the sense I have that other poets are providing Roethke's insights and protecting him from his own. But there is also a real incongruity in combining Eliot and

Stevens as Roethke does. To follow the Gerontian note of the old man with his feet before the fire (exactly the sort of detail one does *not* want) by the Stevenish phrasings about robes of green (not the colour of adieu for Stevens, by the way, and I don't see what relevance the colour has to Roethke's poem) makes the lines look merely factitious. And if you pause to think about the old man with his feet before the fire turning towards the sea in his green robes they also become unintentionally comic. Besides, there are too many inert phrases, and Keats stole Coleridge's 'pure serene' so successfully as to make further borrowing impossible. And the line 'A scent beloved of bees' is absurdly literary in its wished-for resonances; it makes the speaker's resigned magnanimity of spirit seem about three hundred years old.

What is noticeable about this and other poems of 'North American Sequence' is that they do not rage against old age. Apparently, Roethke told Ralph Mills that he expected *The Far Field* would be his last book and unmistakably he is concerned to make a good end. That may sound disrespectful, but 'The Far Field', 'The Rose' and most of the other poems of the opening section seem very much projections of an 'image'. This is not true of 'Meditation at Oyster River', which with nearly total success authenticates a mood of reverie, of some longing for renewal and finally of acceptance of imminent death. Interestingly, at the end it returns to the image of 'The Premonition'; the poet's spirit is lost in the maze of water, but the rhythms stabilise this awareness:

> And the spirit runs, intermittently,
> In and out of the small waves,
> Runs with the intrepid shorebirds—
> How graceful the small before danger.
> In the first of the moon,
> All's a scattering,
> A shining.

Yet though 'Meditation at Oyster River' is a fine poem, there is no doubt that it is a minor one. The feeling is clear and thin; it is a poem from which the mire and blood have been drained away; and without being impertinent, it does seem to me that Roethke here is not only settling for death but settling into it. Acceptance is very nearly a matter of relief:

> No sound from the bay. No violence.
> Even the gulls quiet on the far rocks,
> Silent, in the deepening light,
> Their cat-mewing over,
> Their child-whimpering.

He is so obviously talking about himself there.

The poems of 'North American Sequence' open the volume, but I am reasonably certain that they must have been written after the 'Sequence, Sometimes Metaphysical'. For in the fourth section of *The Far Field* there is still an effort to cope with human involvement. But the poems are muddled; they are looking for a way out of the involvement, even if they don't recognise this. To put it brutally, the agony of suffering himself in another being has simply become too much for Roethke to bear. The two key poems of the section are 'In a Dark Time', probably the most widely praised poem he ever wrote, and 'The Marrow', also much admired.

'In a Dark Time' presents perhaps the easier problem. As I see it, either you believe what Roethke says or you don't, and I don't. It seems to me that so much in this poem has to be taken on trust that we need to have absolute faith in Roethke's honesty, and I am not sure he warrants it. He says:

> I know the purity of pure despair

and for all Stanley Kunitz's defence of the 'oracular abstraction' of the style I am not persuaded that anyone who felt such despair would put it quite that way. Nor would he be likely to go on to ask rhetorically:

> What's madness but nobility of soul
> At odds with circumstance?

Madness can, after all, be a good many other things. This is not to deny that the poem has impressive lines, nor is it to underrate the intensity of Roethke's personal anguish. It is, however, to argue that he has too readily converted his psychological difficulties into a rather book-worn language of mystic intuition. The language of

Dante and St. John of the Cross feels too easily adopted:

> And in broad day the midnight come again

and:

> Death of the self in a long, tearless night

and:

> Dark, dark my light, and darker my desire

and:

> The mind enters itself and God the mind
> And one is One, free in the tearing wind.

These and other lines read to me as the language of a poet who is determined to convince himself that he has shared an experience for which he produces little actual evidence., I accept the last line, 'And one is One, free in the tearing wind', because that honestly admits that the wind may destroy rather than cleanse and that freedom terrifies. At this point we come upon the familiar theme, which, as we have seen, is customarily expressed in terms of the terror of launching forward from the grip of the past. It would be crude to say 'In a Dark Time' repeats the confusion of 'The Lost Son', in substituting reconciliation with a heavenly father for an earthly one, but I do think that essentially the same problem and confusion undermine both poems.

'The Marrow' is a more difficult case. Donoghue calls it one of Roethke's greatest poems, but then Donoghue seems far less concerned with poetry than with God. At least, he appears to think that he can justify his judgement of a poem by saying what it is about; problems of tone, if they occur to him, certainly don't bother him. Neither do problems of interpretation. But this will be clearer if I quote the poem and then Donoghue's gloss:

> 1
> The wind from off the sea says nothing new.
> The mist above me sings with its small flies.

From a burnt pine the sharp speech of a crow
Tells me my drinking breeds a will to die.
What's the worst portion of this mortal life?
A pensive mistress and a yelping wife.

2

One white face shimmers brighter than the sun
When contemplation dazzles all I see;
One look too close can take my soul away.
Brooding on God I may become a man.
Pain wanders through my bones like a lost fire;
What burns me now? Desire, desire, desire.

3

Godhead above my God, are you there still?
To sleep is all my life. In sleep's half-death,
My body alters, altering the soul
That once could melt the dark with its small breath.
Lord, hear me out, and hear me out this day:
From me to Thee's a long and terrible way.

4

I was flung back from suffering and love
When light divided on a storm-tossed tree.
Yea, I have slain my will, and still I live;
I would be near; I shut my eyes to see;
I bleed my bones, their marrow to bestow
Upon that God who knows what I would know.

According to Donoghue:

the first stanza is all alienation—from nature and man and the self. The second is preparation for prayer, a relation with God as the light of light, source of the sun. The third is with the prayer itself to the Ground of All Beseeching. In the fourth and last stanza the loss of selfhood is associated with the break-up of light on a storm-tossed tree, the emaciation of the human will; and then the last gesture, voiding of the self, restitution, atonement.

I take it that the alienation from man to which Donoghue refers us is to be found in the last line of the first stanza. To me that line almost collapses the stanza; the tone drops from sardonic and tight-lipped control to comic self-pity. A paragraph after the one I have quoted, Donoghue tells us that Roethke writes about himself because he assumes that he is 'a representative instance, no more if no less'. How many men find a pensive mistress and a yelping wife the worst portion of their mortal lives? If the line is meant to suggest alienation from 'man' then it is absurd. But more probably it is the old disgust with sexual involvement that shows, and it may link up with the last line of the second stanza and the first line of the fourth. I am far from sure about this, however, because the language is hardly enough in control for us to know. All we can be certain of is that in the second stanza Roethke makes some connection between God and desire, but I do not understand whether this is because he desires God, or thinks that sexual desire blocks his way to God. The ambiguity is less than fruitful—he can't really have it both ways—and I find it difficult to rid myself of the suspicion that the stanza is carelessly written (a suspicion strengthened by the reversal of rhyme scheme, which seems done for mere convenience). Why Donoghue should think he has satisfactorily accounted for the stanza is beyond me.

The problems become more extreme in the final stanza. If Donoghue is right, the poet is to be seen as approving his being flung back from suffering and love and slaying his will, since these presumably are connected with selfhood. Malkoff, on the other hand, argues that 'gathering together his waning powers [the poet] envisions himself as a tree struck by lightning, by all the love and suffering involved in human existence'. That is clearly wrong in so far as '*from* suffering and love' can hardly mean '*by* suffering and love'. But Malkoff's reading is none the less more probable, since it is characteristic of Roethke to feel afflicted by suffering and love (love is suffering), and that would make sense of the pain of desire that burns him. Moreover, if we take up the clue offered us in the last line of the third stanza we can perhaps say that the poet finds the way to God long and terrible because he is flung back by his being human. (If Donoghue is right, we have somehow to convert 'was flung' into an active verb, or 'have slain' into a passive one). The confusion arises because Roethke also wants to suggest that suffering and love go with the desire for God. No doubt they do, but such suffering and love have nothing to do with the pain of *human* desire, which in the poem is focused on a pensive mistress and a yelping wife which breeds self-disgust. On the one hand, he cannot bear the involvement; on the other, he feels it is what he is seeking in God. 'The Marrow', that is, is a confused poem for precisely the reason we might expect, that Roethke has tried to see a pyschological problem in metaphysical terms.

No account of Roethke that pretends to adequacy can avoid discussing 'In a Dark Time' and 'The Marrow', but equally, I believe, no discussion can avoid the fact that they suggest a turning away from that look at the worst he believed he had taken in 'The Pure Fury'. The very ease with which he grasps at the possibility of mystical intuition is a clue to this. Only very rarely did he break through to the severest self-knowledge. But this is not to belittle his accomplishment. It does no good to overpraise Roethke if only because that leads to an unfair reaction against his work. But whatever we can say against him, the fact is that at his best he is a wonderful and original poet, who has produced some of the most distinguished work to have come out of America since the second world war.

Notes

1. M.L. Rosenthal, *The New Poets: American and British Poetry Since World War II* (New York: Oxford University Press 1965).
2. *Five Poets of the Pacific Northwest: Poems by Hanson, Hugo, Kizer, Stafford and Wagoner*, ed. Robin Skelton (Seattle, WA: University of Washington Press 1964).
3. When *The Lost Son* was originally published, the poems appeared in the order in which I discuss them here. However, when Roethke brought out *Praise to the End*, he began the second part with 'The Lost Son', 'The Long Alley', 'A Field of Light' and 'The Shape of the Fire'. This order was retained in the volume *Words for the Wind*, where the fifth section of 'The Lost Son' received a title. The sequence then ended with 'O, Thou Opening, O', which had been published in *The Waking*. In the *Collected Poems of Theodore Roethke* (New York: Doubleday, 1965), which is the text I have used, the poems are returned to their original positions.
   The poetry of Roethke is also available in a Faber edition, *Collected Poems* (London: 1968).

4

Arriving at Acceptance: Randall Jarrell

Robert Lowell famously remarked that 'Eulogy was the glory' of Randall Jarell's criticism, and it is so. Yet he is equally remarkable for his way with absolutely telling quotation and with the remarks that precede or follow it. It means that his critical judgements feel unerring and final. This is the more remarkable when you realise that most of his criticism is about contemporary writing. You have only to think of the standard names of English literary criticism of this century—of, shall we say, F.R. Leavis, Kenneth Burke, T.S. Eliot, I.A. Richards, R.P. Blackmur, Yvor Winters, William Empson—to realise the comparatively small amount of time they gave to writing about their contemporaries. As a receiver and literary journalist, Jarrell was constantly called upon to write about first books by unknown writers and new books by the famous. The wonder is how right he nearly always proved to be. It is almost impossible to catch him out. To be sure, there are individual statements with which we might want to quarrel, but they count for very little compared with the marvellous, swift and untroubled certainty of his critical judgements.

Jarrell was not bothered by reputations. When he reviewed E.E. Cummings's *Poems* 1924-1954, he said, among other things: 'What I like least about Cummings's poems is their pride in Cummings and their contempt for most other people; the difference between the *I* and *you* of the poems, and other people, is the poems' favourite subject.' We might all think that nowadays, but who else would have thought or dared to say it in 1954? Who else, a year later, would have said of Stephen Spender's *Collected Poems*:

When the muse first came to Mr. Spender he looked so sincere that her heart failed her, and she said: 'Ask anything and I will give it to you', and he said: 'Make me sincere.'

If you look at the world with parted lips and a pure heart, and will the good, won't that make a true and beautiful poem? One's heart tells one that it will; and one's heart is wrong.

There are countless other examples that one could give of the truthful clarity and wit that one loves and honours Jarrell for. It is impossible to imagine him being taken in by the fake or the tawdry. In 1945 he reviewed a collection of *Five Young American Poets*, one of whom was Tennessee Williams, and about him Jarrell wrote that Williams 'must be one of those hoaxes people make up to embarrass *Poetry* or *Angry Penguins*: no real person—no fictional one except Humpty Dumpty—would say about poets, "For others, I know, the Army has offered a haven." (That haven, Dachau).' Yet in the same review Jarrell remarked of Lowell's *Land of Unlikeness* that Lowell 'is a promising poet in this specific sense: some of the best poems of the next years ought to be written by him'. Ten years later he wrote of Elizabeth Bishop that 'the people of the future... will read her just as they will read Dickinson or Whitman or Stevens'.

Jarrell was not only invariably right, he was quite fearless. How else would he have dared to say of a collection of poems by William Carlos Williams that his 'limitations are neither technical nor moral but intellectual'? Or remark apropos of *The Age of Anxiety* that 'The man who, during the thirties, was one of the five or six best poets in the world has gradually turned into a rhetorical mill grinding away at the bottom of Limbo, into an automaton that keeps making little jokes, little plays on words, little rhetorical engines, as compulsively and unendingly and uneasily as a neurotic washes his hands'? Now, one might of course argue that *Scrutiny* said something very similar about Auden, or would have done if any of its contributors had possessed a shred of Jarrell's wit; but then no contributor to *Scrutiny* was capable of seeing and explaining why Auden had been one of the five or six best poets in the world, and none of them was able to speak with a proper generosity and understanding of *The Shield of Achilles*, where Jarrell could remark of Auden's technical mastery that when another poet confronts it, he 'is likely to feel, "Well back to my greeting cards."' And how impossible it is to imagine the Scrutineers—or anyone else for that matter—saying of Wallace

Stevens's *Collected Poems* that 'One might as well find fault with
the Evening Star as find fault with so much wit and grace and
intelligence'.

It is proper to bring in *Scrutiny* and the New Critics here
because they did, after all, promise to survey the field of
contemporary literature and pass judgement on what was fit for
human consumption. In fact, they managed comparatively little in
this respect, and their few judgements have not worn well. Jarrell,
on the other hand, did a great deal. He is a marvellous close critic,
quite at home in the world of the New Criticism, as anyone who
has read his analysis of Frost's 'Home Burial' will agree. (I take it
that Jarrell's championing of Frost was of great importance for
that poet's reputation, and who but Jarrell could have wanted to
preserve Frost from his admirers on the grounds that 'they like his
best poems almost as much as they like his worst'?) In a typically
mordant essay, 'Poets, Critics and Readers', he remarked that
'Unless you are one critic in a hundred thousand, the future will
quote you only as an example of the normal error of the past, what
everybody was foolish enough to believe then. Critics are
discarded like calendars'.

It is true, they are. But not Jarrell. And this is not merely a
matter of how well his judgements have worn. It also has to do
with that extraordinary wit, which allowed him to tell the truth in
the most unforgettable of ways, so that he could describe a book
by Oscar Williams as giving the impression 'of having been written
on a typewriter by a typewriter', or suggest that 'The people who
live in a Golden Age usually go around complaining how yellow
everything looks', or say of Matthew Arnold that, far from his age
missing out on great literature, he 'didn't know what he was
having'. Anyone who has read Jarrell will be in a position to supply
his own dozen or so favourites. Often they come in the form of
similes, for Jarrell was a master of the unexpected, truthful, simile.
Who, having read it, can ever forget his remark about how a
collection of critics would be unlikely to show any interest in
Wordsworth's views of his own poetry? 'In the same way, if a pig
wandered up to you during a bacon-judging contest, you would
say impatiently, "Go away, pig! What do you know about
bacon?"'

A wonderful critic, then. Yet he has his limitations, hateful
though it is to admit to the fact. What did Jarrell actually want of

literature? When you ask this question, you find that you come up with a very odd, old-fashioned answer: that he wanted it to be like or about 'life'. In *Poetry and the Age*[1] he has an account of Richard Wilbur's poem 'The Death of a Toad', in which he says of the opening lines that 'you stop to shudder at the raw being of the world... *that* toad is real, all right. But when you read on, you think with a surge of irritation and dismay, so it was all only an excuse for some Poetry.' Jarrell takes it for granted that poetry should possess imitative form (no wonder he was so caustically witty about Yvor Winters). In a review of Roy Campbell's *Selected Poems* he says that 'when I looked for the life in Campbell's poems all I could find was literature'. There are many other such moments scattered through Jarrell's critical writing, and as is perhaps inevitable, the word 'life' seems vaguer the more you look at it, or try to understand what he might mean by it—much as it does, of course, in *Scrutiny*, where writers are regularly commended for being 'on the side of life': but 'What is life?' as Shelley's poet cried. Perhaps the nearest one can come to understanding what Jarrell had in mind is by way of his disappointing essay, 'On Preparing to Read Kipling'. For there he quotes with absolute approval some words of William James's:

> The lunatic's visions of horror are all drawn from the material of daily fact. Our civilization is founded on the shambles, and each individual existence goes out in a lonely spasm of helpless agony. If you protest, my friend, wait till you arrive there yourself!

'A lonely spasm of helpless agony': the phrase is so Jarrell-like that it might almost have been written by him. In the same essay, trying to define what it was he thought Kipling lacked, he pointed to Turgenev and Chekhov and remarked that beside them Kipling reveals 'a lack of dispassionate moral understanding, perhaps... the ability both to understand things and to understand that there is nothing to do about them'. Such a statement might on the face of it seem grandly stoic, a rephrasing of Spinoza's granite-like pessimism; and yet reading Jarrell in bulk, his poetry as well as his criticism, you realise that he doesn't have the massive, assured calm of Spinoza. I don't doubt that Spinoza would have appealed to Jarrell, much as he appealed to Matthew Arnold; but in the end Jarrell is more like Arnold in that he accepts the eternal sadness of things and too swiftly arrives at the position of a helpless, wry dismissiveness about his world; he assents to being a sad heart at the supermarket. Indeed, there are occasions when Jarrell positively luxuriates in his melancholy, and this can infect even his best poems. The line between luxuriating and an energising verve is a difficult one to draw but is vital; sometimes Jarrell falls on one side, sometimes on the other. The fine, late poem 'Well Water' is a case in point:

> What a girl called 'the dailiness of life'
> (Adding an errand to your errand. Saying,
> 'Since you're up ...' Making you a means to
> A means to a means to) is well water
> Pumped from an old well at the bottom of the world.
> The pump you pump the water from is rusty
> And hard to move and absurd, a squirrel-wheel
> A sick squirrel turns slowly, through the sunny
> Inexorable hours. And yet sometimes
> The wheel turns of its own weight, the rusty
> Pump pumps over your sweating face the clear
> Water, cold, so cold! you cup your hands
> And gulp from them the dailiness of life.

It's a lovely and lovable poem. Yet as you register that typical Jarrell run-on line, 'the sunny/Inexorable hours', you feel that it's surely too much the planned surprise, too much in the nature of a wished-for Chekhovian irony. *Why* inexorable? (One way of answering that question is simply to recall the story of Jarrell and Lowell meeting and discussing contemporary English poets by whom they'd been impressed: Lowell said he liked Hughes, Gunn and Larkin: Jarrell replied that his favourites were Larkin, Larkin and Larkin.) Then you notice that for Jarrell it is inevitable that people are a 'means to'—that they should be caught up in ways that typically require them not so much to act as to be acted upon. It would be wrong to assume that this can claim kinship with Spinoza's laconic agreement to conspire with necessity. Jarrell's sense of people being the helpless agents of fate is a softer thing. He lacks what he beautifully identifies in the Psalms as the 'almost physiological dialectic of suffering, with its opposites struggling into a final reconciled, accepting ecstasy'. His sadness is more enervate, more to do with a compassion that only just avoids sentimentality.

That is why, I think, he was obsessed by the Second World War—and 'obsession' is not too strong a word. It comes out not only in the many poems he wrote about soldiers and airmen but also in his critical writing. For example, he has an unusually severe note on Marianne Moore's war poem 'In Distrust of Merits'—though it is typical of Jarrell that he should have been an early and acute admirer of her work—in which he says that she does not remember 'that most of the people in a war never fight for even a minute—though they bear for years and die forever. They do not fight, but only starve, only suffer, only die: the sum of all this passive misery is that great activity, War.' Also included in the present volume is an extraordinary eulogy for the war correspondent Ernie Pyle, where you sense such empathy between Jarrell and his subject that it is as though he is saying, 'I was the man, I suffered, I was there'. (Jarrell did not in fact get overseas during the war.) Thus he remarks that because of Pyle's despatches 'most people of a country *felt*, in the fullest moral and emotional sense, something that had never happened to them, that they could never have imagined without it—a war'. He adds that Pyle's writing, 'like his life, is a victory of the deepest moral feeling, of sympathy and understanding and affection, over circumstances as terrible as any men have created and endured'. It is impossible to avoid the feeling that at such moments Jarrell is projecting something deeply near the heart of himself into his account of the war correspondent. The result is that he succeeds in making Pyle sound like his version of Chekhov and Turgenev; more, he makes him sound like his own poetry. 'For Pyle, to the end, killing was murder: but he saw the murderers die themselves.' I do not see how you can read that sentence and not immediately think of Jarrell's own poem, 'Eighth Air Force':

> If, in an odd angle of the hutment,
> A puppy laps the water from a can
> Of flowers, and the drunk sergeant shaving
> Whistles O *Paradiso*!—shall I say that man
> Is not as men have said: a wolf to man?
>
> The other murderers troop in yawning:
> Three of them play Pitch, one sleeps, and one
> Lies counting missions, lies there sweating

Till even his heart beats: One; One; One.
O *murderers* ... Still, this is how it's done!
This is a war ...

The helpless agents of fate: it was a perception that could produce
marvellous poems, as in 'The Death of the Ball-Turret Gunner',
and a handful of others; but it may also help to explain why, in an
otherwise unaccountable lapse, Jarrell found nothing of worth in
the poetry of Isaac Rosenberg. For Rosenberg's best poetry has
precisely that sardonic quality which would make Jarrell acutely
uncomfortable. He would not be able to call it heartbreaking, one
of his most overused and most revealing terms of critical approval.
By comparison he found it easy to praise Owen because his poetry
'has shown to us one of those worlds which, after we have been
shown it, we call the real world'. Owen's world is, of course, one
above all 'pity', of the 'eternal reciprocity of tears'. It is guaranteed
to appeal to Jarrell.

In a fine moment in *A Room with a View*, E. M. Forster describes
Lucy Honeychurch playing the piano so that 'the sadness of the
incomplete' throbs through her phrases—'the sadness that is often
life but which should never be Art'. There is that in Jarrell which is
solidly in favour of the incomplete. Karl Shapiro was probably right
when he said that 'Jarrell is the one poet of my generation who
made an art out of American speech as it is, who advanced beyond
Frost in using not only a contemporary idiom ... but the actual
rhythm of our speech. Here Jarrell is unique and technically radical.
No other poet of our time has embalmed the common dialogue of
Americans with such mastery ... He listened like a novelist'. This is
true to the extent that Jarrell often uses the stumbling, cliché-
strewn inadequacies of speech to convey important truths about
the speakers of many of his poems. (It is notable that his warmest
praise for W. C. Williams was reserved for Book I of *Paterson*, and
that he singled out for special mention the passage about the two
girls gathering willow twigs, one of whom says to the other, 'ain't
they beautiful'. Jarrell comments, 'How could words show better
than these last three the touching half-success, half-failure of their
language?') The novelist in Jarrell is less importantly represented by
the strung-together jokes of *Pictures from an Institution* than by a
large number of poetic monologues.[2] But the trouble with these
monologues is that although different people may speak, they all

seem to be variations of one person, and that one person—whether it is in 'The Woman at the Washington Zoo' or 'The Lost Children'—has a sad heart which isn't necessarily the fault of the supermarket so much as of, well, *life*. And it is that, every bit as much as Jarrell's lack of concinnity, of the canorous, which prevents him from being a major poet, though he is certainly a very fine minor one.

Several of the essays in the present collection, *Kipling, Auden and Co.*, were first published in *A Sad Heart at the Supermarket*, and the justification for reprinting them here is that that book is out of print. Why not reprint all of them? I imagine the answer is that the English and American editions are different, so that to include all the essays from both versions would take an unwarrantable amount of space. But this is to point to the fact that the state of Jarrell's published criticism is in something of a muddle—as is the *Complete Poems* for that matter.[3] I hope that someday someone will straighten these muddles out: the whole of Jarrell ought to be made properly available. In the meantime, *Kipling, Auden and Co.* contains much of the best work of a critic who is essential reading for anyone wishing to take to heart the rhetorical questions he threw out to his fellow-critics: 'Criticism *does* exist, doesn't it, for the sake of the plays and stories and poems it criticises? ... Brothers, *do* we want to sound like the *Publications of the Modern Language Association*, only worse?'[4]

Notes

1. Randall Jarrell, *Poetry of the Age* (London: Faber 1973).
2. Jarrell, *Pictures from an Institution* (New York: Avon 1980).
3. Jarrell, *Complete Poems* (London: Faber 1981).
4. Jarrell, *Kipling, Auden and Co.: Essays and Reviews, 1935–1964* (Manchester: Carcanet Press 1981).

Part Two

SOME MODERNS

5
Meredith as Poet

When Oscar Wilde called Meredith a prose Browning, he was no doubt thinking of the novels, but his remark can be applied with equal justice to the poetry. For there is an undeniably prosaic quality about much of Meredith's large output of verse; it seems to have no inner compulsion or buoyancy, and above all it is unnatural. Anybody who sets himself the task of reading the collected poems is bound to come away from them recognising that Meridith too often forced himself into the role of poet, that only a very small amount of his poetry repays close attention, and that even his best poems are not entirely free from his characteristic vices. In an age of careful craftsmen Meredith stands out as extraordinarily slipshod, not so much by design as through indifference. It took considerable art to be as cavalier as Browning often chose to be; but where Browning is deliberately outrageous, Meredith is merely inept. Browning's experiments with metre have about them an air of swaggering abundance, but Meredith's are at best resolute (The galliambic measure he tries out in 'Phaeton' provides a good example of stiff determination).

His ear for rhythm is mostly dull and liable to be appalling. Indeed, more often than not he sticks doggedly to metre in a way that works well enough for the ballads, but which becomes obtrusively mechanical in the meditative poems. As for his handling of rhyme, he seems to have been deaf to, or unaware of, his customary badness. Characteristically, he makes use of intricate stanzaic and rhyming schemes, with the result that he has to fracture syntax in order to manipulate the rhyme words into position. (Much of Meredith's reputation for being a 'difficult' poet comes from his inability to handle rhyme without overtaxing his hold on sense.) The failure cannot be attributed to the impetuosity of youth or the fatigue of old age: at any point in his writing career, you can find verse made horridly turgid by his effort to manufacture such rhymes a cloud/endowed, burned/discerned, renewed/food, saith/death, fore/roar, hurled/world. And the inadequacy of these rhymes is made more marked by the distortions of syntax, intricacy of stanza-form in which they so frequently occur, and remorseless end-stopping of lines. In addition, Meredith's defective ear shows in cacophonous phrasing typified by the first line of 'Meditation under Stars':

> What links are ours with orbs that are.

Such flaws occur too often for us to disregard them. It is not that Meredith sometimes writes carelessly, but that he rarely writes well.

This extends to his handling of imagery. Much of it has a reach-me-down staleness, as where, in 'Meditation under Stars', he speaks of stars giving 'radiance as from a shield'. I think we can probably reconstruct how Meredith came to this phrase, and it reveals how derivative and literary his verse can be. I would guess that his first thought, of stars as flashing, led him to recall Wordsworth's great image of gleams like the flashings of a shield. But since he could not take over the whole phrase, he retained 'shield' and substituted 'radiance' for 'flashings'. The result is that all the surprise and precision of the original is lost and we are left with a phrase that is vague and dull. This is typical. Equally typical is the piling of one conventional or derivative image on another to the confusion of both—another reason for the 'difficult' reputation. For instance, Meredith addresses the Comic Spirit as one who

> darest probe
> Old institutions and establishments,
> Once fortresses against the floods of sin,
> For what their worth; and questioningly prod
> For why they stand upon a racing globe,
> Impeding blocks, less useful than the clod.
>
> (402)[1]

How do you prod a fortress? Do fortresses exist to turn back floods? What has happened to the floods? If the globe is racing, what do the blocks impede? Such imprecisions of thought and language are not bolstered by the rhetorical grandiloquence with its too obvious Miltonic echoes. Indeed, almost throughout the

'Ode to the Comic Spirit' Meredith reveals enough incompetence in the handling of language to make even the most sympathetic of readers wonder whether his poetry merits serious attention at all. I think it does, which is why I want to anticipate the likely objections. For the admirer of Meredith cannot pretend that there are not serious charges to be brought against him. The only valid way of rescuing him from neglect is to maintain a proper critical severity, which means virtually dismissing a vast amount of his poetry. But to do this fairly means that I must provide some critical examination of it, no matter how tedious and embarrasing this may turn out to be—doubly embarrassing, really, because I am well aware that the first part of this essay reads as though it is intended as an unremitting hatchet job, and that this comes rather oddly from a professed admirer. I can perhaps defend myself by saying that I think the task of clearing away dead growth is essential if we are to see the good poems plain, and that doing this will in the long run be better for Meredith's reputation—at least among readers who actually like poetry—than the sort of tactic employed by contributors to such magazines as *Victorian Poetry*, who assume that Meredith is unarguably a classic, that all of his poems are equally fine, and that the only relevant task for the critic-scholar is to unravel a poem's meanings, sources and variants. No: I think we have to be severe, and that we must resist the temptation to plead a special case.

Remorseless explication is a fate worse than death for Meredith, because it encourages the pretence that he is always and justifiably a 'difficult' poet. Yet his failures do not stem from his being an intellectual writer. The 'Ode to the Comic Spirit' may be an ambitious performance, but there are any number of modest ones whose flaws are disquieting. 'The Wisdom of Eld', for example, is a slight enough sonnet, and on the whole it is competently written. Even so, Meredith manages to speak of an old man who with 'tottering shank/Sidled'. In one poem he images France as a Maenad:

Ravishing as red wine in woman's form

(Are you supposed to drink it or take it to bed?) In another poem, 'The Sage Enamoured and the Honest Lady', image breeds image in an uncontrollable riot:

Though past the age where midway men are skilled
To scan their senses wriggling under plough,
When yet to the charmed seed of speech distilled
Their hearts are fallow

This is nothing like Browning's apparently similar habit of letting one image disclose another so that meaning progressively unfolds as you are led from image to image (stanzas 4–5 of 'By the Fireside' provide a good point of comparison). Indeed, it must be said that if Meredith is a prose Browning, Browning is much more than a poetic Meredith. Of course, Meredith's lines make a sort of sense; you can see what he means. But for all their show of wit and intelligence they will not bear the weight of close scrutiny. Under it, the images collapse into muddle.

Much of Meredith's failure to control language arises from his mistaken belief that he had a real ability in the handling of epithet, that his gifts naturally tended towards the epigrammatic. In fact, he is at his worst when reflective or sententious, and that perhaps explains why his ballads emerge as so much better than most of his poetry. In 'Phantasy' (his Dream of Fair Women), in 'Archduchess Anne', 'Jump to Glory Jane' and a handful of others, Meredith tells a tale, and he does so with welcome pace and directness. Indeed, what are inadequacies become advantages here, the obedience to metre speeding you over the poorer rhymes. With the exception of 'Archduchess Anne', which I shall have cause to mention again later, these ballads are sport poems, and they demonstrate a measure of the necessary virtuosity that elsewhere Meredith struggled to achieve. It is also to be found in the ballad monologues of 'Juggling Jerry', 'The Old Chartist', 'A Stave of Roving Tim', and 'Martin's Puzzle'. Yet although this group of poems deserves to be praised, I would say that to indicate their comparative ease of movement, consistency of language and deft handling of narrative is to say all that is necessary. They lack both the psychological insight and social attentiveness we find in the verse of such a minor figure as John Davidson, and taken as a whole, they feel curiously pointless. This is because Meredith seems to have written most of them to show off his powers as a virtuoso poet; and the fact is that he has demanded too little of himself in the poems for us to find the powers very remarkable.

This introduces an important point. Meredith, I am suggesting, wrote a great deal of poetry without really knowing what he wanted to do or say. In the last analysis it exists as an assertion of his right to be taken seriously as a poet, and no doubt for this reason it is so varied in genre, style and form. The poetry declares the poet. And yet for all the variety of this verse—and of all his contemporaries, only Browning and Hardy can match his wide choice and invention of forms—there is a very disturbing anonymity about much of Meredith's verse. No matter how various it may be, Browning's and Hardy's poetry is immediately recognisable as their own. But Meredith's is not; it does not seem to have been written by anyone in particular. To read Meredith in bulk is to become aware that he commonly lacked both a style and a subject.

Here, however, we come upon a highly problematic issue. Allowing that the poems I have so far mentioned were written in order to assert Meredith's claim to serious attention, we have to explain the presence of others for which the same excuse seems hardly applicable. After all, the poems I have spoken of can be regarded as occasional verse. Yet Meredith is also, perhaps more importantly, a didactic poet. And although we may say that the faults of a large proportion of his verse are due to his lacking a subject, it is difficult to see how this can be true of 'The Woods of Westermain', 'A Faith on Trial', 'The Test of Manhood' and many others. Even so, I do not think that the didactic poems provide any more proof of Meredith's talent than the occasional verse does, and, as with that verse, they seem to me to owe their existence to his desire for serious attention. Admittedly, this may seem little more than speculation; but we have somehow to explain the existence of a large body of didactic poetry that is plainly forced and for the most part bad, and it is at least possible that Meredith shared or hoped to capitalise on the common Victorian assumption that the poet with a philosophy to offer his audience was the poet who best deserved serious consideration. At all events, when his novels finally brought him to general fame, it was the didactic element in his poetry that was most earnestly attended to. It is no accident that what is still the best-known book on Meredith's poetry should have been written by someone who shared the assumption that the best poets are sages, nor that he should have called it *The Philosophy and Poetry of George Meredith*. As photographs and portraits of the later years sufficiently attest, the sage of Box Hill was born in the late 1880s.

Inevitably, his poems were prized for their 'message', and they
tended to be revered as a body of received truths.

  It is not difficult to see why at the end of the nineteenth century
Meredith became so significant as a didactic poet, nor why he
meant so much to young men of the Edwardian era. For Meredith
was a robustly anti-Victorian iconoclast. He was anti-religious,
anti-imperial—he hated war and the physical bullying of the
imperial ethos and spoke out against them in two sonnets,
'Warning' and 'Outside the Crowd'—and he championed the
private virtues of love and friendship, the emancipation of women
and the cause of sexual equality. True, he also insisted on the
supreme importance of duty and selflessness, but those positivistic
watchwords can stand many interpretations. Whatever difficulties
lay in the way of creating a consistent and understandable
philosophy out of the poetry, there can be hardly any doubt that
Meredith's appeal lay in what he said, not the way he said it. The
point may be made by reference to a late poem, 'With the
Persuader'. From our vantage point it looks almost distressingly
adolescent in its pagan sensuality:

> A single nymph it is, inclined to muse
> Before the leader foot shall dip in stream:
> One arm at curve along a rounded thigh;
> Her firm new breasts each pointing its own way;
> A knee half bent to shade its fellow shy,
> Where innocence, not nature, signals nay.
> The bud of fresh virginity awaits
> The wooer, and all roseate will she burst:
> She touches on the hour of happy mates;
> Still is she unaware she wakens thirst.

(533)

This is altogether too much like Leigh Hunt versifying Sir
Frederick Leighton. Yet it is obvious that Meredith's poems could
recommend themselves to a generation in studious revolt from
high-toned Victorianism. The attitudes of 'Love in the Valley' and
'With the Persuader' become ethical norms in *Where Angels Fear
to Tread*, *A Room with a View* and *The Longest Journey*; and
Forster also copies from Meredith the tactic of translating figures
from Greek mythology into a contemporary English setting. The
spirit of classicism defies the conquering spirit of the pale Galilean.

Verses on the delights of earthly love do not exhaust Meredith's stock of didactic poetry. He also writes about Nature and man's relationships with it; history and progress, and social morality. None of the didactic verse strikes me as any good, and the worst of it is appalling.

Meredith's didactic poems about social morality seem understandable in terms of his allegiance to altruistic thought in the latter half of the nineteenth century. In particular, we may feel that his 'placing' of sexuality is recognisably akin to the attitudes of George Eliot, Frederic Harrison and John Morley. Yet there is also reason to feel that his readiness to urge that the pleasures must not on the passions browse has a more personal, or at least obsessive, meaning than can be accounted for in terms of positivistic ideas. I would guess that he turned with relief to a dogma which stressed the need for transcendence of the flesh. The guess hardens towards a certainty when we consider a remarkable group of poems to be found in *Ballads and Poems of Tragic Life*, from which I would select 'Archduchess Anne', 'King Harald's Trance', 'The Young Princess', 'A Preaching from a Spanish Ballad' and 'The Nuptials of Attila'. Here we approach the core of Meredith's achievement as a poet. For his best work, I would submit, ranges itself round a single subject, the incommunicabilities, deceptions and violent treacheries of love. Given this subject, and with fewer natural endowments than any of his important contemporaries, he was still able to produce a handful of remarkable and perhaps unique poems. The tragedy is that they should be nearly hidden under the dead wood of his didactic and occasional verse. The great poem is, of course, 'Modern Love'. But before I turn to that I want to say a little about the others I have mentioned.

With the exception of 'The Nuptials of Attila', they are all ballads. All of them dramatise relationships through a series of acutely perceived moments, and in their different ways they all are concerned with the violent and uncontrollable emotions of outraged love. There are local failures, but what chiefly draws the attention is Meredith's ability to find the language he needs, itself proof of an unusual degree of engagement. The language of these poems is customarily bare, terse and rapid. It is intensely dramatic, and it makes striking use of similes: I think, for example, of Kraken's eyes like 'spikes of spar' ('Archduchess Anne'), of

Archduchess Anne's 'heart swung like a storm-bell tolled/Above a
town ablaze' and of this description of King Harald:

> Smell of brine his nostrils filled with might:
> Nostrils quickened eyelids, eyelids hand:
> 　　Hand for sword at right
> 　　Groped, the great haft spanned.
>
> Wonder struck to ice his people's eyes:
> Him they saw, the prone upon the bier,
> 　　Sheer from backbone rise,
> 　　Sword uplifting peer.
>
> Sitting did he breath against the blade,
> Standing kiss it for that proof of life:
> 　　Strode, as netters wade,
> 　　Straightway to his wife.
>
> 　　　　　　　　　　　　　　　　　　　　　　(284)

In each of these poems death is the outcome of love: it is the price
people pay for deep personal involvement. And if the involvement
is occasionally made to serve a social theme—as in 'A Preaching
from a Spanish Ballad', which is about male tyranny—it is more
frequently regarded with fear, almost horror. This is particularly
evident in 'The Nuptials of Attila'. The horror here is intensified,
and is perhaps betraying, because we are never allowed to know
why Attila died. We are told of his army's prescient fear for him,
since a woman 'holds him fast'. When soldiers break into his room
the morning after his nuptials, they find him dead and his wife
mad:

> Humped and grinning like a cat, teeth for lips

She destroys not only him but the army's male comradeship, its
unity: some want to kill her, others defend her:

> Death, who dares deny her guilt!
> Death, who says his blood she spilt
> . . . . . .
> She, the wild contention's cause,
> Combed her hair with quiet paws.

'The Nuptials of Attila' is a poem which centres on a fearful unknowableness about love and, in particular, sexual passion. At its heart is the mystery of Attila's death, and although this can be fitted to the theme of social duty—Attila shouldn't have slipped back into a private life—it will not explain the poem's urgency, its obsessive feeling for the horror of personal involvement. It is a strange and compelling poem, and a deeply disturbing one. This is partly because it seems to have come from something deep inside the poet that he hardly knew how to handle or control. A good deal of the detail is gratuitous and hints at Meredith's own uncertainty, his uneasiness as to what he was trying to write about. But the poem is also disturbing because it fends off all explanation; we simply do not know what went on inside that room. 'The Nuptials of Attila' is a statement, not an exploration; it turns its back on the mystery. For that reason its achievement is limited, though still real enough. But on a previous occasion Meredith had dared exploration, in the poem that is his one undoubted major triumph.

'Modern Love' comprises fifty sixteen-line sonnets (Meredith's own term), of which the first five and last two are spoken by a narrator, and the remainder by the husband with the narrator's occasional interpolations. The husband's sonnets are not all spoken in the first person; on one or two occasions he becomes a narrator himself, seeing himself from the outside, and the tactic, which is not overworked, allows for some brilliantly exploited ironies. Meredith's choice of form is extremely tactful. The sonnet is a definite enough structure to curb his impulse to sprawl as he does when he invents his own irregular metres; yet it is not so demanding as to force him into the weaknesses I have already pointed out. But the sonnet form is also a crucial and positive achievement. For Meredith has invented in the husband a person who has to be consistently realised and yet has to be shown in the process of the fluctuations, reversals and modifications of his relationship with his wife and with the Lady whom he takes up as a part retort to his wife's lover. The invented form is ideal for this. Each sonnet in 'Modern Love' presents a considered point of view, which the firm rhyme-scheme reinforces, and each is surprised and upset by subsequent sonnets. By dispensing with a concluding couplet, Meredith remains in control of his material while avoiding the sort of pat or epigrammatic finality which would turn his characters into mere puppets for his comic spirit. I make this point in order to note that we do 'Modern Love' a serious injustice if we try to see it as a thesis poem. In spite of its title, which feels better if we assume it to be the narrator's choice, 'Modern Love' is not trying to argue a case about the collapse of moral values in the post-Darwinian world. Nor is it a study of that egoism which later engaged Meredith's attention in his *Essay on Comedy*. There, Meredith envisaged comic art as presenting a moral pattern of retributive justice; sooner or later the egoist will come unstuck, and his sins of self-deception and ignorance will rebound upon his head. But there is no point in looking for a moral pattern in 'Modern Love'. Only the narrator comes near to finding one, and it is clear that his Manoa-like, pious inanities are not meant to provide the definitive judgement on what is a beautifully sane study of the flow and recoil in a personal relationship.

Yet although we are not to identify the narrator with Meredith, I realise that the opening sonnets may encourage us to do so. In them 'poetry' wins, and with predictable consequences. It would be only too easy to show that the first four sonnets are badly flawed. They are challengingly complex in image and phrase, they puzzle and perplex; but if we take up the challenge they seem to offer, we find ourselves unravelling cliché and inconsistency. There is not much point in trying to blame the narrator rather than Meredith for all these faults, not only because they are so characteristically Meredithian, but because they are irrelevant to the narrator's function. On the other hand, they should not obscure the fact that there are intended faults which do belong to the narrator. Of course, this only makes Meredith's lapses more irritating. But having said that, I would add that it is not worth making too much of these flaws, because after Sonnet IV they more or less disappear, and although we can find failures later on, their effect is minimal; pointing to the flaws of 'Modern Love' becomes an increasingly trivial exercise.

The opening sonnet introduces us to the man and woman:

> Upon their marriage tomb
> . . . .
> Each wishing for the sword that severs all

We are later to find that the narrator has, as is typical with him, put the matter far too bluntly; the couple also desire each other. But for the moment we stay with the narrator as he goes on to speak of the husband's jealousy and sympathetically identifies himself with what he assumes to be the husband's point of view. Indeed, we may note that the narrator is much more sympathetic to the husband than our own viewpoint allows us to be. In Sonnet II his feeling for the husband goes with a simplistic moralising about the wife:

> But, oh, the bitter taste her beauty had!
> He sickened as at breath of poison flowers

If this is true it is only partially so, and the husband sees as the narrator does only when he is acting a part of outraged innocence, as in Sonnet VII:

> Yea! filthiness of body is most vile,
> But faithlessness of heart I do hold worse.
> The former, it were not so great a curse
> To read on the steel-mirror of her smile.

Not the least of the successes of 'Modern Love' is its ability to catch the note of the literary moralism of Victorian England with its grandiose and unearned echoes of the Bible. 'Modern Love' exposes the cant which the husband tries out in these lines and from which the narrator never wavers. 'There is nothing personal in morality', Mr Pecksniff told his daughters. A good deal of the narrator's moral ardour depends on that impersonal language which the husband occasionally shares. At the heart of the achievement of 'Modern Love' is a near reversal of Pecksniff's remark. Its scrutiny of personalities leaves little time for moralising. It is just this scrutiny that the narrator avoids, as Sonnet IV makes evident. Here we are taken as far as possible from what may be called the human situation Meredith treats of:

> Cold as a mountain in its star-pitched tent,
> Stood high Philosophy, less friend than foe:
> Whom self-caged Passion, from its prison bars,
> Is always watching with a wondering hate.
> Not till the fire is dying in the grate,
> Look we for any kinship with the stars.

These lines provide one of the few instances in the opening sonnets where we can be certain that the badness is the narrator's alone. For it is not merely that the rhetoric is inept but that what follows makes the didacticism absurdly beside the point. Sonnet VI helps to show how. Here, the husband tries out various roles, of horror, grief, magnanimity, and in doing so he takes on the narrator's tone of voice. The sonnet rehearses most of the attitudes, bar love, that we are to find in the poem; and it introduces the dramatising dialectic of the husband–wife relationship:

> It chanced his lips did meet her forehead cool.
> She had no blush, but slanted down her eye.
> Shamed nature, then, confesses love can die:
> And most she punishes the tender fool
> Who will believe what honours her the most!
> Dead! is it dead? She has a pulse, and flow
> Of tears, the price of blood-drops, as I know,
> For whom the midnight sobs around Love's ghost,
> Since then I heard her, and so will sob on.
> The love is here; it has but changed its aim.
> O bitter barren woman! what's the name?
> The name, the name, the new name thou hast won?
> Behold me striking the world's coward stroke!
> That will I not do, though the sting is dire.
> —Beneath the surface this, while by the fire
> They sat, she laughing at a quiet joke.

Reading this, it is easy to see why Harley Granville-Barker thought Meredith would have made a great comic dramatist. The sonnet is about the husband's inner posturings, comically contained, as the structure shows, by casual domesticity. There can be no doubt of the debt to Browning; but it is justified. What we have in this sonnet is a variety of *dramatis personae*, as the husband seeks to discover a likely role for himself. In Sonnet II olympian detachment (3–5) yields to racked and forlorn love (6–9) and this gives way to anger (11–12) and finally to magnanimity (13–14). As for the last two lines, they neatly place the impressive absurdity of that invitation to 'Behold me'. It is the husband who beholds himself, as Sonnet IX cleverly shows:

> He felt the wild beast in him betweenwhiles
> So masterfully rude, that he would grieve

To see the helpless delicate thing receive
His guardianship through certain dark defiles.
Had he not teeth to rend, and hunger too?
But still he spared her. Once: 'Have you no fear?'
He said: 'twas dusk; she in his grasp; none near.
She laughed: 'No, surely; am I not with you?'

The effect of this transition to the third person is to make clear the husband's inability to acknowledge his own frustration. If only she *would* fear him. But what is he threatening: 'Had he not teeth to rend, and hunger too?' Judging by her laugh, No and Yes is the answer to that two-pronged question. It would be crude to say that this line is about thwarted sexuality alone; it is also about the impotence of the husband's own desires, which he partly, and perhaps unconsciously, conceals from himself by rhetorically violent language and the indirections of the third-person narrative. It is as though he sees himself as another person.

In Sonnet IX incommunicability reaches towards a final point. It shows something of that psychological acuteness that helps make 'Modern Love' so remarkable. It also testifies to the entire poem's integrity, since the sonnet cannot be lifted from context without losing most of its force. If we do not see it in its relationship to the sequence as a whole, we shall miss the point of the switch from first to third person, we shall settle for a simplistic reading, and in addition we may well take the sonnet as a 'key' to the poem. Indeed, most commentators make just this mistake: of pointing to one sonnet or group of sonnets as the centre of the poem's meaning. They do not realise that 'Modern Love' can have no centre; it is a ceaseless discovery of fluctuations; change is its only constant.[2] Yet although Meredith is fully alive to the comedy of this, the husband and wife are not formulated, sprawling on a pin. He has an interest in them which is very different from the narrator's and only open to him because he knows so much. In his case compassion depends on knowledge, whereas the narrator has merely the ignorant and complacent pity that goes with his dismissive attitude towards the woman and her lover: ('If he comes beneath a heel,/He shall be crushed until he cannot feel,/Or, being callous, haply till he can'. Sonn. III.) For this reason, Meredith's attentive rendering of the way the husband dramatises his roles has a justification that goes well beyond the comic—in the reductive

sense in which he himself came to define the word. The shift of
feeling and attitude between Sonnets XV and XVI show how.
Sonnet XV presents the husband as Othello ('The Poet's black
stage-lion of wronged love'), entering his wife's bedroom with
proof of her guilt:

>   'Sweet dove,
> Your sleep is pure. Nay, pardon: I disturb.
> I do not? good!' Her waking infant-stare
> Grows woman to the burden my hands bear:
> Her own handwriting to me when no curb
> Was left on Passion's tongue. She trembles through;
> A woman's tremble—the whole instrument:—
> I show another letter lately sent.
> The words are very like: the name is new.

So obvious an involvement with his melodramatic role reflects
oddly upon the husband's earlier vow of magnanimity; it also
implies not only a desire to push sympathy to the limits—he dares
the response of disgust—but a compulsive need to be hateful, as
self-protection against other feelings. These exist right enough, as
we discover in the next sonnet. It opens with a sentimental memory
of happiness:

> In our old shipwrecked days there was an hour,
> When in the firelight steadily aglow,
> Joined slackly, we beheld the red chasm grow
> Among the clicking coals. Our library-bower
> That eve was left to us: and hushed we sat
> As lovers to whom Time is whispering.

I would say that such sentimentality is the husband's tacit
admission of his inexcusable behaviour. It anticipates the reader's
contempt. 'Don't blame me. I used to be happy, she's made me
what I am'; this is the feeling that prods the lines into being. But we
recognise it only by seeing the two sonnets in their connection with
each other. The self-pitying sentimentality of Sonnet XVI is a
transparent attempt to ward off the self-disgust that Sonnet XV
caused, and the shift from one sonnet to the next enacts something
of the complexities and uncertainties of a relationship from which
love is not absent. I also think that the sonnets typify an effect that

'Modern Love' has, of disallowing a simple analysis or definition of any one moment or line; seen in the context of other phrases, lines and sonnets, self-pity masks self-disgust which hints at love and its opposite. In this poem nothing is certain, nothing simply true; it is no more or less valid to suggest that the husband hates himself for pretending that his wife has killed their love than it is to say that he loves her. Sonnet XV, for example, says that it's her fault; Sonnet XX says it's his:

> I am not of those miserable males
> Who sniff at vice and, daring not to snap,
> Do therefore hope for heaven
>
> . . . . . .
>
> I have just found a wanton-scented tress
> In an old desk, dusty for lack of use.
> Of days and nights it is demonstrative,
> That, like some aged star, gleams luridly.
> If for those times I must ask charity,
> Have I not any charity to give?

The sonnets contradict each other and in doing so testify to the poem's recognition that absolute terms of love and hate fail to make contact with what necessarily changes minute by minute and is never clearly one thing. The recognition is psychological and observational. The constant modulation of standpoint, together with subtle modifications of echo and prolepsis from sonnet to sonnet, makes 'Modern Love' one of the few Victorian poems to show a formal advantage over the achievements of the great nineteenth-century novel.

Indeed, Meredith deliberately challenges comparison with the novel. Sonnet XX introduced the Lady, and the next nineteen sonnets are mostly taken up with the husband's relationship with her. In Sonnet XXV this is seen in terms of a French novel: 'These things are life.' But they are also predictable, and one of Meredith's most brilliant strokes is to introduce so 'shocking' an idea as the foursome of husband–Lady, wife–lover, and then play off its predictable complications against the deeper and unpredictable muddle of the husband-and-wife relationship. To a large extent, the husband's affair with the Lady is a response to his wife's affair. As shown in Sonnet XXVII, on the one hand it is an attempt to forget:

Distraction is the panacea

On the other hand, as seen in Sonnet XXVIII, it is an attempt to
salve wounded pride:

> I must be flattered, the imperious
> Desire speaks out

But, *pace* Trevelyan and others, the affair is fully consummated. It
moves from 'the game of Sentiment' (Sonn. XXVIII) to sexual
involvement, a transition marked by the truly astonishing Sonnet
XXXIII:

> 'In Paris, at the Louvre, there have I seen
> The sumptuously-feathered angel pierce
> Prone Lucifer, descending. Looked he fierce,
> Showing the fight a fair one? Too serene!
> The young Pharsalians did not disarray
> Less willingly their locks of floating silk:
> That suckling mouth of his upon the milk
> Of heaven might still be feasting through the fray.
> Oh, Raphael! when men the Fiend do fight,
> The conquer not upon such easy terms.
> Half serpent in the struggle grow these worms.
> And does he grow half human, all is right.'
> This to my Lady in a distant spot,
> Upon the theme: *While mind is mastering clay*
> *Gross clay invades it.* If the spy you play,
> My wife, read this! Strange love talk, is it not?

In Sonnet II (9–10) we are drawn to notice the husband's apparent
struggle with conscience over those hungers of gross clay which
have so disturbingly invaded the language of the first eight lines.
Yet the sexual language is directed as much at the wife as at the
Lady; the trap in the last lines is so self-consciously aware of its
taunt. It is also an attempt to deny the dramatised guilt of Sonnet
XXIII:

> I know not how, but shuddering as I slept,
> I dreamed a banished angel to me crept

and to deny the torturings of lust in Sonnet XXIV:

> that nun-like look waylays
> My fancy. Oh! I do but wait a sign!
> Pluck out the eyes of pride! thy mouth to mine!
> Never, though I die thirsting. Go thy ways!

The lust is more easily identified than its object, however; she could
be Lady or wife. The idea may seem ridiculous or horrible, but then
this study of a human relationship acknowledges the existence of
both, as Sonnets XXXIV and XXXV make clear. In Sonnet
XXXIV we are led to understand that the wife has indeed played
the spy, and that the husband will brazen it out:

> Madam would speak with me. So, now it comes:
> The Deluge or else Fire! She's well; she thanks
> My husbandship

But neither deluge nor fire occurs, with the result that the husband
is cheated out of his planned performance. Insted, in Sonnet
XXXV, he is forced to recognise that:

> It is no vulgar nature I have wived

Sonnet XXXV is one of genuine compassion, but it invites the
simplification to which the husband retreats at the end, where he
speaks of 'this wedded lie!' Sympathy shades into self-justification.
Once he has spoken of the lie, he can return to the Lady. This is a
characteristic perception of the poem.

So is the language of Sonnet XXXIX, where the husband tries to
convince himself he is happy with what he's got. In Sonnet
XXXVIII he speaks of his relationship with the Lady in Platonic
terms, but the next sonnet makes plain what has actually happened:

> She yields: my Lady in her noblest mood
> Has yielded; she, my golden-crowned rose!
> The bridge of every sense! more sweet than those
> Who breathe the violet breath of maidenhood.

But the emphatic language we find here quickly gives way to the
doubts of Sonnet XL:

> Helplessly afloat,
> I know not what I do, whereto I strive.

In the next sonnet he returns to his wife, and pretends that for decency's sake he will forgo his deep love for the Lady:

> We two have taken up a lifeless vow
> To rob a living passion.

It is a typical piece of dramatization and self-deception. Sonnet XLII destroys the act. It opens with the husband following his wife to their bedroom. 'I am to follow her.' But nobody is making him go; it is merely that putting it that way allows him to pretend he cannot help it. The sonnet ends:

> Her wrists
> I catch: she faltering, as she half resists,
> 'You love ...? love ...? love ...?' all on indrawn breath.

As the wife's half-resistance shows, it is in fact the husband who is the pursuer; and her question applies equally to herself and the Lady. She wants reassurance before she yields. From a lifeless vow we have passed to a renewed sexual relationship. And in Sonnet XLIII we move part-way back again, as we are told of 'the unblest kisses which upbraid/The full-waked sense'. *Post coitum, omne animal triste est.* In Sonnet XLV the regression is complete:

> Here's Madam, stepping hastily.

This sonnet is less successful than most because it is too predictable; the point about the impossiblity of emotional stasis is a bit crude in its irony. But the next two sonnets more than make up for the lapse.

These sonnets establish a rare moment of rest, of quietness, though it cannot be sustained. Sonnet XLVI is about failures and mistakes of love. The husband's 'disordered brain' leads him to suspect his wife of continuing her liaison with the lover, but he triumphs over the moment of jealousy and in taking her arm becomes assured of her trustworthiness. He even finds it possible to tell her this, although he notes at the beginning of the sonnet that they are 'so strangely dumb/In such a close communion'. Speech destroys communication:

> I moved
> Toward her, and made proffer of my arm.
> She took it simply, with no rude alarm;
> And that disturbing shadow passed reproved.
> I felt the pained speech coming, and declared
> My firm belief in her, ere she could speak.
> A ghastly morning came into her cheek,
> While with a widening soul on me she stared.

This discovery of incommunicability through communication is not merely ingenious; it is persuasive in its psychological attentiveness. The 'dumb' linking of arms creates that moment of trust in which the husband is able to speak the words of love that the wife mistakes for pity. All the same, there is a weakness to do with the last two lines, since if the husband has registered his wife's look, it is difficult to understand his unobservant complacency in the next sonnet. This, the most frequently anthologised of all the sonnets of 'Modern Love', is about a presumed companionableness:

> We saw the swallows gather in the sky
> . . . .
> Our spirits grew as we went side by side.
> (XLVII)

The sonnet catches well enough the note of quietness, but it loses its full force unless it is seen in context. As a Nature poem or love-lyric it is unremarkable, but it becomes remarkable as soon as we recognize that the moment of communication is also the moment of betrayal, which is what sonnet XLVIII reveals:

> We drank the pure daylight of honest speech.
> Alas! that was the fatal draught, I fear . . .
> (XLVII)

Though the husband thinks he is offering love (and why should we trust him?), the wife sees only pity, rejects it and flees the house:

> For when of my lost Lady came the word,
> This woman, O this agony of flesh!

Jealous devotion bade her break the mesh,
That I might seek the other like a bird.

(XLVII)

Then we return to the narrator. Sonnet XLIX tells us that the
husband brings the wife home, that she believes his love, and that
she commits suicide out of terror:

lest her heart should sigh,
And tell her loudly she no longer dreamed

—dreamed, that is, that her husband now loves her. The last sonnet
is predictably pious.

I am not sure that the wife's suicide is the best way of ending
'Modern Love'. For one thing, it is misleadingly liable to hint at a
progressiveness of her relationship with the husband. I also think it
perhaps too readily falls into the mode of reversal and
unpredictability, which Meredith handles with so much human
awareness elsewhere in the poem. The suicide comes perilously
near to lending itself to the narrator's tone:

Thus piteously Love closed what he begat.

On the other hand, I recognise that 'Modern Love' can only really
end by being cut short, for once Meredith has created this
incessantly shifting dialectic of the relationship, he needs the
intervention of the arbitrary to halt the poem. I suppose the suicide
makes a further point: that such a relationship cannot be resolved; it
can only stop. But however successful we think it, the ending of the
poem must be discussed in this way; we can only regard it as a
triumph of comic art if we take a Popeian view of the comic, which
is not the view Meredith officially took. For this reason I think it an
unforgivable mistake to try fitting 'Modern Love' to theories
Meredith was later to elaborate. If we do, we merely lay the poem
open to F.R. Leavis's charge that it is 'the flashy product of unusual
but vulgar cleverness working upon cheap emotion'. As I have tried
to show, that charge can be met. But we need to take it seriously.
Not to do so is a disservice to Meredith, whose reputation as a poet
will not be restored in any way that matters while admirers find
themselves so little capable of tackling the problematic issues his
poetry as a whole presents. In particular, we must be able to account

for the nature and level of the achievement of 'Modern Love', recognising that it is not equalled elsewhere in his work and that only very occasionally is it approached.

Notes

1. My text is taken from *The Poetical Works of George Meredith*, with some notes by G.M. Trevelyan, 1912. Two collections of Meredith's poetry are currently in print: *Selected Poems*, ed. Graham Hough (London: Greenwood Press 1980) and *Poems*, ed. P. Bartlett (New Haven, CT: Yale University Press 1978).

2. I have not wanted to burden the text of my essay with references to the critics who have discussed 'Modern Love' because although the poem customarily receives high praise I do not think its complexities have been properly appreciated. The comments by Swinburne and Arthur Symons are generous and just, but they do not pretend to be more than general remarks (Swinburne praised the poem in his famous letter to *The Spectator*, 1862, protesting at the vulgar review of the poem that had appeared in its pages; Arthur Symons's essay was collected in his *Figures of Several Centuries*, 1916); Trevelyan, Jack Lindsay and Siegfried Sassoon stick far too closely to the biographical aspects, and as a result fail to notice how distanced Meredith is from the husband's point of view. (Trevelyan's remarks are made in his notes to the *Collected Poems of George Meredith*, 1912, Sassoon's are in his *Meredith*, 1948, especially pp. 64-7, and Lindsay's are in his *George Meredith, His Life and Work*, 1956, especially pp. 83-7.)

   Norman Kelvin, it is true, half-sees his way to how the poem dislodges any effort at a simplistic reading, but he tries to find a moral core to it. Predictably it turns out to be the one offered by the narrator and involves Kelvin not only in a highly unlikely interpretation of some lines from the closing sonnet but also in the disastrous course of trying to identify the narrator's voice with Meredith's. Kelvin claims that the marriage is a failure because husband and wife 'have approached each other as barbarian aggressors. They are not individuals transformed by reason and capable of passion without destruction' (*A Troubled Eden; Nature and Society in the Works of George Meredith*, 1961, p. 26, and *see* pp. 25-35). Such a view is woefully moral.

   Probably the best account of the poem is C. Day Lewis's. He recognises that the movement of the poem is best seen as a 'series of impulses and revulsions proceeding from the conflict within the husband's mind, which swings wildly from jealousy to generosity, from pity to indignation, from hysterical egotism to civilised sympathy, from regret to cynicism, from cursing to blessing' (Introduction to his edition of 'Modern Love', 1948). My main quarrel with Day Lewis's argument is that he separates out the series of impulses too schematically and ignores the role of the narrator, whom he seems to feel speaks for Meredith; at least, verse which I find appallingly (and deliberately) bad, he thinks is good and offers a valid point of view.

6
Thomas Hardy, Donald Davie, England and the English

I

Over the last twenty or so years Thomas Hardy's reputation has risen at an astonishing rate. I can indicate the nature of this rise by saying that if I think back to the latter half of the 1950s, when I was an undergraduate, I recall how very cool were the literary and academic worlds towards 'the good little Hardy'. Indeed, James's famous remark was thought to say it all. There were few critical studies of the novels or the poetry, and I do not imagine that Hardy was taught on many undergraduate courses. You might know why R.G. Collingwood thought that the ending of *Tess of the d'Urbervilles* spoilt an otherwise impressive novel, and any anthology of twentieth-century poetry would be likely to include 'The Darkling Thrush' and a few other poems; but that was more or less that. Not any more, however. Hardy has replaced Jane Austen as the novelist students will have read all or most of, the critical studies pour from the presses, and as for his poetic work, it is almost certain to feature prominently in any course on modern poetry.

Yet here of course the difficulties start. Is Hardy really a modern poet at all? Is he a great one? Or even a master? and if he has had an important influence on later English poets (and Auden and Larkin, at least, have been quick to insist on his significance for them), has that been a good or a bad thing? More particularly, does Hardy offer a valuable challenge to these and other poets, or is he their excuse for not doing better, working harder, struggling with great intensity to make it new? These questions are at the very heart of Donald Davie's *Thomas Hardy and British Poetry*, a book which, like everything else that Davie has written, is packed with interesting, challenging ideas.[1] It is also often muddled and infuriating. Yet perhaps this has to be so. For the book is very much a personal record of Davie's fight to establish what he wanted (and wants?) to be his own priorities; and I strongly suspect that it was written at a time of some crisis, a crisis which was certainly within Davie himself, and which he thought was also within England. Hence the muddle. For Davie is compelled to speculate on links between the two which may not always be there, or which, if they were there, were so in ways different from the ones he imagined. As a result, the priorities he seeks to establish don't emerge with any great clarity, they can't be easily defended, and it is even possible that they can't be fully understood.

I grant that to say this may seem merely impertinent, an intrusion into areas which are strictly private. Yet one can hardly avoid the fact that *Thomas Hardy and British Poetry* must have been written at the period when Davie was deciding to leave England in order to work in the United States; and it is clear from pronouncements he made at that time that he saw England as somehow finished. America called because in America he could practice his art as poet and critic with a seriousness and dedication which in England had become virtually impossible, since in England the very terms 'seriousness' and 'dedication' would be likely at best to provoke a wry smile, at worst a hoot of dismissal. Is this to state the matter too baldly? I do not think so. For if we recall the time when the book had its inception, the late 1960s, we will remember that it was among other things the period of student unrest, of sit-ins, riots, book-burnings; it was the period of Danny the Red, of Tariq Ali and *Red Mole*, of Oz and its trials; it was a period in which, if the worst seemed to have all the passionate intensity, then some of the best had to demonstrate conviction. And Donald Davie's conviction was that if the great Anarch was about to let universal darkness fall on England, he must escape to a world elsewhere. It is this, I believe, which explains the almost hysterical note that sometimes intrudes into the book. To give just one example, Davie speaks of 'English intellectuals of the Left making the late Stephen Ward (one of the minor actors in the Profumo scandal) into love's martyr, happy to overlook the squalid tastelessness of his life as a procurer for the sake of the humaneness that (arguably) shone through it'.[2] Now this won't at all do. It is true that Ward—whom I may say I never heard an intellectual of

the left refer to as love's martyr—*ought* to have been a minor actor
in the scandal. But in fact his desertion by the rich and famous who
had used his services turned him into the fall-guy and caused his
suicide. (Whereas they themselves were well enough protected by
the establishment to be able to escape). That they could do so
understandably angered many people, and not, I believe and hope,
merely those on the left. Davie goes on to say that you won't find
'moral fastidiousness' in British politics of the left or the right, not
until you get to the far right—'as the case of D.H. Lawrence
shows'. I think the kindest way to treat that remark is to assume it
was written in haste and out of great anger.

Much of the anger is quite justified. Donald Davie was writing at
the time when many intellectuals felt a sense of acute dismay at the
goings-on of the Wilson government. This government had, after
all, come to power mouthing the words of the great men of the
British labour movement, and what had resulted? A shallow, largely
cynical or philistine acceptance of tawdry glitter in civic life; a
materialism which found expression in the high-rise blocks of
town-planners and the bulldozing of inner cities; above all, perhaps,
an open contempt for the ideals of education and the life of the
mind which had been at the heart of the socialism identified with
R.H. Tawney. The 1960s witnessed a disaster for English
education, one we are still living through and from which we may
never entirely recover. I write as a socialist, and I cannot look back
on the 1960s without thinking that during these years a great
tradition was systematically betrayed. 'The tigers of wrath are wiser
than the horses of instruction'. Blake's proverb was everywhere
spray-gunned or chalked on walls. It meant that all respect for
learning, for wisdom and its concomitant, memory, were suspect,
derided. What made it worse was that this was being done in the
name of socialism! This appalling preference for ignorance was
actively encouraged by well-meaning liberal educators who were
terrified of alienating the young by requiring them to *know*, to
remember, to fill their minds with *facts*.

The nature of this disaster is conveniently indicated by the
famous debate between F.R. Leavis and C.P. Snow about the two
cultures, and in Harold Wilson's promise of 'a technological
revolution'. (Snow became a member of Wilson's government.) In
many ways the debate was trivial, but in one way at least it proved
crucial for the 1960s. Snow and his supporters looked forward to

the displacement of the humanities from the centre of education. For Leavis, on the other hand, and *his* supporters—among whom Davie would surely want to be included?—such a displacement must be ruinous because, *pace* Snow and Wilson, technology had already been tried and had been found wanting. It had proved insufficient to nourish the creative human spirit. I do not mean to say that I agree with this, or even with the terms of the debate, but I think it important to note that such a conviction is deeply embedded in *Thomas Hardy and British Poetry*. For Davie's procedure is to identify some symptoms of what he believes to be England's serious, even terminal, malaise, and then look for a root cause. The result is that when he writes about Hardy, it is as though he sees him as the poet-spokesman of the technological revolution; an embodiment of all those forces whose sudden-as-it-might-seem eruption in the 1960s spelt anarchy. Such anarchy could be literal and take political shape—as it did, for example, on Davie's own university campus at Essex—or it could be implicit, as it was, or was held to be, in the general capitulation before youth culture and the acceptance of 'pop' in art, poetry, and music. But no matter what shape it took, the anarchy didn't so much presage the technological revolution as show itself to be that revolution's malformed child. Only a society which did not take humane education at all seriously could encourage the illiterate in their illiteracy, or say that anyway none of it mattered, the important thing was to get rid of elitist, outmoded views of art in favour of a cultural free-for-all of doing your own thing.

Now all this may seem very strange. Does the road from Hardy lead to Roger McGough? Well, in perfectly obvious senses, no. But in one sense at least it does, or so Donald Davie implies. He takes Hardy as the starting-point for an investigation of the dangerous consequences that modesty breeds. Hardy is absolutely different from Yeats, Eliot, Pound, Lawrence, not simply because his politics aren't of the right, as theirs are, not merely because unlike them he is anti-elitist, but because he never claimed very much for his poetry—'all we can try to do is to write a little better on the old themes' he famously told Robert Graves, because he did not make large claims for art as criticism of life, and because he did not write 'great' poems. In other words, Hardy encouraged an acceptance of the scaled-down, he thought that small could be beautiful as long as you didn't make too much of the beautiful, and he was prepared to put up with the second-best. This, at least, is what Davie argues, and he goes on to assert that it is this which has bedevilled English poetry throughout the twentieth century and which reaches its logical conclusion in the fulsome praise accorded to the Liverpool pop poets and the fact that Larkin put them into his *Oxford Book of Twentieth-Century English Verse*. (Davie doesn't say that in *Thomas Hardy and British Poetry*, but he has argued it subsequently, and the argument fits perfectly well with all he says in his book.)

It is easy to imagine Davie agreeing with Nietzsche's Zarathustra, who gazed at a row of new houses and asked himself what they meant:

> Verily, no great soul put them up as its likeness ... And these rooms and chambers—can *men* go in and out of them?... And Zarathustra stood still and reflected. At last he said: 'Everything has become smaller! Everywhere I see lower gates: those who are my kind probably still go through, but they must stoop. Oh, when shall I get back to my homeland, where I need no longer stoop—no longer stoop *before those who are small?*'[3]

On this reading, Davie's homeland would be America, because there he can find the matter of art taken with that passionate intensity which frees it from the grasp of trend-spotters, philistines and media-men: all those who degrade its worth. (I imagine the very different reception of Charles Tomlinson in the two countries has always been much in Davie's mind.) It would help to explain why he so frequently invokes the name of D.H. Lawrence in his book. For Lawrence was also a self-imposed exile, one who could be said to have left an England which he saw as given over to littleness and essentially buried under anarchic darkness.

An acceptance of littleness; a taste for modesty—one could not accuse contemporary American poets of living with such things. Self-deprecating modesty is an alien mode for any serious poet writing in America today, as one can see if one looks at an interview with Anthony Hecht that appeared in the magazine *Quarto*. Hecht is a fine poet and in no sense a self-advertiser; and yet in reply to a question about the nature of a writer's responsibility, he says:

The life of a writer is a life of an extraordinary sort of dedication, and it's worth saying that and repeating it often because most non-writers have no sense of what's entailed in terms of dedication. It becomes more and more, what shall I say, almost religious (though of course I cheapen the word when I use it, I don't mean really religious). But it's a desperate and terrible kind of dedication, the more desperate and terrible because it's so little appreciated.[4]

'A desperate and terrible kind of dedication'. Imagine Philip Larkin talking like that, or—and here's the nub of the matter—Thomas Hardy. Thus if something is badly wrong with English poetry—and Davie is sure that there is—the root cause can be traced back to the particular kind of modesty which Hardy's poetry embodies:

On every page, 'Take it or leave it', he seems to say; or, even more permissively, 'Take what you want, and leave the rest'. This consciousness of having imposed on his reader so little is what lies behind Hardy's insistence that what he offers is only a series of disconnected observations, and behind his resentment that he should be taken as having a pessimistic design upon his reader, when in fact he so sedulously respects the reader's privilege not to be interested, not to be persuaded. It is on this basis—his respect of the reader's rights to be attentive or inattentive as he pleases—that one rests the claim for Hardy as perhaps the first and last 'liberal' in modern poetry.[5]

But Davie hardly means those last words, I think; not unless he specifically wishes to distinguish between the modern and the contemporary. The truth is rather that Hardy inaugurates an attitude to poetry that is harmful both to its practitioners and its readers and which again may be thought to have come to a head in the 1960s. (For when Davie speaks of Hardy 'permissively' allowing his readers to take what they want and leave the rest, we can hardly avoid hearing an echo of the 1960s cliché about the permissive society.) The final judgement on him has therefore to be a severe one:

it begins to look as if Hardy's engaging modesty and his decent liberalism represent a crucial selling short of the poetic vocation, for himself and his successors. For surely the poet, if any one, has a duty to be radical, to go to the roots. So much at least all poets have assumed through the centuries. Hardy, perhaps without knowing it, questions that assumption, and appears to reject it. Some of his successors in England, and a few out of England, seem to have agreed with him.[6]

Hardy's failings do not end here. Davie contrasts the skills of a craftsman (he seems to believe that Hardy trained as a stone-mason) with those of the engineer; and what he claims to detect in much of Hardy's work is a harsh, metallic brilliance that belongs with the world of engineering. Thus he remarks of 'Overlooking the Rover Stour':

> The 'cunning irregularity' which heedless readers have taken for clumsiness may be in a touch like the crowded stresses and consonants in 'the pane's drop-drenched glaze'. But once we have taken Hardy's word for it that such effects are the result of 'choice after full knowledge', the poem becomes throughout, and all too shiningly, the work of 'a superb technician' who dismays us precisely by his *superbia*. The symmetries, stanza by stanza, are all but exact to begin with; once we know that the occasional inexactitude is no less engineered, 'engineered' seems more than ever the only word to use. Once again there is an analogy with Victorian civil engineering, which topped off an iron bridge or a granite waterworks with Gothic finials, just as Hardy tops off his Victorian diction with an archaism like 'sheen' or 'alack'. Within its historically appropriate idiom, the poem is a 'precision job'; that is to say, its virtuosity is of a kind impossible before conditions of advanced technology.[7]

I do not wish to ask whether Davie is fair to this particular poem. (Some of his points have been very well answered by Tom Paulin in *Thomas Hardy: The Poetry of Perception*[8]). I will, however, say that his knowledge of Victorian engineering leaves a good deal to be desired, not simply because waterworks were more often built of brick than of granite, but because they were staggeringly triumphant responses to huge problems of water cleansing and distribution and were the product of wonderful creative energies. Besides, the claim that Hardy's kind of ingenuity is impossible before conditions of advanced technology looks dubious as soon as one thinks of such highly artificial forms as the Pindaric ode (popular in England at the time of Palladianism, so there isn't much of a link there unless one cites the dubious claims of Vanburgh), or of those stanzaic patterns with which major and minor seventeenth-century poets liked to struggle.

Why then should Davie want to see Hardy's poetry in terms of engineering 'brilliance'? ('What one hears is not the chip-chip of a mason's chisel, but a clank of iron girders swung down from a crane', he says of 'Lines to a Movement in Mozart's E-Flat Symphony'.) The answer, clearly enough, is that to do so clinches the argument for Hardy as progenitor of all that is wrong with the spirit of contemporary England and its poetry. It is bad enough that he should be modest and a liberal, but what makes it far worse is that he is on the side of the technological revolution! Driving the final nail into the coffin, Davie calls Hardy a 'scientific humanist'. Coming across that phrase, and thinking also of his insistence that Hardy was 'ambitious technically, and unambitious in every other way', and recalling his account of Hardy's mechanical skills, I find it inevitable that one should make a connection with the young Yeat's passionately voiced hatred of the scientific humanism of Huxley and Tyndall, of his nightmare of the endlessly chattering sewing-machine, and of his view of modern life as a condition where 'opinion crushes and rends, and all is hatred and bitterness; wheel biting upon wheel, a roar of steel or iron tackle, a mill of argument grinding all things down to mediocrity'.[9] Yeats has modern Dublin specifically in mind in the passage, but what he says there clearly applies to what he thinks of modern life in general. I do not know whether those words were lodged somewhere in the back of Donald Davie's mind when he came to write his account of Thomas Hardy, but they could well have been. Indeed, he has virtually taken over Yeats's terms: for Davie, every bit as much as for Yeats, modern life is characterised by the spirit of scientific humanism, reducing all things, by and because of mechanical means, to an acceptance of the second-best; what we have is a society where littleness and mediocrity triumph, and which is able to claim a modest liberalism as midwife if not parent.

II

So far I have tried to reconstruct the underlying argument of Davie's book and to explain what its hidden implications are. For it has to be repeated that the argument is very much one to be inferred and is by no means lying out in the open. But now a

further problem arises. Just how accurate or telling is this account
of Hardy's poetry and of its influence on later poets? (I am not at
all clear as to why Davie uses the word British, by the way, since he
speaks exclusively of Hardy's influence on English poets, and it
would be difficult to imagine how Hardy could have influenced
Scottish, Welsh or Irish poets. I know that Dylan Thomas said
that Hardy was his favourite poet, but that isn't the same thing.)
The truth is that Davie's account is both tendentious and
procrustean. In the first place, I do not believe that Hardy, any
more than any real poet, can adequately be thought of as a
scientific humanist. As it happens, Davie no longer believes it to be
so. For in a great essay, 'Hardy's Virgilian Purples'. which was
published in a number of the magazine *Agenda* that was devoted
to Hardy,[10] Davie convincingly refutes his earlier contention that
Hardy 'appears to have mistrusted ... the claims of poetry to
transcend the linear unrolling of recorded time',[11] just as he puts
paid to the assertion voiced in his book that the ghost of Emma in
those late, great love poems is 'only subjectively real'. is no more
than a psychological fancy. In view of what he says in the essay,
there is really no point in taking issue with the book's untenable
argument, that the love poems:

> instead of transforming and displacing quantifiable reality or the
> reality of common sense, are on the contrary just so many glosses on
> that reality, which is conceived of as unchallengeably "given" and final.
> This is what makes it possible to say (once again) that he sold the
> vocation short, tacitly surrendering the proudest claims traditionally
> made for the act of the poetic imagination.[12]

It is, however, worth suggesting that here again Davie may well be
prompted by his own concerns. For in the poem, 'Or, Solitude',
published in *Essex Poems* (1969),[13] he writes:

> The transcendental nature
> Of poetry, how I need it!
> And yet it was for years
> What I refused to credit.

But when the poem was first published, in, I think, the *New
Statesman*, I recall that the first line was 'The metaphysicality/ Of

poetry'. In replacing 'metaphysicality' by the more insistent word 'transcendental', Davie is utterly rejecting that tradition of commensensical scientific humanism to which he himself had belonged, and which he saw as reaching back to Hardy.

But not any longer. For in the *Agenda* essay Hardy is specifically linked with Dante and Virgil as a poet of metaphysical insights. What, though, of Davie's other claim that Hardy sold the poetic vocation short? It falls into two parts. The first, which I have already touched on, is that Hardy is too much the engineer and too little the craftsman. I have said why I think it is that Davie chose to level this charge at Hardy; but it isn't at all clear that the charge can be sustained. I agee that there are poems where Hardy's pursuit of form—or rather his determination to make a poem come out in a certain form—may seem perverse. But the fact is that being perverse in this way is undoubtedly an habitual delight for a certain sort of poet—Donne, Browning and Auden come immediately to mind—and to scold them for it feels rather pointless. Besides, Davie himself generously acknowledges that as a prosodist Hardy 'was immensely learned, with a learning that seems to be lost beyond recovery'. Yet he fails to see that Hardy's characteristic genius is therefore to be accounted for, not by means of analogy with architecture or engineering, but through his extraordinarily subtle ear, his attentiveness to cadence and the pull of narrative through time. Time rather than space is the element in which Hardy's poems exist, at anyone surely knows who reads them aloud. Davie utterly misses the point when he says that Hardy's 'symmetrical stanzas *lie on the page* demurely self-contained'.[14] They don't lie there at all, I submit, to anyone who can *hear* the poems, and who can therefore respond to Hardy's 'cunning irregularity'.

'Cunning irregularity'. The phrase comes from a passage in *The Life of Thomas Hardy*, which Davie quotes, but which he doesn't seem fully to understand. This is what Hardy wrote:

> He knew that in architecture cunning irregularity is of enormous worth, and it is obvious that he carried on into his verse, perhaps in part unconsciously, the Gothic art-principle . . . of spontaneity, found in mouldings, tracery, and such like—resulting in the 'unforeseen' (as it has been called) character of his metres and stanzas, that of stress rather than syllable, poetic texture rather than poetic veneer; the latter

kind of thing, under the name of 'constructed ornament', being what he, in common with every Gothic student, had been taught to avoid as the plague. He shaped his poetry accordingly, introducing metrical pauses, and reversed beats; and found for his trouble that some particular line of a poem exemplifying this principle was greeted with a would-be jocular remark that such a line 'did not make for immortality'.[15]

Stress rather than syllable. It is of the utmost importance, and yet how many commentators of Hardy's poetry have in fact done justice to the subtlety of his ear, have understood his ability to make his poems voice or breathe their meanings through cadences. (It is worth noting that 'breathe' is a good Hardy word: you breathe the air and air is a synonym for song, a condition to which many of Hardy's poems move.) The sad truth is that most critics talk of what Hardy's poems are 'about' as though how the poems sound had nothing whatever to do with the matter. No doubt this in great part due to the fact that many of them either began teaching or were taught in the 1960s, when proper respect for, and attentiveness towards, how a poem *sounds* became a matter for scorn. (It is no paradox that that was the decade of large-scale public readings: anyone who remembers the mangling of great poems and the chanting of rubbish that formed the matter of such read-ins will know what I am talking about, just as he will recognise its consequences when he asks any of his students or, God help him, many of his colleagues, to read a poem aloud.) But however one may explain it, the fact is that most critics who write about Hardy are plainly unfit to do so.

I can pinpoint this by referring to a comparatively slight poem, 'I look into My Glass':

> I look into my glass,
> And view my wasting skin,
> And say 'Would God it came to pass
> My heart had shrunk as thin!'
>
> For then, I undistrest
> By hearts grown cold to me,
> Could lonely wait my endless rest
> With equanimity.

But Time, to make me grieve,
Part steals, lets part abide;
And shakes this fragile frame at eve
With throbbings of noontide.

I had known and loved the music of this poem for years when I had to endure hearing it read by an academic who chose it as an example of Hardy's grim pessimism, and for whom its dignified emphases meant nothing at all. Thus he read the middle stanza with a leaden, metronomic thump, producing a series of steam-hammer iambs. Yet anyone with half an ear must surely notice how in the first line of that stanza the pause on 'I', created by the punctuation, requires that one stress it and so lighten the force of 'undistrest'; so that one gets a lovely, quizzical balancing of distress and its opposite—a balancing that can be heard in the echoing vowel sounds ('*grow*n cold' is echoed in '*lonely*', '*end*less *rest*' in '*eq*uanimity'). Of course, the stanza comes to rest with the last word, which takes all three stresses of that line, and in its unhurried calm actually embodies what it's about. There are other felicities which one might dwell on: the hovering stresses on 'part steals', for example, or the spondee with which the poem concludes and which gives a queer, almost uncanny pulse at its very end. But I will say only that perhaps the most cunning thing about this little poem is that it is written in poulter's measure, that stanza form which we have always been assured—by C.S. Lewis and others—cannot be effectively handled in serious poetry. It is true that if you look at those Elizabethan poets who used the form, the results are mostly dire, though Gascoigne, Turberville and Googe all produced honourable exceptions. And it is also true that if you look at those eighteenth-century hymn-writers to whom the form was known as 'Short Metre' and who used it for a good many of their hymns, the results are not much better. ('Hosannah to the Son/ Of David and of God,/ Who brought the news of pardon down,/ And bought it with his blood' is a typical example.) But this at least shows where Hardy took much of his inspiration from, and how he modified it. Behind his poetry lies the absorption of, and appeal to, folk-song, ballad and hymn, to a tradition which is anything but those architectural products of engineering that Davie claims to detect an analogue and even inspiration.

The fact is that more than those of any other nineteenth-century poet, more than Hopkins even, Hardy's poems are for the ear. Ignore that and you lose everything. The man who thumped his way through 'I look into My Glass' could ignore it because he was helplessly ignorant of how to read poetry. Yet that can hardly be the case with a critic as sensitive and intelligent as Davie. So that if one asks how he came to speak of Hardy's poems as 'lying on the page', one can only reply: by the same route that allowed him not to notice how impossible it is to identify as a scientific humanist the man who wrote such poems as 'Friends Beyond' or 'Paying Calls' or 'During Wind and Rain' or ... But of course there are *hundreds* of poems that should have told Davie that his argument was hopelessly awry. If, then, he pressed ahead with it, it must be because the real object of his attack is not Hardy at all, but the plight of English poetry, and beyond that, of England. And this brings us to another major change he levels at Hardy, that of an improper modesty, a readiness to put up with the second-best, whether in himself or in others, or in what he sees around him.

'Except in the ill-starred and premature *Dynasts*, Hardy the poet comes before us as the "honest journeyman", highly skilled indeed but disablingly modest in his aims'.[16] There is not the space here to challenge that dismissive phrase about the Dynasts. But I do need to take up the more general and indeed familiar accusation that Hardy's modesty is a selling short of his vocation. Thus when Hardy 'rises dutifully to public occasions, like an unofficial poet laureate', we get 'Drummer Hodge', which Davie says is 'esteemed by some who would castigate Rupert Brooke's "1914" though the senselessness of war is glossed over by the same means in the one poem as in the other'.[17] No, it isn't. For Brooke's 'The Soldier', which I assume is the poem to which Davie refers, speaks patriotically of his 'richer dust' being forever England in some foreign field; Hardy, on the other hand, speaks with a kind of awed, comic wonder (the tone is difficult to pin down but it certainly *isn't* Brooke's tone), of Hodge's 'homely breast and brain' growing to some southern tree. This is the oddest of transformations, in other words; and there is a genuine and proper slyness in Hardy's handling of his 'official' subject, which is certainly not to be found in Brooke's sonnet. The poem's modesty therefore implicitly demystifies the glorification of war. Such modesty is hardly disabling; on the contrary, whatever else the poem achieves, it plainly undercuts conventional patriotism and sees the death, casual burial and transformation of a common soldier in a deeper, and perhaps darker, comic context.

What is the strategy that lies behind Davie's argument? It amounts to this, I think: that Hardy's modesty is a mode of acceptance, a putting-up with life in England as he finds it. He is a kind of poetical Erastian, whereas the poet with claims to greatness should be a radical, should want to go to the roots and thus confront and question the society he finds himself in. The very first sentence of Davie's book reads: 'I have taken it for granted that works of literary art are conditioned by economic and political forces active in the society from which those works spring and to which they are directed, forces which bear in on the solitary artist as he struggles to compose.' Hardy, the implication is, struggled too little, was too ready to stand aside and let the forces rush past him. And he has bequeathed the tendency to his followers, so that much English poetry of the twentieth century is bedevilled by its readiness to accept second-best, to duck the awkward questions, confrontations, the really radical issues. Again, I have to add a note of caution. For the truth is that Davie never quite puts this argument together, and it may be that he will protest that I am not being entirely fair to him. Nevertheless, it seems to me that one has to infer such an argument from his book, as is I hope clear from the following astonishing statement, where Davie says that 'One recalls the cries of satisfaction with which the modern reader approaches that one of Wordsworth's nature poems, 'Nutting', in which the imagery conveys a submerged metaphor of rape. "All value is in the human, and nowhere else." It is a possible point of view, and may be sincerely held.' (I have to say that I don't recall hearing such cries, but if they exist it is surely for a reason opposite to the one Davie gives: namely, that the rape is seen as a violation of nature, not as confirmation of the overwhelming importance of the human, and therefore Wordsworth has correctly identified an improper human aggressiveness.) But, Davie goes on, this acceptance of the overwhelming importance of the human

for the English ... has the great advantage of anaesthetising them to the offensiveness of their own landscapes and removing any sense of guilt at having made them offensive. It is D.H. Lawrence's constant guilt and horror at what the English had made of England which makes it certain that, breeder as he was of his own symbolic horses ...

he certainly counted the cost and mostly he thought it extortionate
... either we accept that we deserve no better than the gracelessness of
scene which surrounds us, or else we shut ourselves off from our
neighbours who seem to ask nothing better and are doing their best to
make it worse. Like Richard Hoggart as regards literature, Larkin, as
regards landscape and architecture and indeed literature also, agrees to
tolerate the intolerable for the sake of human solidarity with those
who don't find it intolerable at all. Rather than put up with the
intolerable, Lawrence forfeited the solidarity—and with a clearer sense
of what he was doing, of the price he was paying.[18]

We may seem to have come a long way from Hardy in this series of
ill-argued assertions, but we haven't; not really. For it was Hardy,
so the submerged argument runs, who initiated a readiness to
tolerate the intolerable; and who therefore led English poetry into
shared acceptance of that awfulness from which Lawrence recoiled
(and Davie after him, we are surely to assume).

Well, it was of course Hardy who famously remarked that
natural scenes were of small importance compared with the wear on
a threshold made by a human foot, and who to that extent thought
that the human must claim primacy over the natural. And Auden,
Hardy's admirer, remarked in his 'Letter to Lord Byron' that:

> To me Art's subject is the human clay,
> And landscape but a background to a torso

But was Lawrence so different? And if so, did he have a clearer sense
of the price he was paying? I do not think so. For the pictue that
emerges of Lawrence during the war years, when he was planning to
leave England, is of a man almost out of control, swayed by angers
and contradictory impulses that pushed him to what can only be
called the brink of insanity.[19] This is not to say that Lawrence
claimed to be unaware of the implications of his decision, but it is to
argue that in the event matters turned out to be far more
complicated than he persuaded himself they would be. The result
was that during those long years of self-imposed exile, when he
wandered the world ceaselessly and restlessly, he found himself
unable to be at peace in his mind about the England which in
Kangaroo he had claimed to leave with little or no pain:

It was a cold day. There was snow on the Downs like a shroud. And as he looked back from the boat, when they had left Folkestone behind and only England was there, England looked like a grey, a dreary-grey coffin sinking in the sea behind, with her dead grey cliffs and the white, worn-out cloth of snow above.

(Ch. 12)

There it may seem easy for Lawrence to accept that he was seeing the last of England. But one has only to think of the letter he wrote to the young David Chambers in 1928 to realise how little he was able to come to terms with forfeiting that solidarity which Davie says he knowingly and willingly surrendered:

Whatever I forget, I shall never forget the Haggs—I loved it so. I loved to come to you all, it really was a new life began in me there. The waterpippin by the door— those maiden-blush roses that Flower would lean over and eat and trip floundering around. —And stewed figs for tea in winter, and in August green stewed apples. Do you still have them? Tell your mother I never forget, no matter where life carries us . . . Oh, I'd love to be nineteen again, and coming up through the Warren and catching the first glimpse of the buildings. Then I'd sit on the sofa under the window, and we'd crowd round the little table to tea, in that tiny little kitchen I was so at home in . . . If there is anything I can ever do for you do tell me. —Because whatever else I am, I am somewhere still the same Bert who rushed with such joy to the Haggs.

There is surely a pain in that letter which can hardly be thought of as belonging to a man who has a clear sense of what he is doing, of the price he is paying—except in a tragic sense.

Where Lawrence does attempt to be clear-sighted, what emerges is a series of simplistic generalisations that imply either an attempt to ease a troubled conscience or that he has abandoned the difficulties and stresses of real thinking. Such matters are deeply involved in the writing and rewriting of *Lady Chatterley's Lover*, the novel on which he was working during the latter years of the 1920s and in which he raged at what the English had made of England. In the published version of that novel one has a very powerful and betraying example of Lawrence's wish to trace to one source what he has detected as the symptoms of a terminal malaise. I am thinking in particular of that passage which describes Connie's drive through Tevershall, a journey which fills her with despair over

England and its people, 'In whom the living intuitive faculty was dead as nails, and only queer mechanical yells and uncanny will-power remained'. The passage has been extravagantly admired by F.R. Leavis and others; and it is certainly a clear-sighted statement about the condition of England. Davie could obviously cite it as an—or perhaps *the*—instance of Lawrence's decision not to put up with the intolerable. But to say that is immediately to point to what is wrong with the passage. For the important question is whether Connie's despair amounts to vision. The truth is rather, I suggest, that the clarity of her point of view, which is undoubtedly also Lawrence's, depends on wilful simplification of the actual. This is in no sense radical art; on the contrary, it is simple-minded rant. How can she *know* all this about Tevershall? How can anyone?

Interestingly enough, in the first version of the novel Lawrence deliberately undermines Connie's clear-sighted certainties. For in that version she has no sooner thought her worst of Tevershall than she remembers that it is where her lover—Parkin, in that version—comes from. Moreover, she doesn't think of the people as being 'dead as nails'. How can she? Her knowledge of Parkin's belonging with them acts as decisive rebuke to her outsider's view of the matter. Instead, the scene 'gave her a certain feeling of blind virility, a certain blind, pathetic forcefulness of life'. Lawrence is very careful to make clear that Connie's thoughts are those of a particular individual; they are not to be taken as the truth. Indeed, he stresses how, given her class prejudices, she *would* think as she does. (Discussions of class and its ideologies play a large part in the novel.) The first *Lady Chatterley's Lover* seems to me far and away the best of the three versions that Lawrence wrote, and this is at least partly because Connie's viewpoint isn't allowed there to operate as an objective account of the truth about England, one in which we can place unquestioning trust. Of course, she feels deeply about England, and her feelings drive her into generalisations. But she is made to see just how rashly simplistic some of them are. Because of that, one therefore has the sense of a real novelistic intelligence at work. In the published version, on the other hand, Lawrence allows Connie's viewpoint to be authoritative, and inevitably you realise that a number of crass simplicities have taken the novel over and reduced it to rant; and they are such simplicities as may be found in Davie's statements about 'the gracelessness of scene around us ... [and] neighbours who seem to ask nothing better and are doing their best to make it worse'. As soon as you put the matter that way you have outlawed yourself from a due seriousness of purpose. For now everything can be seen—clearly, no doubt—as a series of distemper-board headlines.

If we need further evidence that this was the way that Davie was thinking during the latter part of the 1960s, we can turn to his poem 'Thanks to Industrial Essex', a poem which invokes the 'hatred' that infects *Lady Chatterley's Lover*:

> Thanks to industrial Essex,
> I have spun on the greasy axis
> Of business and sociometrics;
> I have come to know the structures
> Of public service
> As well as I know the doves
> Crop-full in mildewed haycocks.
> I know that what they merit
> Is not scorn, sometimes scorn
> And hatred, but sadness really.
>
> Italic on chalky tussocks,
> The devious lovely weasel
> Snakes through a privileged annex,
> An enclave of directors.
> Landscapes of supertax
> Record a deathful failure
> As clearly as the lack
> Of a grand or expansively human
> Scale to the buildings of Ilford.
> The scale of that deprivation
> Goes down in no statistics.

If this is to be radical, to go to the roots, then give me Erastianism. For in spite of the last two lines, with their confident, Pound-like assumption that in England quantification of life has now taken over from quality—so that the public services are defined as structures—what we have is a series of bland and blank statements with no particularity to them. Except, that is, for the doves in the mildewed haycocks, which symbolise a lost glory; oh, and the weasel, of course, a last flicker of the natural life that is fugitive in a world of directors. But for the rest, we must make do with the simple, untested *Telegraph*-ese of: 'the lack/ Of a grand or expansively human/Scale to the buildings of Ilford.' The poem's title snarls defiance at thanks: 'Thanks to Essex, *this* is what I have to live with...' I cannot take that seriously, any more than I can take seriously the anger of Charles Tomlinson's poem 'On the Hall at Stowey', which is about the final decay of a great house and what it symbolises:

> Five centuries—here were (at the least) five—
>   In linked love, eager excrescence
> Where the door, arched, crowned with acanthus,
>   Aimed at a civil elegance, but hit
> This sturdier compromise, neither Greek, Gothic
>   Nor Strawberry, clumped from the arching-point
> And swathing down, like a fist of wheat,
>   The unconscious emblem for the house's worth
>
> . . . .
>
> Five centuries, And we? What we had not
>   Made ugly, we had laid waste—
> Left (I should say) the office to nature
>   Whose blind battery, best fitted to perform it
> Outdoes us, completes by persistence
>   All our negligence fails in. Saddened,
> Yet angered beyond sadness, where the road
>   Doubled upon itself I halted, for a moment
> Facing the empty house and its laden barns.

'On the Hall at Stowey' is the kind of poem that would obviously appeal to those who know of the tradition of country-house poems; it is very self-consciously a literary poem. No harm in that, perhaps, but where a tradition is uncritically invoked and set against what 'we' have done, then the dangers abound. For this is not radicalism at all; it is a mere echoing of cliché ('But to have gathered from the air a live tradition'). And if there is to be anger, then it had better be a good deal more self-critical and enquiring than either Davie or Tomlinson shows himself capable of being. It had better be the anger of Yeats ('And maybe the great grandson of that house,/ For all its bronze and marble, 's but a mouse'), which has an acute historical dimension to it, doesn't seek refuge in convenient commonplaces about past and present, and accepts a measure of guilt for what was engendered in the 'great' past. Davie refers to Lawrence's 'guilt and horror', and the horror is there, certainly—not only in Lawrence, but in Davie and Tomlinson too. Hence, no doubt, the anger. But where is the guilt? It does not exist, I suggest, for in Tomlinson's poem 'we' is an unexamined term that may as well be read as 'you'. After all the speaker of the poem knows the greatness of the past and is thus not guilty of ignorant vandalism. Where there is no self-criticism, no enquiry into the adequacy of one's clear-sightedness, there can be no generosity of vision, without which art becomes rhetoric. At the end of his essay on Dickens, George Orwell wrote of how he imagined Dickens's face: 'He is laughing, with a touch of anger in his laughter, but no triumph, no malignity. It is the face of a man who is always fighting against something, but who fights in the open and is not frightened, the face of a man who is *generously angry.*' Generous anger is the very opposite of those commonplace clarities that between them confuse the purpose of *Thomas Hardy and British Poetry*. And although I would not claim Hardy as a poet of generous anger, his modes of acceptance amount to a comprehending generosity of vision that seems to me far more valuable for English poetry than the alternatives that Davie prescribes.

Notes

1. Donald Davie, *Thomas Hardy and British Poetry* (London: Routledge and Kegan Paul 1979).
2. *Ibid.*, p. 71.
3. Nietzsche's italics.
4. *Quarto*, September 1981.
5. Davie, *British Poetry*, p. 28.
6. *Ibid.*, p. 40.
7. *Ibid.*, p. 22–3.
8. Tom Paulin, *Thomas Hardy: The Poetry of Perception* (London: Macmillan 1975).
9. W.B. Yeats, *Autobiographies* (London: Macmillan 1980), p. 231.
10. Davie, 'Hardy's Virgilian Purples' in *Agenda* X, 1972.
11. Davie, *British Poetry*, p. 4.
12. *Ibid.*, p. 62.
13. *See* Davie, *Collected Poems* (London: Routledge and Kegan Paul 1972).
14. Davie, *British Poetry*, p. 36.
15. *The Life of Thomas Hardy* (London: Macmillan 1970), p. 301.

16. Davie, *British Poetry*, p. 36.
17. *Ibid.*, p. 36–7.
18. *Ibid.*, p. 68–9.
19. This is thoroughly documented in Paul Delany's remarkable book, *D.H. Lawrence's Nightmare: The Writer and His Circle in the Years of the Great War* (Brighton: Harvester Press 1979).

7

For Ever England:
The Case of Siegfried Sassoon

With the appearance of *Sherston's Progress* in 1936,[1] Siegfried Sassoon completed what Howard Spring, writing in the *Evening Standard*, called 'the most satisfying piece of autobiography to be published in our time'. Other reviewers and commentators, then and later, seem to have agreed with Spring's assessment. Not Hugh MacDiarmid, however. In a poem which contrasts those who went to fight in 1914 with the International Brigaders, MacDiarmid writes:

> Despite the undeniable honesty, the little literary gift,
> What is *Sherston's Progress* but an exposure
> Of the eternal Englishman
> Incapable of rising above himself,
> And traditional values winning out
> Over an attempted independence of mind.

MacDiarmid is both right and wrong. *Sherston's Progress* is undoubtedly an exposure of the eternal Englishman, at least as Sassoon imagined that Englishman. But the Memoirs are really more fiction than fact, and the publication of his war diaries now allows us to understand just how carefully Sassoon created his image of Sherston as Englishman out of chaotic material and experiences which threatened his sense of identity.[2] In his celebrated book *The Great War and Modern Memory*, Paul Fussell claims that the trilogy of Memoirs 'is in every way fictional ... it would be impossible to specify how it differs from any other novel written in the first person and based on the author's own experience.'[3] That is astute but it oversteps the mark. After all, nearly all first novels are by writers about whom nothing is known. If they become famous it is because of their novels. Sassoon, on the other hand, was already famous. Everyone knew that he was the war hero who in 1917 had chucked his medals into the Mersey and written a public letter of protest about the conduct of the war. *Sherston's Progress* is about a war hero who lives with the consequences of having chucked his medals into the Mersey and written a public letter of protest about the conduct of the war. How can that be fiction? The truth is that Sassoon wants it both ways. He invents, suppresses, adapts, not so much to make a pure fiction as to make sense of a life. He is remaking himself. And in the Memoirs he finally produces an image of that kind of Englishman with which, as MacDiarmid saw, his later self can be at ease:

> It is not that Sherston was either
> A weak or a cowardly person.
> It is rather that his rebelliousness was only
> Superimposed on his profoundly English nature.

Sherston's Progress completes the image which first appeared in *Memoirs of a Fox-Hunting Man*.[4] The cheerful if shallow sportsman becomes the tearaway scapegrace of the middle volume, living by and for values formed on the sportsfield, worried that those values are becoming warped, and then modulates into the repentant veteran, ready to accept that his protest against war was not quite the thing: that it could indeed look a bit like throwing away your wicket because you disapproved of your captain's tactics. As reported in *Sherston's Progress*, the meeting with Rivers, the famous psychiatrist, becomes the crucial episode in recalling Sherston to himself. He now accepts that it is not necessary to approve of tactics which he may simply not understand, and after a brief spell in the pavilion—'retired hurt'—he plays on until the match is over, wicket intact. For all the possible irony of its title, *Sherston's Progress* finally endorses Pilgrim's journey towards the Celestial City which can be attained only by hard slog and which, when it is reached, looks very like the England of sun-drenched meadows, good sport and flannelled gentry.

There is an obvious element of self-parody in the creation of Sherston, and this is hardly surprising. It is one way of fending off criticism, of coping with unresolved difficulties. Or rather, it resolves them by adopting a pose of wry detachment. Looking back from 1936 at that young and callow infantry officer, the author can

allow himself the luxury of mockery. Yet in 1917 matters had been
very different. What the Diaries record is the muddle of a man who
chose an identity and then found that he could not function within
it. Infantry Officer Sassoon is undoubtedly one kind of eternal
Englishman. That is to say, he takes on values and a tone of voice
which in the early years of the war seemed appropriate to the great
adventure. In December 1915 he is full of zest:

> I want a genuine taste of the horrors, and then—peace. I don't want to
> go back to the old inane life which always seemed like a prison. I want
> freedom, not comfort. I have seen beauty in life, in men and things . . .
> the last fifteen months have unsealed my eyes. I have lived well and
> truly since the war began; now I ask that the price be required of me.

Similar sentiments are on show in some of the early poems.
'Absolution' (April–September 1915) sees the soldiers as

> the happy legion, for we know
> Time's but a golden wind that shakes the grass.

In its vague uplift this is close to Herbert Asquith's poem of 1915
about the 'Volunteer' who is rescued from a life of humdrum
clerking and who in death is described as having his lance 'broken in
life's tournament'. War is a chivalric affair: although in 'The Prince
of Wounds' (27 December 1915) Sassoon sees a road 'that's dark
with blood', the blood has spilt from the bodies of soldiers 'on
warfare's altar sacrificed'. In its way, 'The Prince of Wounds' is as
inept, if not so offensive, as Owen Seaman's 'To the Shirker: A Last
Appeal', which ends by telling the reluctant soldier to go and serve
his country:

> Come, then, betimes and on her altar lay
> Your sacrifice today.

Seaman's poem was written in late 1914, and its exhortations were
quite unnecessary. Men were offering themselves in such huge
numbers that the Army simply couldn't cope. Many of them had
read Brooke's famous sonnets and saw themselves as swimmers into
cleanness leaping. Sassoon was one of hundreds of thousands who
entered the war ardent for some desperate glory.

By the latter half of 1916, however, his attitude had changed, as had that of the vast majority who lived through the promises and muddy failures of the Somme, and who were coming to realise that the war which was supposed to bring them 'Home by Christmas' was lengthening to no apparent end or purpose. On 16 July 1916 Sassoon writes:

> I'm thinking of England, and summer evenings after cricket-matches, and sunset above the tall trees, and village-streets in the dusk, and the clatter of a brake driving home. Perhaps I've made a blob, but we've won the match, and there's another match tomorrow ... So things went three years ago; and it's all dead and done with. I'll never be there again.

It is, of course, a very partial view, a pastoral dream dear to English hearts which MacDiarmid almost certainly had in mind when he spoke of those

> traditional values winning out
> Over an attempted independence of mind

He could not have known how close Sassoon came to achieving that independence.

By 1917 the sweet dream of England had turned utterly sour. There is an extraordinary diary entry for 30 March of that year. Under the title 'Dream Pictures', Sassoon imagines writing a book of 'Consolations for Homesick Soldiers in the Field':

> I would turn them loose in some dream-gallery of Royal Academy pictures of the late 19th century. I would show them bland summer landscapes, willow and meadowsweet reflected in calm waters, lifelike cows coming home to the byre with a golden sunset behind them; I would take them to gateways in garden-walls that they might gaze along dewy lanes with lovers murmuring by the moss-grown sundial; I would lead them 'twixt hawthorn hedgerows, and over field-path stiles, to old-world orchards where the lush grass is strewn with red-cheeked apples, and even the wasps have lost their stings. From the grey church-tower comes a chiming of bells, and the village smoke ascends like incense of immemorial tranquility. And at the rose-grown porch of some discreet little house a girl in a print-dress is waiting, waiting for the returning footsteps along the twilight lane, while the last blackbird warbles from the may-tree.

Two years previously, Ernest Rhys had put out an anthology for soldiers, called *The Old Country*. It included an introduction by Sir Arthur Yapp of the YMCA which spoke of the soldier in imagination seeing 'his village home' (most soldiers came from industrial cities); and the contents supplied an England of fields, hedgerows and village steeples. Sassoon's 'Dream Pictures' is a ludicrous parody of the kind of anthology that *The Old Country* typifies. Moreover, he now sees the England with which he had identified becoming a parody of itself. In May 1917 Sassoon goes to stay with Lord and Lady Brassey. Lord Brassey is 'a pattern Englishman, no doubt, very wise in the ways of his generation, a useful servant of the State, but a strange figure to Youth in Revolt, and Youth torn by sacrifice. His wisdom has had its day ... Death presses him hard.'

Very interestingly, as Sassoon begins to distance himself from this England, he begins to practise fiction. The diary for 15 May has an entry called 'A Conversation', which I have no doubt is based on talks he had with Lady Brassey, but which is presented as third-person dialogue:

> She was a Great Lady. And he was only a poet; but he knew that life was taking shape within his heart ... For a while he thought that she understood ... 'But death is nothing', she said ... he was struck dumb: he had forgotten that he spoke to an alien intelligence, that would not suffer the rebellious creed that was his.

It is as though Sassoon is unable to acknowledge his own rebellion. Perhaps this should not surprise us. For the rebellion was against all he had chosen to believe in and identify with. In short, it was against himself. The following day he reports a release from 'the furies that pursued me. I am an Orestes freed from the tyranny of doom.'

It is also interesting to discover that as soon as the famous letter of protest is written, on 15 June, and he is posted first to Litherland and then to Craiglockhart War Hospital, the diary stops. Hart-Davis does not make it clear whether Sassoon destroyed any diary he might have kept at that time. He says merely that 'from this point there is no surviving diary until December', and he adds that the outline of the missing months can be sketched in by reference to the Memoirs. This strikes me as disingenuous. For if we look at *Sherston's Progress* we find that the tone of the narrative is radically different from the frenzied, muddled rage of the Diary. Rebellion is now seen as faintly ridiculous, a boyish peccadillo:

> Once, when I saw that one of my best friends had been killed, I lapsed into angry self-pity, and told myself that the War was 'a sham and a stinking lie', and succeeded in feeling bitter against the unspecified crowd of non-combatants who believed that to go through with it to the end was the only way out.

Succeeded in feeling bitter: as soon as the matter is put that way, and once the protest is pinned between quotation marks, the narrator emerges as an older, wiser man presenting for our amused scrutiny his ironic account of a youthful self whose anger can be put down to insincerity or blamed on others. (Sassoon was nearly thirty-one when he wrote his letter.) 'Of course the weak point about my "protest"', the narrator goes on, 'had been that it was evoked by personal feeling. It was an emotional idea based on my war experience and stimulated by points of view which I accepted uncritically.' Well, it is certainly true that the Diaries show the Infantry Officer outraged by his personal experience at the front, and that his clearest, most reasonable argument against the war emerges in the letter—in the composition of which he was undoubtedly helped by the Garsington set, particularly by Bertrand Russell. Yet the version of events which the narrator of *Sherston's Progress* chooses to set down hardly does justice to those same events insofar as they can be recovered from the Diary. The reason is clear. The later text consistently revises in order to create an image of a sardonic but essentially good-humoured man who, with the help of others, managed to overcome a series of petulant, selfish outbursts against matters he did not really understand.

What finally brings Sherston to his senses, we are told, is his encounter with the pacifist Doctor Macamble. Macamble comes to see Sherston at Slateford Hospital, and advises him to abscond:

> I had only to take a train to London, and once there he would arrange for me to be examined by an 'eminent alienist' who would infallibly certify that I was completely normal and responsible for my actions . . . I suppose I ought to have waxed indignant, but all I thought was, 'Good Lord, he's trying to persuade me to do the dirty on Rivers!' Keeping this thought to myself, I remained reticent and parted from

him with the heartiest of handshakes. Did I ever see him again, I
wonder? And have I been hard on him? Well, I can only say that
nothing I can do for Doctor Macamble could be worse than his advice
for me—had I been imbecile enough to act on it.

But why is Macamble's advice so absurd? To answer that question is
to open up the large and probably unbridgeable gap between the
Sassoon of the Diaries and the narrator of *Sherston's Progress*. It is
clear that in the later text the narrator does not wish us to take his
protest seriously. At all events, he isn't serious about it. That is his
way of coping with what would otherwise seem a fearful solecism, a
shocking offence against his Englishness. Yet, to his credit, Infantry
Officer Sassoon had been entirely serious when he wrote his letter.
Robert Graves and other friends understood that much, which was
why they were so keen to get Sassoon certified as insane. If he was
mad, he could not be held responsible for his actions. So
Macamble's advice makes perfectly good sense. For Sherston to be
proved sane would be bound to cause the authorities the maximum
embarrassment. Unfortunately, it would also cause the later
Sassoon great embarrassment. The advice is therefore dismissed as
imbecilic.

But the episode becomes even more revealing once we look at
some of the letters which Sassoon wrote between June and
December 1917 and which Hart-Davis puts into the Diaries to help
plug the gap left by an absence of entries for that period. For we
then find that the imbecilic idea had in fact been Sassoon's own. On
19 October he reports to Graves that Rivers says: 'I've got a very
strong "anti-war" complex, whatever that means. I should like the
opinion of a first-class "alienist" or whatever they call the people
who decide if people are dotty.' A week later tells Lady Ottoline
Morrell frustratedly that 'they will *never* court-martial me. The
only chance would be—after being passed fit—to get an outside
opinion from a man like Mercier. I don't quite know how they'd act
if he said I was normal.' (Hart-Davis refers to Mercier as a 'physician
for mental diseases'.) There is no mention in either letter of anyone
who corresponds to Macamble, and it seems safe to conclude that
Sassoon invented him. He would form a strong contrast with
Rivers, on whom he plans 'to do the dirty'. We are told that
Macamble was 'a doctor not of medicine but of philosophy ...
which may have been the cause of his being so chock-full of ideas

and adumbrations'. Very like a Cambridge philosopher of marked pacifist tendencies, it may be.

In this reading, Rivers becomes the wise physician who brings young Sherston to his senses—there is a good deal in the *Progress* about schoolboyish pranks at Slateford—and who cures his muddled protest against the war. Sherston can therefore explain his protest in terms that look like explaining it away: 'the fact that it was everybody's business to be prepared to die for his country did not alter the inward and entirely personal grievance one had against being obliged to do it.' That deflective 'one' shows how difficult Sassoon finds it to cope with a protest which, as his letter makes absolutely clear, was *not* personal, but was written 'on behalf of those who are suffering now', and was directed against the 'political errors and insincerities for which the fighting men are being sacrificed'. 'The necessary supply of heroes must be maintained at all costs', Sir Edward Carson announced early in 1917.

In view of all this it seems reasonable to suppose that the war poems of Siegfried Sassoon would prove an embarrassment to the author of *Sherston's Progress*. Yet reading them through I can see that they fit with the image of the eternal Englishman which the Memoirs promote.[5] Some years ago D.J. Enright remarked that although most of Sassoon's satires hit the mark, the target he aimed at was usually a sitting duck. It is true. The poems operate from a standpoint of decency, and that is both their strength and their weakness. Sassoon attacks Blighters, warmongers, the Junkers in Parliament and incompetent generals, and he speaks for soldiers who

> went arrayed in honour. But they died,
> Not one by one: and mutinous I cried
> To those who sent them out into the night.
>
> The darkness tells how vainly I have striven
> To free them from the pit where they must dwell
> In outcast gloom convulsed and jagged and riven
> By grappling guns.

The language is both vaguely metaphoric (with the coming of war darkness has fallen on Europe) and literal. Sassoon and his men were forced to do much of their work by night: crawling across no man's land in order to check wire installations, recover bodies of the dead and wounded and spy on enemy movements, and they often had to take cover in shell-holes ('the pit where they must dwell' is both the hell of war and a crater). The poem does its best to give off a sense of pity and anger for the men, but the language is weak, repetitive and fatally betrayed by the notion that war ought really to have been a glorious adventure. The soldiers went 'arrayed in honour', very like those crusaders whose images were repeatedly used for recruiting posters and popular propaganda art of the period. They should have been allowed to fight and die in single combat (one by one). Sassoon's poem clings to the feeling, so common in 1914 and for some time afterwards, that the war somehow offered an escape from modernity: it provided a chance to turn from a world that Brooke had stigmatised as 'grown old and weary', and choose a life which Julian Grenfell imagined would be one of 'colour and warmth', where the soldier would discover:

> when fighting shall be done
> Great rest, and fullness after dearth

In short, it was to be a cavalry war, a springtime of opportunity to test sporting and individual skills. But the fox-hunting man became an infantry officer, the war turned out to be a machine-war and thus a confirmation of modernity, and it is *that* which Sassoon protests against in 'To Any Dead Officer':

> I'm blind with tears,
>   Staring into the dark. Cheero!
> I wish they'd killed you in a decent show.

There is a great deal to be said for decency. The case against it, as MacDiarmid saw, is unwittingly set out in *Sherston's Progress*.

Notes

1. Siegfried Sassoon, *Sherston's Progress* (London: Faber 1983).
2. *Siegfried Sassoon Diaries 1915–1918*, ed. Rupert Hart-Davis (London: Faber 1983).

3. Paul Fussell, *The Great War and Modern Memory* (New York: Oxford University Press 1983), p. 183.
4. Sassoon, *Memoirs of a Fox-Hunting Man* (London: Faber 1960).
5. *The War Poems of Siegfried Sassoon*, arranged and introduced by Rupert Hart-Davis (London: Faber 1953).

8
Edgell Rickword

There still seems to be a commonly held view that Edgell Rickword gave up writing poetry in the early 1930s either because the Communist Party of Great Britain—which he had newly joined—told him to, or because his own political conscience made him regard poetry as a bourgeois luxury and therefore an unworthy pursuit for a committed writer. Clive James holds this view, and it has been voiced by writers a good deal more cautious than James. Thus Roy Fuller, in his excellent introduction to Rickword's *Fifty Poems: A Selection*,[1] remarks that Rickword's career in the 1930s makes sense only if we assume that he had decided to 'devote himself to the regeneration of society rather than the regeneration of literature', presumably choosing to allow Leavis and *Scrutiny* to try to bring about the latter regeneration; and Fuller mourns 'the truncation or deformation of a talent so outstanding'. Fuller, however, adds a note of caution that is unlikely to recommend itself to a man of James' brash absolutes: 'How far the Marxism he embraced led to his abandonment of poetry we cannot say, but his verse anyway quite quickly began to develop towards satire, epigram, and the kinds of topicality that only a few great poets—a Pope or a Swift—have been able to make of permanent interest'.

I met Edgell Rickword only once, in the winter of 1975, when he was already old and physically frail. But there was nothing wrong with his mind, and he made a very firm reply to my hesitant question about whether being a Party member had had much to do with his giving up poetry:

> No, not at all. It was just because I hadn't any impulse to write poems. I would have quite liked to, but I was getting into rather a different mood, less subjective I suppose, and I think poetry must have much of the subjective in it. I had stopped writing poetry well before I became a Party member so all that stuff about how being a communist killed me off as a poet is nonsense ... My acquaintance with Marxism didn't act

as a psychological brake on my writing life. Lyric poets tend to finish early, you know.[2]

I think we need to weigh these words carefully, because they do much to dispel the simplistic argument that Rickword's decision to give up poetry may be explained in terms of his political commitments. The hidden point of such an argument is to deny that art and politics can ever have anything to do with each other, which is and ought to be seen as nonsense. Dangerous nonsense, too, for it finally implies that art ought to be indifferent to ideas. Yet in a sense Rickword seems to be in agreement with it. 'Lyric poets tend to finish early, you know'. Yes, but Rickword was never an entirely lyric poet; and as Fuller says, he quickly began to develop towards satire. On the other hand, it is undeniably the case that certain poets do exhaust all they have to say in a comparatively brief span; the entire combustible world of their poetic material swiftly burns itself out. (Of poets roughly contemporary with Rockword we might note William Empson and Kenneth Allott, whose *oeuvres* are even slighter than his, and whose prolonged silences have led to much speculation; e.g. Christopher Ricks on Empson and Donald Davie on Allott.)

It is in the nature of things that speculation cannot be other than tentative, provisional. Nevertheless, a careful reading of Rickword's work, poetry and prose, may go some way towards helping us grasp the probable reasons for his decision to give up poetry. And in case it should be thought that I beg the question in speaking of a decision— for mightn't it simply be that poetry deserted him rather than he poetry, that he had no choice in the matter?—I should add that in his interview with me he remarked that he didn't try very hard to write poetry in the 1930s because 'for some time I had had the news that it had ceased'. Which, if it admits that the necessary fire was out, also makes it clear that he chose not to hammer cold iron.

Rickword published three separate collections of poetry: *Behind the Eyes* (1921), which contains some of the most remarkable poems to have come out of the First World War, poems which are still under-estimated; *Invocation to Angels* (1928), which, I agree with Fuller, contains his finest work; and *Twittingpan* (1931), which is dominated by satirical verse. There is in addition a so-called *Collected Poems* of 1947, which omits a good many poems, and

Fifty Poems, already mentioned, which restores fifteen poems
withheld from the 1947 volume and adds two which had been
previously uncollected.

Anyone coming to Rickword's work for the first time is bound
to be struck by the fact that he belonged to the generation for
whom Grierson's great edition of Donne acted as the discovery of a
new-found land. 'Our ears have been opened', Rickword wrote in
the course of a savage review of a bad critical study of Donne, 'and it
would be profane now to think of [him] as less than a master of
English verse ... If we are to compare 'purest utterances', those of
Donne on sacred and profane love are, it has been granted, excelled
by no poet in the language.' Those sentences were written in 1924,
and the extent of Rickword's debt to Donne is plain to see in
Behind the Eyes, which appeared in the same year as Eliot's famous
essay on 'The Metaphysical Poets'. It is customary to assume that
Eliot defined those poets for his generation; and to an extent he did:
'A thought to Donne was an experience; it modified his sensibility
... The poets of the seventeenth century, the successors of the
dramatists of the sixteenth, possessed a mechanism of sensibility
which could devour any kind of experience'. I do not deny that
Rickword would wish to assent to those words, and it is certain that
some of his own work exemplifies the hope for poetry which they
embody. His poems can glitter with brilliantly deployed ideas,
handled with a grace that is perhaps justifiably described as toughly
lyric. (Rickword's skill in handling ideas in verse gives him the right
to attack Wyndham Lewis's irresponsible way with them. As he
justly remarks, 'To have a lot of ideas is no more to be a good
thinker than to have a lot of soldiers is to be a good general').

Yet this side of Rickword's work always seems to me somehow
sport; it is more than merely dutiful because the nature and scope of
his gifts never allow him to write a dull or unmusical verse. But in
the last resort Donne surely matters to Rickword less for the
reasons that appealed to Eliot than for his love poetry (which was
also why he appealed to Empson). So that when Rickword writes,
in 'Beyond Good and Evil':

> Her thoughts haunt that duplicity
> and perch alike on tree and star,
> in calm, white-winged simplicity,
> innocent as angels are.

> Since, in those blissful powers at least,
> thought and act are identified,
> it is a part-angelic beast
> sleepily smiling by my side

—when he writes this, he is not merely asking us to remember Nietzsche's famous remark that whatever is done out of love takes place beyond good and evil, he is also identifying with Donne the spaceman, in Empson's famous formulation; he is emotionally and intellectually at one with the poet who insists that lovers create their own universe, free from the moral and religious considerations of a post-Lapsarian world. And this is the voice that speaks in 'Intimacy':

> Since I have seen you do those intimate things
> that other men but dream of; lull asleep
> the sinister dark forest of your hair
> and tie the bows that stir on your calm breast
> faintly as leaves that shudder in their sleep;
> since I have seen your stocking swallow up,
> a swift black wind, the flame of your pale foot
>
> . . . .
> I have not troubled overmuch with food,
> and wine has seemed like water from a well

But here another comparison inevitably suggests itself. The tone of these lines echoes the work of English poets of the decadence, of Symons and Dowson, perhaps; and behind them, of course, loom the greater figures of certain French poets, above all Baudelaire. For although I would not wish to place undue stress on an isolated phrase, that 'sinister dark forest' may well signal woman as Salome, as fatal attraction; and in its characteristic deployment of such images Rickword's love poetry is the nearest thing I know in English verse to an attitude, a habit of mind, that one finds in much of Baudelaire's poetry. Indeed, although Fuller notes qualities that link Rickword to the characteristic virtues of seventeenth-century verse, it is the French connection I would rather stress. Poems such as 'Obsession', 'Chronique Scandaleuse' and 'Necropolis':

Decayed fertility now wraps me close
in darkness of no-more-desire,
in damp and fusty sheets of fallen rose
rust-edged at touch of fire
expired, and staring coldly as the moon
. . . .
The essence ravished from the pubic rose
oozes from Memory's fallen flask

—such poems are inconceivable without those French poets of the decadence whose work Rickword knew and about whom he wrote—Baudelaire, Laforgue, Corbière and Rimbaud. Whether he knew equally well the work of the English decadents is unclear, but it is at least likely.

I do not mean to say by this that Rickword set out to imitate such poets. But I think it obvious that they meant a great deal more to him than even Donne, and I suggest that they did so because his modern sensibility was more attuned to their sardonic, disillusioned view of love than to the one he found and cherished in Donne. The only poem of Rickword's which utters an unqualified Yes is a remarkable lyric, 'The Cascade', which is, or so I think, at once a brilliantly ingenious description of a waterfall and also a metaphoric evocation of the female orgasm. And even this poem ends with a bitter twist:

The iron beaks that seek her flesh
vex more her lovers' anxious minds,
in whose dim glades each hunter finds
his own torn spirit in his mesh.

If I understand this stanza aright, and the conceits are uncomfortably compacted, Rickword sees man as both aggressor and victim: he is in fact hurt by his own lusts, tortured by his own flesh.

Now this sad, sour account of love has to be set beside Rickword's sense of universal disorder that finds expression in such poems as 'Earth and Age' and the wryly named 'Regret For the Passing of the Entire Scheme of Things':

Whilst now in dusky corners lovers kiss
and goodmen smoke their pipes by tiny gates—

these oidest griefs of Summer seem less sad
than drone of mowers on suburban lawns
and girls' thin laughter, to the ears that hear
the soft rain falling of the failing stars.

Such accidie is unmistakably modern; which is to say that it is of the 1920s. It is easy to forget how that decade was marked by deep-rooted cynicism, a feeling, (and perhaps no more than a feeling, since the best lacked all conviction) that life had become a kind of posthumous existence without purpose or value. If we are tempted to dismiss such feelings as youthful excess, or indulged rancour, we ought to remember that they were shared by most of the best writers of the time. 'The man of today has inherited a nervous system which cannot withstand the present conditions of life'. That is Montale. And this is Rickword, on Corbière. '[His] is the poetry of rhythmic agitation of the subconscious'. The point I wish to make is simply this, that Rickword's sensibility was one that made it impossible for him to be other than grievously shaken by the world he came into and fought through—and although he was physically injured in the Great War, the poems that come out of that experience record the equivocal mastering of a deeper hurt. His finest work expresses a rhythmic agitation of the subconscious in which delight and disgust are blended in about equal proportions, but in which the equilibrium always threatens to give way to vicious cynicism, hatred and self-loathing. That is to say, Rickword's poems have an outer suavity and almost dandaical control of cadence, which he was almost certainly helped to discover through his reading of French poets, and which at a very deep level he needed because his formal orderliness helped him cope with the otherwise intolerable disorder he found about him. Although love might seem to offer a stay against confusion, in fact it proved to be a further, or even major, source of confusion—yet further evidence of a world falling apart.

Rickword, in short, found himself deeply divided. On the one hand, there was the promise that Donne's poetry seemed to epitomise, a promise of a world elsewhere, which makes one little room an everywhere; on the other, the fact of disillusion, of 'spirit sunken, girls undone' ('Complaint After Psycho-Analysis'). How far was he prepared to face the fact of that division? 'It is often in the artist himself that the enemy to creation is most deeply entrenched, in distrust of his own intuitions; in fear of, resulting in contempt for, aspects of his own emotional life'. Rickword wrote those words in the course of an essay on Wyndham Lewis which is of stunning brilliance; and I think they may tell us a good deal about himself. They may, that is, explain why he began to move towards satire and away from the more lyric, though guarded, personal poetry of his early period. For it is at least possible that Rickword came to feel that he had to direct his attack towards the outer world, to find in its horrors an explanation for disorders within:

> The churches' sun-dried clay crumbles at last,
> the Courts of Justice wither like a stink
> and honourable statues melt as fast
> as greasy garbage down a kitchen-sink

Those lines come from 'Luxury', and if we recall the earlier meaning of the word as well as its modern one, we can, I think, gain some sense of Rickword's seeing in the sins of the flesh a releasing metaphor for a distinctively modern malaise. Given this, he was bound to turn towards satire, and to the wish for 'explosions of the spleen', as he put it in his fine essay on 'The Re-Creation of Poetry', where he makes it plain that such explosions are of value because they 'bring about that relief and cleansing of the mind which is one of the functions of expression'.

Why then did Rickword stop writing? Because he had sufficiently cleansed his mind? Perhaps. Yet I think it truer to say that the best of his work answers to his claim that 'We need a poetry in which the moods (of pure ecstasy and sheer revulsion) are subtly balanced'. The difficulty comes in holding that balance once you have achieved it. Rickword achieved it in a handful of lyrics that are of a quite unique value. I do not know that we have the right to expect any more.

Notes

1. Edgell Rickword, *Fifty Poems: A Selection* (London: Enitharmon Press 1970).
2. The interview can be found in John Lucas, *The 1930s: A Challenge to Orthodoxy* (Brighton: Harvester Press 1978).

9

Yes, But Hang On a Minute:
F. R. Leavis

It was said of Hall Caine, the indefatigable biographer of Victorian men of letters, that he came in with the undertakers. I don't suggest that William Walsh is so quickly off the mark in publishing this book on F.R. Leavis, who died in April 1978, but I do think that perhaps his book shouldn't have been written.[1] Not yet, anyway; not now. The problem is an obvious one. It is that the very mention of Leavis's name arouses such strong feelings, both for and against, that it is very difficult for a critic to find the appropriate tone in which to write about him. Certainly, Walsh hasn't succeeded. He often seems to be a mere hagiographer, and on occasions his prose becomes so Leavis-like that one almost feels that, in a way not usually intended by the cliché, this book is a ghosted production. I am not merely thinking of the number of times the word 'profound' makes an appearance, though there's no doubt that Leavis used it to such unique effect in his prose that, for the moment at least, it ought to be banned from anyone else's vocabulary. More to the point are the constant parentheses, the Leavisian turns of phrase, the recommendation of 'tart wit' and so on—all of which suggest that Walsh has found it impossible to stand at a proper distance from his subject.

Not only that. Walsh says that he doesn't intend to 'hark back over old controversies, or to engage in new ones'. In fact, he does; and whenever he does, he so absolutely takes Leavis's side that one begins to have the gravest suspicions about his fitness to estimate Leavis's achievement properly. For example, in his opening chapter, he mentions the Richmond Lecture in which Leavis attacked C.P. Snow's famous account of the Two Cultures. According to Walsh, Snow

offered no more than some superficial observations about the mutual

151

incomprehension of scientists and non-scientists, cast in a characteristically unrigorous way and expressed with insensitive vulgarity ... Snow's rather bumbling complacencies ...

Walsh may be right, but he ought at least to do Snow the justice of quoting him. Instead, he merely assumes the argument to be settled in Leavis's favour. Too often we are asked to accept that Leavis has carried the day in controversy and that the worth of his ideas and convictions are beyond dispute.

One of the many odd contentions apparently taken for granted by Walsh is that Leavis 'was Johnsonain in temperament'. True, Johnson could be violently disputatious, and his magisterial dismissal of Soame Jenyns may recall Leavis's of Snow; but Johnson was intensely gregarious and loved London—characteristics which scarcely describe Leavis, whom one cannot imagine agreeing with Johnson that a tavern seat is the throne of felicity. Yet these are important aspects of Johnson's temperament. And for all his violent repudiation of such an old friend as Mrs Thrale (a repudiation he regretted, suffered for and humbled himself over) Johnson was a most lovable man. Can the same be said of Leavis? It is obviously difficult to answer such a question without being impertinent; all the same, I find it difficult to envisage Leavis exercising the kind of strong hold on our affections that Johnson so readily commands.

Still, many of his pupils would disagree; or they would say that, if not lovable, he was a man to revere. There is no doubt that generations of his students admired him very deeply indeed, and the testimonies Philip French gathered for his radio portrait include many by distinguished former students. D.W. Harding recalls that he and fellow undergraduates

> would be partly exhilarated, partly somewhat subdued and rueful perhaps—exhilarated by the fresh insights he gave us, the fine discriminations he made and the fresh vistas he opened up: sobered because his standards of insight were extremely high, making us realise how unskilled we ourselves were as readers, how ignorant and immature in general

D.J. Enright remarks that Leavis was one of the few teachers 'who treated one absolutely as an equal', and Walsh himself remembers Leavis as 'a most attractive teacher, very witty and amusing'. It would be absurd to downgrade the importance of these memories, but what about the implicit claim they make for Leavis's uniqueness? I remember with the deepest affection a very great scholar and historian of ideas who taught me, and if I were asked to list his qualities as a teacher I would probably use the identical words that Harding, Enright and Walsh use about Leavis. After all, undergraduates are, in the nature of things, ignorant and immature, so it isn't surprising that a mixture of gratitude and humility is their response to teachers (admittedly rare) who make them understand what it is to want to take possession of their subject. Perhaps, too, the praise given to Leavis as teacher tells one as much about Cambridge as it does about him, and in that case one of the important beneficial effects of his skill and manner may be that it has encouraged a new openness of intellectual relationship between academics and students.

This is perhaps a point to argue over. Incontrovertibly, though, Leavis was at his best a great literary critic, and for me that best is to be found in the essays that make up *Revaluation* and *The Common Pursuit*. I don't think it sensible even to begin to question this fact: those who have tried, including the egregious George Watson, are quite clearly motivated by pique, jealousy or, more understandably but no more productively, by dislike of Leavis's literary personality. For there is no doubt that, even through what is usually the distancing medium of the printed page, Leavis does make a very strong impression. There can be very few students of literature who haven't found themselves incensed by one or the other of his implied judgements, contained in a throw-away parenthesis. And yet it's because of the power of his customary critical argument that one becomes enraged by the unargued assumptions. The *ex cathedra* pronouncements of the majority of critics, academic or otherwise, are of no interest whatsoever.

Even so, I think one has to regret this side of Leavis and to wonder why he so repeatedly indulged it. If style is the man, then one has to say that over the years Leavis's style hardened in a way that suggests a growing intolerance of argument and an increased readiness to make do with pronouncement. Walsh will not concede this. For him, Leavis had

an amazing thing, when one thinks of our age of uncertainty, anxiety and doubt, a swift and untroubled, a positively Augustan, self-

confidence about his deepest judgements of value and an unworried
certainty in their application to the exercise of his craft.

Unintentionally, Walsh allows us here to recall the Johnsonian way
of putting an end to argument: 'I'll have no more on't.' Yet Walsh's
words and their rhythms remind me of a nineteenth-century
fictional hero, whom the later Leavis much admired:

> A composed and unobtrusive self-sustainment was noticeable in
> Daniel Doyce—a calm knowledge that what was true must remain
> true, in spite of all the Barnacles in the family ocean, and would be just
> the truth, neither more nor less, when ever that sea had run
> dry—which had a kind of greatness in it, though not of the official
> quality.

That, it seems to me, is how Walsh wants us to see Leavis. And to
some extent at least it is how Leavis saw himself. 'We were, and
knew we were, Cambridge—the essential Cambridge in spite of
Cambridge.' That claim was made for *Scrutiny*, and during
Scrutiny's formative years in the thirties, Leavis undoubtedly
gathered about him a prodigiously talented group of critics and
collaborators—including Harding, L.C. Knights and James
Smith—who helped him to make it a literary journal of quite
outstanding importance. Again, this seems to me so obviously true
that the proposition does not need to be defended. But it is equally
obvious that by the time *Scrutiny* came to an end, in 1953, the sense
of collaboration had quite gone. Leavis apparently felt himself
betrayed by virtually all his former friends, and the younger
students who identified with him were not so much collaborators as
unquestioning disciples, with those who found themselves posts in
the educational world operating as *Gauleiters*. In this context,
Leavis's critical judgements, which in repetition had by now
hardened into a kind of dogma, were harmful. In the thirties the
collaborative spirit had allowed for creative disagreement. (An
obvious example is the sharp exchange of views between Leavis and
Knights over *Measure for Measure*). But the later 'collaborators'
were in fact hard-liners. The result was that Leavis's famous critical
touchstone 'this is so, isn't it', became shortened to 'this is so'. For
those of us new to literary matters in the fifties, there was no
possibility of discussing with those who had been taught by Leavis

whether Milton was best thought of in the way that he had suggested, or whether Meredith was as meretricious as he had reported, or Browning as vulgar. They were and—'I'll have no more on't.'

Some years ago, for instance, I met a fairly well-known Leavisite at a conference and invited him to join a group of us who were, as it happened, arguing about Shelley. 'I can only read Shelley', he said, 'if I suspend my critical intelligence.' Which Shelley had he in mind, someone asked. 'Any', he replied. *Julian and Maddalo*, perhaps? 'I was thinking of the lyrics', he said. Yes, but what about *Julian and Maddalo*? Silence. It was clear that he'd never read it. Nor could he be expected to. Leavis had pronounced on Shelley, and that was enough.

There must be many people who have had similar experiences which demonstrate that Leavis's very powerful personality did, harm and indeed often led to the opposite of that enquiring spirit he wanted to encourage in his students. Much of the blame for this must lie with him. He can't perhaps be blamed for the quality of the students he attracted after the thirties—those who found it comforting to take on his air of certainty without going through the process of hard, original thought that had brought him to his conclusions. But I do blame him for the air of insufferable moral self-righteousness attached to all he said, so that, if you disagreed with him about Shelley, you were not only a bad critic but the kind of person who would steal money from a blind man's tray.

Eric Bentley, in his essay, *The Importance of Scrutiny*, published as early as 1948, tried to forestall exactly this charge, but he clearly felt that there was a charge to answer:

> those who do not know Leavis sometimes think of him as one who hands out opinions to the young. They miss the point. It may be a fact that some young people have 'stolen' their opinions from Leavis. How could he stop them? The important thing to remember is that such stealing is clearly contrary to Leavis's principles.

Agreed, but principles and practice simply aren't the same thing. Can anyone avoid recognising that during the post-war years you were thought to be either wholly for Leavis or wholly against him? Thus Walsh refers to a journal which, according to Leavis, aimed 'not the less so for deferential shows, at the undoing of all one has worked for'. The journal in question must be the *Cambridge Quarterly* (which I am not here to defend), yet to an outsider like myself, the one thing clear about it, at least in its early days, was that it was precisely modelled on *Scrutiny*.

I bring this up because it hints at something seriously wrong with Leavis, namely his belief in 'the essential Cambridge'. That Cambridge—no matter how anti-establishment—had, I suspect, to measure up in his mind to a platonic concept as absolutely unattainable as Arnold's dream of the aliens. Behind it is a simplistic, demagogic reading of history. Civilisation is a mess and can be saved from its own worst mistakes only by the intervention of the few. So the reading goes. Perhaps demagogic is the wrong term, but I am trying to define a quality of mind that is shared, for example, by Carlyle and Ruskin, and which is typical of the later Leavis. In the last analysis this cast of mind is non-collaborative, since the few have to think as one (and not just anyone either), and it produces uninflected statements such as the following:

> The industrial revolution, which by the end of the eighteenth century was well-advanced, worked and went on working inevitable destruction upon the inherited civilisation of the people. Dickens was the last great writer to enjoy anything of the Shakespearian advantage. There will never be another Dickens. What has been achieved in our time is the complete destruction, the completion of the destruction, of that general diffused creativity which maintains the life and continuity of a culture. For the industrial masses their work has no human meaning in itself and offers no satisfying interest. They save their living for their leisure, of which they have very much more than their predecessors of the Dickensian world had, but don't know how to use it except inertly before the telly, and in the car and bingo hall, filling in pools forms, spending money, eating fish and chips in Spain.

That comes from Leavis's lecture 'T.S. Eliot and the Life of English Literature', which he gave at the Cheltenham Literary Festival in 1968. Perhaps the citizens of Cheltenham thought it deep stuff and vaguely assumed that Leavis was an amalgam of Malcolm Muggeridge, Bernard Levin and the ghost of George Orwell. If so, they were wrong, at least to the extent that Orwell's essay, 'The Art of Donald McGill', shows a good deal more understanding of the actualities of working-class life than can be found in Leavis's formulations. 'Industrial masses': once you define people in that way, they can be pinned down by the offensive journalistic clichés that Leavis wheels out.

The only time I heard Leavis lecture was just before I was to begin a series of Workers' Educational Association classes on the nineteenth-century novel. Leavis lectured on *Dombey and Son* and concluded that in our own day the novel would be unlikely to find favour, 'for this is the age of the telly and Tottenham Hotspur'. Yet sixteen years later I can vividly recall the extraordinary excitement of the six-week period during which my W.E.A. class and myself jointly explored and discovered Dickens's great novel. No doubt many of the class watched telly; and for all I know there were some Spurs supporters among them. But thinking of them now, and of Leavis's remark, I feel a cold fury at the glib dismissiveness that's implied in his acidulous sneer.

Leavis was not only an elitist, he was an ignorant one. 'Some may think it ironic', Walsh writes, 'that this great proponent of the necessity for academic and intellectual elites should have felt, as he undoubtedly did, part of the people.' Ironic wouldn't be my word for it, although I'm quite prepared to believe that Leavis's conception of the 'people' is every bit as Platonic and unrealised as his belief in the elite. And they link up with another of his pieces of historical schematising: his notion of 'the organic community'—a concept responsible for Leavis's praise of a dire passage in *Lady Chatterley's Lover*, where Connie, looking out from her car window over Nottingham's industrial landscape, sees

> the utter negation of beauty, the utter negation of the gladness of life, the utter absence of the instinct for shapely beauty which every bird and beast has, the utter death of the human intuitive faculty ... What could possibly become of such a people, a people in whom the living intuitive faculty was dead as nails

Interestingly enough, in the first and vastly superior version of the novel, Connie, having thought most of this, suddenly remembers that this is where her lover (Parkin in that version) comes from. In other words, she is made to recognise the externality of her point of view and has to accept her ignorance of ways of life which she has been so ready to write off. Lawrence omits that chastening recognition in the published version of the novel, and I can't imagine Leavis ever being similarly chastened.

Which is to say that his feeling of 'enjoying a profound unity with ordinary people' (Walsh's words) is contemptible nonsense. So that I find merely funny Walsh's claim that Leavis's attitude to Oxford and Cambridge, as the only universities, 'relaxed when he had more experience of other places', especially since he doesn't appear to realise what this admission entails. Indeed, he goes on to assert that Leavis's position 'cannot be gainsaid ... Unless the democratic axiom that everyone is capable of the highest in education is dropped, then it is, in Leavis's view "a poor look out for liberal education".' That is, of course, a gross parody of the democratic axiom. It *is* true, rather, that any attempt to predict who will benefit most from education at the highest level is foolish, unjust and inhumane. In a democratic society, opportunities must therefore be as widely available as possible. Disagree with that and you are almost certain to end up muttering about an age of telly and Tottenham Hotspur for the industrial masses or, in Walsh's words, identifying 'the social process which now controls us—the saturation of every fragment of life by the spirit of a commercial civilisation, and within that main drive, most emphatically by the influence of the entertainment industry'.

With this in mind, we can understand why Leavis moved from poetry to fiction; for novels, and especially the novels of Lawrence and Dickens, could be used to indicate and diagnose the ills of modern society. In contrast, Eliot, the only modern poet who Leavis thought of as unambiguously great, could be tried and found wanting. Of course *The Waste Land* was a great poem, because it demonstrated Eliot's awareness that in the modern world sex is 'sterile, breeding not life and fulfilment but disgust, accidie, and unanswerable questions', and because this sterility could be traced finally to 'the final uprooting of the immemorial way of life, of life rooted in the soil'. But the *Four Quartets* won't do because Eliot does not take this immemorial way of life with due seriousness. Leavis accuses Eliot of reducing English civilisation, and the language which made Shakespeare possible, to

> lumpish yokels heavily disporting themselves in the passage which presents the people of pre-Industrial England as 'clumsy, crude, gross, and incapable of the spiritual or cultural graces'.

('Rustically solemn or in rustic laughter/Lifting heavy feet in clumsy shoes,/Earth feet, loam feet ...') The explanation is that Eliot—I quote Walsh's gloss—shared with Pound 'an essential blankness about the kind of human world, the living principle, that has vanished'.

What concerns me is not whether Leavis has properly understood the passage from *East Coker*, but whether he is in any position to talk about a vanished 'living principle'. I don't for a moment think he is. Assertion isn't argument, and anyone who writes about Leavis ought to address himself to the question of why Leavis thinks it should be, and why in particular he should make such totemic use of phrases as 'the organic community' and 'the living principle'. It's because Walsh doesn't even see the need for this that his book won't do. And it perhaps explains why he can end by asserting that, like Lawrence, Leavis, 'in a way Eliot is not, is all of a piece throughout', as though that makes Leavis the more considerable figure. Mightn't Eliot's modesty, his knowing that he did not know, be more valuable?

Notes

1.   William Walsh, *F.R. Leavis* (London: Chatto 1980).

Part Three

SOME CONTEMPORARIES

10
The Red Man:
Geoffrey Grigson

In the mid-1950s, when I was beginning to read poetry avidly and, as I thought, with passionate discrimination, there was a nasty man called Geoffrey Grigson. He was nasty because literary editors paid him to attack Dylan Thomas. Someone would bring out a critical study or, more likely, a reminiscence of days and nights with Dylan; or it might be on account of modern poetry with a section on Thomas. Grigson would review the book and would be rude about it. The author could not write, he could not tell a poem from a lamp-post, he was—more or less, a liar—probably an academic, and the world was full of his kind.

Memory distorts. I do not suppose that I read as many Grigson reviews as I now feel to have been the case. But clearly their brisk discharge of venom lodged in my mind. And I do suppose that lazy-minded people in charge of newspaper book-pages or the back half of the weeklies thought Grigson an easy way to provide their readers with controversial copy. 'Another book on Thomas? Give it to Grigson, let's have some damning and blasting.' I would not have known that then, of course; it takes time to understand the ways of literary editors. But I did know that Thomas was poetry. And who was Grigson? Flame-haired, red-faced with permanent rage, or so I imagined him, his name a malignant humour you uttered through clenched, grinding teeth. 'A Thirties man', one of my lecturers told me. He also told me about *New Verse*, Grigson the champion of Ben Nicholson and Henry Moore, Grigson the anthologist, Grigson the poet.

I was not appeased. It is normal to hate the enemies of your heroes. When you are young, the love and the hatred are intense. I found and read a few of Grigson's poems and knew it was safe to hate him. *He* would never be able to write 'After a Funeral', or 'Should Lanterns Shine' or 'Poem in October' or 'Fern Hill'.

Besides, in poetry and prose alike, he was so infuriatingly, hatefully certain about everything. Even in his longer pieces he did not argue; he simply said *this* goes to heaven and *that* goes to hell, and if you think differently then you are a fool or worse. As a university student I knew that you must 'argue for your preferences'. It was, of course, evident that arguments which brought you to see things as your lecturers did were certain to gain you better marks than arguments which implied that your lecturers had missed the point. Still, there was at least a pretence that we were engaged in a common pursuit of true judgement, weeding out the lesser growths so that the deserving plants would have all the light. Grigson was simply trampling wherever he pleased, and without regard for others. (This was before I had heard of the billhook.)

I do not doubt that there is an element of parody in what I have said. But I set the matter down as I remember to have felt at the time when I first came across the name of Geoffrey Grigson. Looking back over *Blessings, Kicks and Curses*[1] and other Grigson pieces which I have kept and which now I would not be without, I see that my memory is correct in this respect at least: that he does not argue, not well, not consistently. The red-faced man says 'this is so' and does not wait for an answer to 'isn't it?' But then the true test of his blessings and curses will be in his anthologies, editions and selections, and as I went on reading—we are now in the 1960s—I found that I was increasingly dependent on, or persuaded by, Grigson's taste. It was his Muse's Library editions that introduced me to William Barnes and John Clare, from him I learnt of Clere Parsons, Landor, Norman Cameron, William Browne, Barton Holyday and others. And this was troubling. For the red-faced man had been rude about both Larkin and Lowell, and how could you trust someone who refused to bow before *Life Studies* or *The Whitsun Weddings*? Aw' a muddle.

It was resolved, this muddle, in 1971. That year Grigson published two anthologies. I bought, read and delighted in his *Faber Book of Popular Verse*, with its tangy, unofficial English and American language, its bawdy, work-a-day subjects, its relishing of private faces often poking their tongues at public faces in public places.[2] *This* Grigson seemed more often red-faced with laughter than with rage. For my children I bought *Rainbows, Fleas and Flowers: A Nature Anthology*.[3] They never got it. (But I did buy them another copy.) Nowadays my own copy looks three times its age: thumb-marked, dog-eared, torn, it has been picked up and put down in so many different rooms that its cover is an impasto of tea rings, wine stains, toothpaste flakes, cigarette burns and the streaked juices of crushed flies. It is not only my favourite anthology, it has no rival. Nor can I imagine one possible. Relish is what it has and gives—of poets (Eastern as well as Western), of past and present, of the things of this world, of flora and fauna (except that such words make abstract what the anthology makes actual). Grigson opens his anthology with the following words:

> It is cheerful to learn, I think, that from space our earth is an exquisite blue. Red Mars, White Venus, Blue Earth. Poets of all the past would be delighted at the news. But it would make them—if they could be persuaded into space—want all the more to turn round, and come down to go on enjoying this world, this Blue World, which is their habitat by nature.

What did that remind me of? Of Frost, saying:

> Earth's the right place for love,
> I don't know where it's likely to go better

Of Cowper, noting that 'A yellow shower of leaves is falling continually from all the trees in the country ... The consideration of my short continuance here, which was once grateful to me, now fills me with regret. I would live and live always.' (The words obviously cut deep for Grigson; he refers to them, quotes them, paraphrases them, on many occasions.) But I suddenly realised that the poet who was closest to the opening words of the anthology was someone Grigson professes not to admire, indeed someone he is customarily scornful of: Wallace Stevens. Stevens's Large Red Man reads from the poem of life, from 'the great blue tabulae', of 'the pans above the stove, the pots on the table, the tulips among them'. He is crowded round by the ghosts of those who have returned to earth, eager for a chance to relish 'this world' from which they had chosen to turn away, preferring until it was too late 'a wilderness of stars' where heavenly meanings, so they hoped, could be found. Now, they

> would have wept to step barefoot into reality
> ... would have wept and been happy, have shivered in the frost

> And cried out to feel it again, have run fingers over leaves
> And against the most coiled thorn
>
> ('Large Red Man Reading')

Grigson as the Large Red Man. Stevens's poem is about 'reality', Grigson's anthology is a packed hive of the real—at least as far as words, plosive and cadenced, can make it. No ideas but in words that keep the closest touch with things—to taste, hear, see, smell, touch: 'To savour or enjoy [an experience] to the full'. To relish.

Two years previously Grigson had published *Ingestion of Ice Cream.*[4] I read it in 1971, at the insistence of Barry Cole, poet and friend. (I had not bought a copy when it first appeared; Barry, who has a Grigson-like certainty about what is good and bad, told me I was a fool.) I read:

> But always up between the two
> On a most narow wall

' "Most narrow", he got that trick from Stevens', I said. Seven pages further on I came upon 'most netted thicket'. 'Stop being a boring academic', Barry said. 'Read the poems.' When I had read them, I went back and read them again. This was the Red Man right enough. The exactness of the eye, matching—making for—exactness of cadence, of phrase, of savoured rhymes: like a spray of cold, salt water, fresh on the skin. From 'Red Dahlias':

> To vanish, after a share,
> if not enough, of the
> yellow fruits of the world,
> sharp, scented and sweet, without
>
> Pain or too much pain to
> those I love and leave.
> But I wake up again:

And for this Red Man, death was, as it must be, the mother of beauty. From 'Old Man by a Lake in June':

> It is hard to climb out
> but at last he stretches at length on his towel,
> adjusts his cloth cap over his eyes and sleeps

before lunch, if you call it sleep, his last summer,
it wouldn't surprise me, under the mountains,
under the freckling sun.

Old also, I wish him no thinking, only
the feel of the sun.

There is red for anger, as in 'I Love You', about an incident in the
Vietnam war, and red for laughter; for, as he writes in 'Yahoos: A
Variation, and Reply', though the world's pros seem hard to find:

> never mind:
> Short as you may suppose their list,
> Sour pessimist,
> They do exist, they do exist.

I do not pretend to know why at the end of the 1960s Grigson
should suddenly become a necessary poet. (*A Skull in Salop*, has the
first hints of what will follow.[5]) There are, and remain, limitations.
Grigson is no good on love. He does not try long poems at all. He
couldn't do so, of course, because his poems start from and are
threaded on the single, singular sighting, the single idea. He is still a
bit heartless. Admittedly the billhook works more neatly, swiftly
and surely in poetry than in prose, where its swishing often turns
into an unintendedly funny noise, but his dandified view of people
as objects can be shallow in its remoteness, and chilling. Grigson is
the poet of surface. He has little to say about process. He is the poet
of moment. He takes a few lines out of someone's poem,
sometimes no more than a phrase and—look, he says, *that* is the
poem. So, nearly always, it is. That poems can come from and be
heading elsewhere is something his certainties don't allow him to
know. If they did, he wouldn't be Grigson. But how, given the
anthologies and the poems of the last fifteen years, could you wish
him to be other than he is?

Notes

1.   Geoffrey Grigson, *Blessings, Kicks and Curses: A Critical Collection*
     (London: Allison and Busby 1981).

2. Grigson, *Faber Book of Popular Verse* (London, 1971).
3. Grigson, *Rainbows, Fleas and Flowers: A Nature Anthology,* (London, 1971).
4. This volume is currently out of print, but *see* Grigson, *Collected Poems 1963–1980* (London: Allison and Busby 1983).
5. Grigson, *A Skull in Salop* (Chester Springs PA: Dufour 1969); *see also Collected Poems, op. cit.*

11
The Bluff Masks of Old Buff:
Roy Fuller

In 'School Time, Work Time', one of the poems in his new collection, *The Reign of Sparrows*,[1] Roy Fuller contrasts the financier inside his chauffeur-driven car, gazing on long-legged school girls, with the girls themselves, who might

> by wild chance
> Glancing inside, see papers spread
> Apropos some cool million.
> Grave nonsense of bonds and bourses:
> Glass case of the mummified dead.

'Grave nonsense'. It's an old buffer's pun, or rather, in its unoriginal knowingness, the pun of someone who is perfectly prepared to play the old buffer's role. Indeed, in one of the poems in the sequence, 'In His Sixty-Fifth Year', Fuller calls himself an 'elderly buffer'. *The Reign of Sparrows* illustrates the state of bufferdom, in phrases, lines and sometimes whole poems; for example, 'In the noddle' and:

> Three and thirty years past I sojourned here

and:

> Yet no one is more aware
> Than I of the Beast-ruled age

and:

> A seven-spotted ladybird
> Toddles across the sheet

and so on.

Coming across such moments I am reminded of Ian Hamilton's comment on an earlier collection, *Buff*, that 'it is perhaps Buff's real distress that ... the style he has to be content with is as insufficiently nourished by direct feeling as the personality, or state of mind, he wants it to express'. Such a style, or tone, is much in evidence at the opening of *Souvenirs*, part autobiography, part memoir, where Fuller fears that his reminiscences may be 'degenerating into an old buffer's chain of consciousness'.[2] But as with 'grave nonsense', so with 'chain of consciousness'. This isn't *quite* an old buffer speaking. Fuller may tell us of a poet's 'Frog ancestry', he may refer to his own 'testy reactionariness', or remind himself not to 'waffle on about gramophone records', or say that 'mere caricature pertains, of course, when the aristocracy is offered to be depicted' (of Dickens). He may even choose to recall John Davenport 'initiating a physical kerfuffle'. Yet for all that, 'old buffer' is something of a mask. Speaking of himself when a young man, he notes, 'I cannot exaggerate my seriousness about the trivialities of life, lack of knowhow, nervousness, shyness —coupled, though of course it is hard to judge how effectively, with masks designed to hide my deficiencies'. Revelation? Hardly, I think. Fuller doesn't like to give much away.

In an early and interesting though badly written poem, 'The Journey', the protagonist finds himself led willy-nilly to a fateful encounter, rather like Childe Roland, except that here there is no possible heroism—instead, defeat that stems from a move too far:

> In his cracking brain, his tortured thews,
> A little world is burning:
> The snow, the treading rooks, the plan
> Of a last mistaken journey.

There are mistaken journeys in *Souvenirs*, outer and inner, but they are all recorded with that conscious inadequacy of style which Hamilton criticised and commended. Reading the book makes for a baffling experience. It is *so* determined to avoid a coherence that could be thought contrived, *so* unwilling to become anything as ambitious or deliberate as an account of the growth of a poet's mind, *so* ready to strike a self-deprecating pose.

Of course, there is much of interest. How could there not be? The maternal grandfather comes across as a Bennettian card, and there are fascinating glimpses of both parents. But we are forced to see by glimpses. Chapter 5 begins, 'For a reason I never knew or have forgotten, phrases applicable to much of these reminiscences'; and it's difficult not to feel that he ought to have remembered, or at least have made the effort. For example, he claims to have no memories of a soon-dead brother's brief life, a failure which he puts down to 'the misunderstandings of childhood but [which] surely has been augmented by self-centred obtuseness'.

Hard to quarrel with such candour, but one does rather wonder why he didn't think it worthwhile to ask his mother about it all. And when he remarks on letters sent to his future wife that they were 'never perused since sent', one is puzzled as to whether that way of putting it is meant to disarm us from asking whether he thinks they should have been, and if not why he mentioned them in the first place.

So it goes. What, for example, is one to make of the remark that when he was asked by a physician whether he was nervous, he answered that he was, although 'In fact my "nerves" were doubtlessly efficiently concealed behind the mask by then perfected for presentation to the ordinary encounters of life'? That prim, teasing elusiveness, those stilted rhythms, almost as though James's Mr Longdon is staging a re-appearance: they define the feeling of *Souvenirs*. (The title itself is borrowed from a once-popular song, genteel, sentimental, a bit absurd.)

When he left school, Roy Fuller went in for law, for which he claims he wasn't fitted, although he largely exonerates his headmaster from 'the blame for my entering a profession which called for talents I neither possessed by nature, nor by education thus far'. Yet *Souvenirs* seems to me very much a product of the legal mind: canny, utterly astute in its 'candid' admissions of weaknesses—'I spent much of my childhood (and later life) missing connections in human affairs, obvious to others' and 'my dotty and priggish devotion to authority'—bufferish and game-playing to its own advantage in its use of (*pace* Hamilton's praise for 'trim vocabulary') the pedantic and not-quite-but-nearly absurd use of such words as 'rugeous', 'endentulousness', 'obstipated', 'minaciousness', 'oleaginous'. What *is* one to make of them? Reading the book makes one realise afresh why David Copperfield had a hard time of it trying to fathom Mr Spenlow.

In short, it is difficult not to feel irritated by *Souvenirs*. The

bufferdom, apologies for non-existent or faulty memory, the sense
of someone talking, if not to himself then to a few of the family—it
can become a way of shutting off the reader; and a way of
nourishing an improper casualness. For example, speaking of a maid
whom his mother kept on tiny wages, and from whom as a boy he
borrowed a shilling so that he could buy the new *Tom Webster's
Annual*, Fuller confesses:

> As I write this it comes to me for the first time that not only was Amy
> a sterling soul: possibly she also loved me, a benefaction that
> throughout life my character has not counted on.

Is 'my character' apart from 'me'? If so, which of the two is it who
condescendingly refers to Amy as a 'sterling soul'? This is Spenlow
and Jorkins territory. In both *Souvenirs* and *The Reign of Sparrows*
Fuller is liable to put matters in such a way as to suggest that he is
somehow not responsible for his own life or for what goes on in it.
At one point in the reminiscences he remarks that he is now 'more
capable of letting ordinary human feelings govern my actions,
though that is not saying much'; and again one has the sense of the
canny admission, of a move that stays a long way short of danger.

There is a sense in which Fuller's presentation of himself in
Souvenirs comes across as a carefully contrived stoicism. He
remarks that in his early years 'much of what was happening to me
was fundamentally antipathetic, yet such is youth's vigorous
acceptance of existence, I accepted the lifestyle of others without
much protest or attempted avoidance'. And he then goes on to ask
himself whether he was not 'possibly unhappier in early days about
a life far from fulfilling its deepest and truest desires and gifts? Later,
some sort of compromise was achieved and endured'.

Later still, he refers to the 'renewals and developments of
creativity which have sustained—helped to make not
unhappy—my life'. The problem is that he is so reticent about the
desires and gifts, renewals and creativity, that it becomes difficult to
gauge the strength of what has helped to make for a state of not
unhappiness. For one thing, he tells us little about the poets who
must have been early influences on him, or of the Marxism (was it?)
to which he gave allegiance during his green years. For another, we
learn little about his emotional life. It isn't so much that one
demands blinding theologies of fruits and flowers as that one

wonders why, if it all perhaps meant so comparatively little, it
proved worth recording. But then the velleities of *Souvenirs* are
positively Jamesian. Yet, as one of the war poems reminds us, Fuller
has found it necessary to remark that:

> Beyond the word, the chosen images,
> Painful and moving as they are,
> I feel
> Unutterably the epoch's tragedies

It's a way of asking us to take something on trust. At the same time,
the reticence, the development of a style to admit and not admit
how much he knows, can pay off.

But not always, and perhaps not often. Many of the poems in the
new volume are flawed by Fuller's refusal to utter feelings that may
surprise him. For example, the Arnoldian 'On His Sixty-Fifth
Birthday' suffers precisely from its readiness to accept

> these lines devoid
> Of charm, as stuck they are
> With the cares of a Philistine world

What really hurts this poem is not so much the cares of the
philistine world as that Fuller isn't prepared to make a poem that
defies such cares. Why else should we have to put up with the
silliness of 'The heavens sufficiently ope', let alone the reference to
Heine (it must be) as 'the Kraut', or such an unscannable line as:

> For arraigning England he forgave

which can be turned into a three-stress line only by a lunatic game of
ducks and drakes with syllables?

So often with Fuller one notices syntactic inversions which seem
to apologise for their ineptitude on the grounds that there are
things that are important beyond all this fiddle. As in 'Notebook':

> Yet aren't
> To this new world the keys
> Pedestrian particularities?

Or one comes across the arbitrary alteration of rhyme, as in

'Oxford Album', where the last stanza oddly conflates the pattern that Fuller had chosen to establish at the poem's beginning.

Even the better poems suffer from the lawyer's professional modesty, which implies an all-too-English sense that there's no virtue in making a song and dance about poetry. The beautiful, tactfully conversational poem to the dead Bonamy Dobrée, 'Last Dreams', is flawed by the clumsy, would-be Hardyesque line:

> You liked it not those months without your wife

and by the metrically chaotic:

> Apt for the grim not ignoble rite

Bufferdom pops up in 'The Sloth Moth' (successfully) and the 'Cinquains' (less successfully), which surely have for inspirational source the wonderful 'Marginalia' of *City Without Walls*, but which lack the bite, wit and rightness of those miraculous runic utterances.

Still, there are some neat successes among 'Quatrains of an Elderly Man', and '140 Years On' is for the most part a fine tribute to the Tennyson of 'In Memoriam'. But much more important is a poem in which feelings can be and are uttered:

> Evening: the robin silent; trees
> > Dark on a cloudless, still-bright sky
> > The near trees calm, but modestly
> The far stirred by a transient breeze.
> The scene so beautiful perhaps
> > Because unhaltable the hour—
> > As though the extent of summer's power
> Were reckoned by the day's collapse.

"Methinks Buff smiles." "Buff neither laughs nor smiles."

Notes

1. Roy Fuller, *The Reign of Sparrows* (London: London Mag. Edns 1980).
2. Fuller, *Souvenirs* (London: London Mag. Edns 1980).

12
A Claim to Modesty:
Peter Porter

Peter Porter's remark that poetry is 'a modest art' has excited a good deal of comment, most of it unfavourable. There is a general feeling that he is somehow selling poetry short, and that while one might not actually want to mention the divine afflatus nowadays (although some don't seem to mind claiming it for themselves), it's there right enough, and to pretend otherwise is boorish or downright philistine. Yet in an obvious sense Porter's remark seems perfectly just. For although there are excellent poets writing at the moment, it is difficult to see how the achievement of even the best of them can sensibly be compared with that of Solzhenitsyn, or Heinrich Boll, or Nadine Gordimer, for example. As to the claim for 'inspiration', of the poet as *vates*, there are two good reasons for wanting to challenge that. In the first place, to do so clears away the rubble of poseurs and hysterics; in the second, it creates a space in which art can freely stand. More particularly, perhaps, the call for modesty is the satirist's way of reminding us that *his* poetry matters:

> At no time have I sluiced my mouth in the Fountain
> Of Hippocrene, nor (if my memory serves me)
> Have I dreamed ever on two-peaked Parnassus, that I
> Should burst forth, this way, without warning, a poet.
> I leave to them whose busts the fawning ivy
> Favors all claim to the Muses of Helicon
> And the spring at Pirene which imparts pallor: not more
> Than half a member of their clan, I offer my song
> At the bards' banquet.

Persius's mock disclaimer (I quote from W.S. Merwin's excellent version) is of relevance to Peter Porter, and not merely because Persius deeply influenced Martial, one of Porter's favourite poets.

There is the more general point that the kind of modesty to which Persius testifies isn't at all the same thing as hesitancy. Indeed, it carries with it a kind of certainty of judgement which Porter clearly identifies with and which he makes good use of in the opening lines of his volume, *After Martial*:

> Because I don't attempt those modern poems
> like lost papyri or Black Mountain Lyrics
> stuffed with Court House Records, *non sequiturs*,
> and advice on fishing; and since my lines
> don't pun with mild obscenities in
> the *Sunday Times*; nor yet ape Ezra's men
> in spavined epics of the Scythian Marsh,
> The Florentine Banking Scene, or hip-baths
> in Northumberland; nor am I well-fledged
> in the East European Translation Market,
> whose bloody fables tickle liberal tongues;
> despite this I make my claim to be a poet.

Like Martial, who went to Rome in early manhood from his home near Barcelona, Porter is an outsider. He has the provincial's sour relish in attacking the absurdities and vices of the world he comes into, including its immodesty, and there is a deliberate tastelessness about much of his work, a witty refusal to accept the values which that world lives by. Yet at the same time, he knows just how attractive it is—why otherwise leave home for it?—so that envy and distaste, and a mocking awareness of both, touch and move apart in his satiric writing. At the end of a fine early poem, 'Forefathers' View of Failure', Porter notes of Australia that:

> In this new land the transplanted grasses root,
> Waving as sulkily as through old falling soot

The substituted word—'sulkily' for 'silkily'—neatly catches the note of dour, grudged, wry self-dramatising he so often has when he is writing well.

Porter enjoys being the malcontent. Indeed, there were times in the earlier poems when you felt that the role came too easily. In spite of the conscious self-parody of 'Metamorphosis' ('This new Daks suit, greeny-brown,/Oyster-coloured button, single vent, tapered/Trousers, no waistcoat, hairy tweed'), he seemed about to turn professional as the Rancorous Digger, as in 'John Marston Advises Anger':

> Love goes as the M.G. goes.
> The colonel's daughter in black stockings, hair
> Like sash cords, face iced white, studies art,
> Goes home once a month. She won't marry the men
> She sleeps with, she'll revert to type—it's part
> Of the side-show: Mummy and Daddy in the wings,
> The bongos fading on the road to Haslemere
> Where the inheritors are inheriting still.

Good, rough, knockabout stuff, but redeemed from journalese only by the sharpness of Porter's eye and phrase-making ability ('sash cords' is exactly right). Even the celebrated sequence 'The Sanitised Sonnets' in *The Last of England*, suffers, I think, from never being able to shake entirely free of knowingness. And the fact that Porter candidly admits to such knowingness doesn't really help: it's Chinese-boxy. Still, the sonnets have that scabrous wit which is one of the immediately recognisable features of Porter's writing and which makes him so enjoyable a poet, even when he writes clumsily.

The clumsiness is an odd matter. I am not merely thinking of such journalistic language as 'she'll revert to type', though there is rather too much of that in the earlier work; nor of those occasional heaps of words that scrape against each other like jag-edged flint (again, they occur more often in the early work). More troublingly, there are strange moments when a poem's movement, and its controlling cadences, simply disappear. An example occurs in 'Between Two Texts', from *Preaching to the Converted*, where stanzas of adroitly-handled iambic pentameters suddenly collapse at the line:

> Gesture alarm at premature burial

which has no discoverable rhythm at all. (It should perhaps also be pointed out that 'burial' is made to rhyme with 'Ariel', and that Porter's rhymes are by no means always the best.) Or there is the stumbling first line of a stanza from 'The School for Love':

> Meanwhile, a schoolmaster is heard
> Praising the egotistic sublime
> And I demur. We live, I fear, in time
> And death is a big thing and bigger word.

In the new volume, *English Subtitles*, a poem called 'About on the Serchio' begins with the lines:

> Shelley's unfinished poem
> must have been written
> on the flat dull stretch to Pisa.

You can't get much flatter or duller than that.

These clumsy, awkward or careless moments may be accounted for as the bad side of modesty. They may even look like the provincial's determination not to take the values of the centre seriously, to see art as artificial. Yet this can hardly be so. For one thing, in *Preaching to the Converted* Porter has a vicious poem ('The Isle of Ink') about those who favour a feelingful artlessness at the expense of art and intelligence:

> Why sod about? Blood's running down the sluice,
> Napalm in the knickers, if I may quote Jeff.
> We need a new art, with angles all obtuse

Also, many of his poems are unembarrassed about their passionate interest in music and painting; and they include some of his best work. For although Porter is a good satiric poet, he is much more besides.

How then to account for these old flaws? I suspect the truth is that they are simply the price Porter pays for his fertility, his teeming inventiveness. And here his being the outsider is a great advantage. He is, after all, the Power the giftie's given us. His 'Story Which Should Have Happened' is the best poem I know about a kind of England that's discoverable in the fiction of Hugh Walpole through to Elizabeth Taylor or William Trevor, and which corresponds to that particular nostalgia for a past which the English still like to pretend is available to them, or perhaps to others, more English even than themselves:

There should have been the Old Manse under creeper
with half a sermon lying on the desk,
the vague light reaching in to touch the roses—
there should have been herb gardens and poppies

Compared with the wit, and insatiable accuracy of detail, in 'Story Which Should have Happened', Donald Davie's much-admired 'The Garden Party' is poorly written and weakly observed.

More important, however, is Porter's language. It is truly an international language, quite simply because it isn't like the language of any native English poet and because he can do things with it that no English poet can. It's dazzingly eclectic sometimes almost too much so; as if Christopher Middleton and John Ashbery had agreed to write a pastiche of, say, Hans Magnus Enzensberger. (See, for example, 'The Workers' in *The Last of England*, too long to quote here. I suspect that the Hamburger-Middleton anthology of *Modern German Poetry*, which was published in 1962, had a more frutiful effect on Porter than on any other poet who began writing in the 1960s.) Yet what I am attempting to describe is perhaps less a matter of language than of what such language can reveal. It is a habit of mind, an attitude, sometimes and quite properly a pose even, that is extraordinarily generous, accessible and responsive to ideas, to art and to music, to the things of this world; and it can therefore move at ease among a whole variety of subjects which English poets typically approach, if at all, with awestruck solemnity or rasping contempt. In short, it is utterly civilised. Yet it is quite without the collusive implications which that word customarily takes on. (This no doubt helps to explain why Porter's civility in defining poetry as a modest art should have been so much misunderstood and should have aroused so much hostility.) This language, this habit of mind, could perhaps be defined as a variety of latter-day Baroque: ebullient, delighting in creativity, and emblematically caught in this stanza from 'The Tomb of Scarlatti':

I hate the idea of Spain, yet for Domenico
I'd round each corner with its urine smell,
tickle the garden fish with a martyr's bone,
sit in the shadow of a cancered priest.
So many slaps of black! The old dust lumps

For American recordings, keyboard clatters
like cruel dominoes—E major fills the afternoon.

One could put the matter slightly differently by saying that Porter
is a fit successor to Auden who, as I think Porter has himself
pointed out, was the first poet to find a language that is both truly
of the twentieth century and unrestricted, and whose wry comment
that 'poetry makes nothing happen' has been as much
misunderstood as Porter's, and even more abused. *The Last of
England* is dedicated to 'the decade of the Nineteen Thirties' and
poems such as 'The Widow's Story' and 'Europe: An Ode' make
very clear the way in which Porter has learned from Auden that it's
possible to have the confidence to see things as a European. He has
acquired a vision which is much more assuredly international than
that of poets who insist on the need to imitate Carlos Williams or
'Black Mountain Lyrics'.

There are, it has to be said, occasions when this easy, delighted
confidence can degenerate into a knowingness which is merely
slick. Several of the 'Postcard Poems' from *Preaching to the
Converted* are too slight a joke to earn their keep. They are notes
about paintings, small enough to fit onto the back of postcard
reproductions of the paintings they are about:

> I look
> as though I've got the collywobbles or
> I've swallowed a Latin Grammar:
> you'd never guess the things I can do
> with my lips. I'm seventeen and bored again.
> (Domenico Veneziano—Profile Head
> of a Young Woman— Kaiser Friedrich
> Museum, Berlin).

This is the kind of jotting one finds in later Auden. It is witty but
essentially trivial.[1]

Porter also shares with Auden a gift for generalisation, for moral
statement. Indeed, there are moments when Porter's gift comes so
near to Auden's that you have to rub your eyes to make quite sure
that you are not in fact reading Uncle Wizz's own words:

> The pity
> Of it, that we are misled. By mother,

    saying her sadness is the law, by love,
    hiding itself in evenings of ethics,
    by despair, turning the use of limbs
    to lockjaw.

Yet these lines, which come from 'The Delegate', one of the poems from *The Cost of Seriousness*, are in fact utterly secure, and 'The Delegate' is a truly marvellous poem.[2] The person who speaks is the dead wife of a poet, and it is worth noting that Porter has been fascinated by the possibilities of dramatic monologue from the outset of his career, and that his convincing ability to inhabit other lives, while it may not prove an ability to 'suffer dully all the wrongs of Man', yet again makes sense of why he should say that poetry is a modest art.

The Cost of Seriousness contains five or six poems that seem certain to last. The same is true of *English Subtitles*.[3] Porter's ability to deliver lapidary statement has never been finer than it is in the new book, nor more telling—(though it is typical of him that he should self-deprecatingly refer to himself as a 'philosopher of captions'). The poems of *English Subtitles* have extraordinary verve and a quite new eloquence, measured but genuine, in which wit is poised against melancholy in ways that are often expressed through taut, graceful rhythms, as in the comparatively slight poem, 'My Old Cat Dances', which ends:

    Moving one paw out and yawning,
    he closes his eyes. Everywhere
    people are in despair. And he is dancing.

There is a major group of poems in the volume concerned with the process and experience of ageing. They include 'Occam's Razor', 'The Future', 'The Story of Jason', 'The Garden of Earthly Delights', 'What I have Written', 'The Imperfection of the World', and 'Returning', all of them good, and three poems of quite stunning achievement. One, 'The Werther Level', brilliantly evokes Werther, that 'pure/cavalier of auto-angst', speaking to the poet who is divided against himself and shared out among the personal pronouns, 'I', 'you' and 'he'. It is a poem which acknowledges its savouring of melancholy and in which knowingness is deployed as intensely serious wit, as it is in 'At Lake

Massaciuccoli', and the wonderful 'The Unfortunate Isles', about which the 'dictionary of discontinuity' finally remarks:

> 'there stands
> the Principality of Childhood reducèd
> to a crumpled letter, there a rain tank
> rusting into canna flowers which marks
> the courtliness of love. Nobody weeps here
> for what he's lost, since everything is home.
> Each is a creature calming himself
> with more anxiety. The prevailing wind
> blows memory in your face, and up the beach
> the harmonies of death return to breed.'

Randall Jarrell would have understood just how well Porter uses run-on lines in this passage.

The other major group of poems in *English Subtitles* have to do with memories of a dead wife. (The groups are in a sense linked by dreams, and the word itself occurs some twenty times in the volume.) The memories are not only of her, they are also hers, as in 'Alcestis and the Poet', which, if it isn't quite as good as 'The Delegate', is nonetheless a poem of urgent authority. The same can be said of 'Good Ghost, Gaunt Ghost' and 'All the Difference in the World'. This latter poem has a bitter truthfulness of statement, a difficult, hard honesty; as the apparently casual title implies, there is all the difference in the world between this and sincerity:

> Between wounds made by words
> and the enduring silence of those
> who can talk of love
> only in the cadences of memory

Other good poems are 'Addio Senza Rancor' and 'Talking to You Afterwards'. The volume closes with a dramatic poem of the utmost command, 'Landscape with Orpheus'. Orpheus is subtly presented as a composite figure, and the landscape through which he moves is at once mythical and modern, a blend of Poussin-like classicism and twentieth-century Australia. The poem itself is a dream rewind as of an old film, a viewing, now distanced, now foreshortened, of Orpheus's eager, reluctant journey into the dark, unknowable, beckoning future, of his wish to return, his wanting and not wanting to take the inevitable step from his beginnings. The theme is familiar, the treatment utterly original, and that is true for several poems of *English Subtitles*. To say that Peter Porter is one of the best poets now writing is not, I think, to make an immodest claim.

Notes

1. Porter, *Collected Poems* (Oxford: Oxford University Press 1983). All of the poems so far discussed can be found here.
2. Peter Porter, *The Cost of Seriousness* (Oxford: Oxford University Press 1978).
3. Porter, *English Subtitles* (Oxford: Oxford University Press 1981).

13

Emphasising the Elegiac:
British Poetry Since 1970

In a prefatory note, the editors of *British Poetry Since 1970* explain that their new book doesn't attempt to be comprehensive: 'Most of the essays are on individual writers'.[1] There is nothing wrong with that, although one is bound to note some striking omissions. Scottish poets come off badly. There is nothing on MacCaig or Mackay Brown, nor on Sorley Maclean, for that matter, even though the publication of *Poems for Eimhir*, in 1971, was surely an event of very considerable importance. Indeed, if one thinks of individual volumes rather than writers, the omissions become even more striking. In their bibliography of poetry published between 1970 and 1980 the editors list, among others, Silkin's *Amana Grass*, Anne Stevenson's *Correspondences*, Derek Mahon's *The Snow Party*, Paul Muldoon's *New Weather*, and Peter Porter's *The Cost of Seriousness*. None of these is mentioned in the essays. In the cases of Mahon and Muldoon this is presumably because, as the editors tell us in their polemical introduction, with the exception of Heaney and Tom Paulin, Ulster's poetic activity 'does not transcend locality'. It is difficult to know whether this remark is the result of blindness or ignorance. Have they actually read 'In a Disused Shed in Co. Wexford', for example, or 'Elizabeth'? Silkin is perhaps omitted because he had a row with Donald Davie, and Porter because Davie doesn't approve of him. (Davie and C.H. Sisson are very obviously the presiding influences over the collection.) But I think it very odd that *Correspondences* should be listed in the bibliography and yet not be thought important enough to merit critical discussion. Still, although this hardly gives one confidence in the editors' critical acumen, it perhaps doesn't finally matter. Good poets eventually make their way, and *The Snow Party*, *Correspondences* and *The Cost of Seriousness* don't lack recognition as being among the best work to have come out of the 1970s.

At the back of *British Poetry Since 1970* is an anthology of poems 'to indicate where we, as editors and publishers, place our emphasis'. One can hardly object to that, but it is surely less than satisfactory that several poets whom the editors and/or contributors praise do not appear in the anthology, so that one cannot always put the rightness of that praise to the test. This is not important in the case of well-established poets. On the other hand, since the anthology is a way of raising the colours, it seems strange that there is nothing by Dick Davis or Tom Paulin, both of whom are spoken of warmly and yet whose work may not be readily known to the 'general poetry reader' for whom the editors intend their book to be of value.

It is a decent enough intention, but I doubt whether it will be realised. There is an unmistakable air of critical drudgery about the majority of the essays, especially those on R.S. Thomas, W.S. Graham, Sisson, Davie, Hughes and Larkin. They are not necessarily bad, but they certainly are not very good, and oh!, they are dull. Andrew Waterman's essay on Geoffrey Hill is so vilely written that the general reader is likely to find himself wondering whether he has not accidentally strayed into the wrong book:

> Much of Hill's poetry is religious, but if less amenable to easy explication than, say, the later R.S. Thomas's religious poetry, this is precisely because Hill gives complex spiritual experience and questioning resonant realization, where Thomas's poems spending most of their time telling us what they are on about instead of getting on with being it, fall towards the mere higher prattle of the metaphysically worried man

and:

> Or, like Eliot with Prufrock, Gerontion, Tiresias Hill masks utterance with personae discrete from the authorial identity: King Offa, or in that oblique fiction 'The Songbook of Sebastian Arrurrez' what Hill's notes tell us is an 'aprocryphal Spanish poet'.

Reading sentences such as those, you wonder whether prose should not be at least as well written as poetry.

What are we left with? In the first place, excellent essays on Thom Gunn and Charles Tomlinson by, respectively, Clive

Wilmer and Michael Kirkham. In the past decade a considerable amount has been written about both poets, but these two essays are ideal introductions: lucid, intelligent and, above all, capable of making the poems discussed seem worth discussing. There is also a note by Thom Gunn on Dick Davis's *In the Distance*, which is perfect of its kind. I do not see how anyone could read it without immediately wanting to buy Davis's volume.

Davis is a young poet. So are Craig Raine, Tom Paulin and Andrew Motion, and Blake Morrison pays particular attention to all three in his essay 'Young Poets in the 1970s'. Since Motion is the only one of these included in the anthology, the general reader will no doubt wish to check his view against Morrison's by turning to the back of the book. He may, however, feel somewhat alarmed by the terms of Morrison's praise. Motion's 'is, of course, a twilight world ... Whatever he sees or touches is dissolved before him'. It sounds a bit like Theodore Wratislaw in crêpe soles. And it is!

> The inland docks
> contain their waste of sky, and lamps
> along the Humber illustrate a map
> I cannot recognise as home tonight.
> Though will, in time. I watch you
> vanish on the last train south
> through districts no one visits.

Motion takes a good deal from Edward Thomas and Larkin—far too much in fact—but the echoes serve to remind one that, after all, both those poets are much tougher, more resilient, than he is. Reading these lines from 'Hull Paragon', with their exquisite but essentially trite cadences, their carefully planted properties (it *would* be a 'waste' of sky) and the lugubriousnes of 'vanish on the last train south', I find that there sound irresistibly in my head the words Byron growled at Tom Moore: 'Don't be so damned poetical.'

Morrison remarks of Craig Raine that there is 'in some quarters strong resistance' to his work. One of those quarters is very obviously occupied by Peter Jones and Michael Schmidt. In their introduction they make three specific charges against him. The first is that he is praised by John Bayley and John Carey: 'Against the general poetic gloom of our best writers, a game rather than a 'game' appeals to some critics. It alleviates the tedium of the severe witness of such writers as Larkin, Davie, Thomas, or the serious levity of Graham.' There are confusions here. The editors imply that Bayley and Carey prefer Raine to the other poets they mention. I am not aware that this is so, but even if it is, it is hardly Raine's fault. Moreover 'general poetic gloom' is a heavy loading of terms and suggests that a particular kind of cultural conservatism must be the truth of the matter. If Raine won't endorse apocalypse then he is clearly no good. But anyway, the chief spokesman for this gloom appears to be C.H. Sisson, who according to John Pilling has an 'unsparing awareness of cultural malaise'. Yet in his own essay Sisson attacks Larkin for helping the malaise forward. I think that one ought to object pretty strongly to his particular 'unsparing awareness', by the way, but it is hardly necessary to do so in order to see that this objection to Craig Raine's work comes out of a very muddled ideological position.

A second criticism of Raine is that his metaphoric dazzle dims our vision rather than, as Morrison claims, helping us to see: 'What we are supposed to *see* becomes more remote: when a gardener stands "tired as a teapot", do we see gardener, teapot, or some steam let off by the connection?' I grant that this is not one of Raine's most distinguished comparisons, but it surely requires no great effort to realise that he is asking us to make a connection between the way the gardener stands and the way a teapot handle and spout are shaped; and that he transfers the epithet from one to the other in order to alert us to the actuality of those shapes. To ask for more is to ask for what words cannot give. 'The lion's ferocious chrysanthemum head' cannot be as precise as a lion's head painted by Le Douanier Rousseau. But it is an odd reader who cannot experience a delighted recognition at the best of Marianne Moore's images, and an odd one who fails to see the wit and justice in the best of Raine's.

The third criticism has more substance, though it's overstated. It is that Raine, and Christopher Reid (with whom he's often linked), lack prosodic skills: 'Interest in and understanding of prosody have not characterised the 1970s.' Agreed, and agreed also that teachers of poetry usually haven't the faintest idea of how a poem should sound. Not long ago I heard a young man from Cambridge lecturing on Hardy's poetry, and his attempt to read 'I Look into My Glass' was rather like what I imagine a concrete mixer would sound like if it tried to sing madrigals. It is shaming that students at all levels can write apparently competent critical essays on poems, and yet simply can't begin to hear what the poems are about. I take it that this is what Jones and Schmidt mean when they say that 'the market for *teachable* poetry is the readiest one', meaning by 'teachable', 'the "well-made poem"', with a discussable or teasing image structure, dramatic progression and climax, paraphrasable meaning and thematic "relevance"'. The trouble is that nearly all poems can be taught in this way, including the greatest. If cultural conservatism means redirecting attention towards prosody, then I am for it. But for Jones and Schmidt it means much more than that, and here their polemic won't do.

They wish to argue that the 1970s lacked 'defining and unifying social issues with "imaginative content"', and as evidence of this they cite George Steiner's end-of-decade contention that now 'even the young have the strong intuition that every hope goes wrong':

> Why did we let ourselves be seduced by the great dreams? They were, I think, enormously creative mistakes, enormously creative fantasies. What really scares me at the moment is: how do we operate without such windows? What happens when there is the insight or the conviction or the instinct that, whatever you do, you'll get it wrong?

The implication behind all this is that, in the editors' words, 'betrayed by the forward dreams of ideology', young poets 'set out to explore that betrayal'. Hence the predominance during the decade of poetry of an elegiac tone, which speaks for a community or place, and hence also the fact that:

> the poet who goes back to the time before we went to sleep and seeks there the source of the dream can help to clarify, if not alleviate, our situation. His poem may be an imaginative analysis and a kind of exorcism. During the trip into the past, he may release old and serviceable prosodic skills, rediscover a now neglected 'nature' as Robert Wells and Dick Davis have done.

There is much more here than can be argued with in a review, but a few points need to be made. What exactly were those enormously creative mistakes, those great dreams? Steiner's journalistic generalisations don't allow of an answer, but they sound suspiciously like the 1960s hippie-style pipedreams of peace and love, which can hardly be thought of as creative at all. Such dreams aren't in any sense ideological, and although ideology implies vision, it is built out of kinds of hard thought and considered intellectual commitment that have nothing to do with Steiner's frivolity. I don't deny that ideology can be adopted as a fashionable mode, but ideas, real ideas, do not make their appearance and disappearance merely to satisfy the shaping whims of trend-spotters; and to pretend that they do is to become a trend-spotter yourself (a charge which *British Poetry Since 1970* can't altogether avoid).

It is therefore quite wrong to say that young poets during the 1970s were betrayed by the forward dreams of ideology, because betrayal requires a commitment which those poets surely never had. True, Steiner imputes it to himself: 'Why did we let ourselves be seduced by the great dreams?' But to be blunt, if you put it like that, you have no conception of what's at issue. And I think the same may well be true of those young poets whom the editors mention, for whom 'a trip into the past' is in fact precisely a fashionable ideology, and therefore a programmatically shallow one. This becomes clear if we look at Robert Wells's 'The Axehandle', which is included in the anthology:

> Calling my eyes back from the sea
> —With adoration I watched the horizon lift
> Above the headlands, far up against the sky—
> And looking instead for a human token
> Even at this distance, to hold me back,
> I noticed the axe where I had put it aside
> —How the balanced ashwood handle
> Was like a limb with its muscle shaped to use,
> An arm graceful and certain with hillside labour
> Evidencing the generations of hands.

The impulse that fuels this poem is presumably one in which the poet opposes the desire for self-annihilating ideality to a 'human token', which will 'hold me back'. Yet the uneasy tone of that phrase and of the word 'adoration' suggests a very self-conscious awareness that this almost Shelleyan desire is a mere pose, is not any sort of felt commitment. And is not, then, the description of the axe-handle as like 'An arm graceful and certain with hillside labour' a piece of programmatic 'medievalising', an expression of that ideological line that runs at least as far back as Ruskin on the nature of gothic and whose unexamined literariness and sentimentality, in Wells's case, become the more noticeable when you consider that the arm is supposed to be shaped by the 'hands' that swing it? ('What we are supposed to *see* becomes more remote.') You have only to think of Frost's 'Mowing' to realise how factitious and cliché-ridden Wells's kind of poem is. Presumably the editors fear as much, for why else should they surround the word *nature* with quotation marks?

One other essay deserves mention. In 'English and American in "Briggflatts"', Donald Davie argues persuasively for the importance of Basil Bunting's poem, and especially for Bunting's objectivist concern with 'ramming his words so hard, one on the heel of the other (object on verb on subject), that no interstices are left through which his eye on the thing to be said can be deflected towards the reader, the person he is saying it to'. But this argument is part of a strange polemic against English poets, who are accused of paying altogether too much attention to their readers. This is how Davie puts the matter:

> The sad fact is that English readers of contemporary poetry—few as they are, and perhaps just *because* they are so few—have got used to being cajoled and coaxed, at all events sedulously *attended to* by their poets. Teachers in English classrooms have for years now persuaded school-children and students to conceive of the reading of a poem as responding to nudges that the poet, on this showing debased into a rhetorician, is supposedly at every point administering to them. And accordingly English readers have taken to their bosoms a poet like the late John Berryman

This is a deeply unsatisfactory way of proceeding. What evidence has Davie that readers are used to being 'attended to' by their poets, or that teachers behave in the way he claims? Is it not odd that, always supposing they do, they are guilty of finding what is not in the poem ('*supposedly* administering to them'), since according to Davie it *is* in the poem, or at least in the work of those English poets who 'sedulously' attend to their readers? And who are these English poets? Berryman, according to Davie. But then he is American, so Davie has to claim that English readers have taken him to their bosoms, which if my experience is anything to go by is as far from the truth as it may be.

I draw attention to this tangled argument because it has to do with Davie's strongly-urged, but I think dangerous, endorsement of the objectivist's 'determination to cut the reader down to size, by making him realise that he is only as it were a bystander'. A bystander is a person present but not involved, and indeed the noun is customarily preceded by the adjective 'casual'. The casual bystander is someone who comes upon, say, a street quarrel, observes it for as long as he pleases, and then walks away. He may have understood little or nothing of what he observed, and he is free to leave whenever he chooses. I do not think that this is a helpful analogy for the reader of poetry, 'general' or otherwise.

Notes

1. *British Poetry Since 1970: A Critical Survey*, ed. Peter Jones and Michael Schmidt (Manchester: Carcanet Press 1980).

Part Four

SOME DOUBTS

14

The Birth of Eng. Lit.

One of the pieces in *Writing in Society*, Raymond Williams's latest collection of essays, reviews and lecturers, is called 'Crisis in English Studies'.[1] Originally a lecture, its starting point is William's intervention in what became known as the MacCabe affair. By an inevitable irony of history, those who had been the beleaguered innovators of English studies at Cambridge in the 1920s and 30s were now appealed to as the guardians of a tradition whose timeless centrality and rightness could be taken for granted. But traditions have their starting points and their histories; and this is what Chris Baldick's book, *TheSocial Mission of English Criticism, 1848–1932*, is about.[2] How did English studies come to exist? When? Why? Dr Baldick's carefully plotted account begins, as it must, with Matthew Arnold. It then works forward, through the promoting of English studies at Oxbridge, the work of Eliot and Richards, to the Leavises and the founding of *Scrutiny*. Much of the material is familiar, but Baldick handles it with good sense; and the ways in which English studies became institutionalised at all levels seems to me to be documented in an exemplary manner.

A point of major importance is just how closely the rise of English studies was tied, often openly, to political considerations. While some of us never doubted that this was the case, it is good to have the matter so neatly spelt out. For example, Baldick has some very interesting pages on the work of the committee which Lloyd George set up after the end of the First World War—its chairman was Sir Henry Newbolt—whose aim was to 'propose rebuilding an entire "arch" of national education round the "keystone" of English'. Such education mattered, not only because it made for better soldiers, but because it could resolve class hostilities. According to the report:

> Literature ... seems to be classed by a large number of thinking working men with antimacassars, fish knives and other unintelligible

195

and futile trivialities of 'middle-class culture' and, as a subject for instruction, is suspect as an attempt 'to sidetrack the working-class movement'. We regard the prevalence of such opinions as a serious matter, not merely because it means the alienation of an important section of the population from the 'confort' and 'mirthe' of literature, but chiefly because it points to a morbid condition in the body politic which if not taken in hand may be followed by lamentable consequences.

Professors of English literature in the modern universities therefore become 'ambassadors' or 'missionaries' sent out into 'every important capital of industrialism in the country'. They have an obligation not merely to their students but 'still more towards the teeming population outside the university walls, most of whom have not so much "heard whether there be any Holy Ghost"'. Hence the extension lecture, adult education, the introduction at home and abroad (i.e. empire) of examination syllabuses in English—in schools, colleges and universities.

If this seems messianic, we need to remember that from the beginning—that is, from Matthew Arnold—the study of literature was seen as providing a stay against political and cultural anarchy. For Arnold took the purpose of such study, or 'criticism', to be an acknowledgement of the best has been thought and written. Its function was disinterestedly to test all would-be literature at the bar of approved wisdom, to judge it by timeless or classic ideals. Criticism makes culture prevail; and culture is both a means to and an expression of harmony, poise, balance. Moreover, it can be served and brought to bear only by those who abstain from practical matters and quarrels, and who will not allow themselves or their language to be 'blackened by the smoke of the market place'. Thus spring the aliens, those recruits from all classes, who somehow belong to none, who are therefore culture's only true ambassadors; and who in due time mutate into professors of literature at provincial universities or into the 'essential Cambridge' of the Leavises' formulation.

There is, of course, an unstated problem in all this, which at times lurches into plain contradictoriness. (I leave aside the question of who decides what is wisdom.) On the one hand, culture as class-dissolvent or agent of reconciliation will save us all; on the other, for Arnold and Leavis at least, only a few may profit from it or have access to it. Mass civilisation and minority culture are implacably opposed. Arnold, with his appeal not merely to the classic spirit but to the literary heritage of Greece and Rome, accepts that culture is denied to most of his contemporaries. As for Leavis, 'it must be obvious' that only a few can benefit from the study of literature. Still, the literature he had in mind was by no means the same as Arnold's and here I think Baldick's narrative won't do.

When did the study of literature become the study of *English* literature? Baldick suggests that the change came after the First World War. Patriotic pride plus contempt for all things German meant that Teutonic scholarship, and especially philology, could be dismissed. In its place came the study of the classics of English literature. And such study could be protected from the sneer of 'soft option' because of 'practical criticism'. This brainchild of I.A. Richards was both rigorous and 'objective'; and it had the additional advantage of offering itself as yet another saviour of mankind. In Baldick's words, 'for Richards, literary critics, and possibly a further small layer of discerning readers, are the most valuable people in society'. If students cannot respond adequately to poems, Richards asks, 'How far can we expect such readers to show themselves intelligent, imaginative and discriminating in their intimate relations with other human beings?' The implied answer is, not at all.

What Baldick has to say here is true as far as it goes, but it doesn't go far enough. In particular, it doesn't go far enough back. The invention of 'English literature' happened well before the First World War. It is surely inseparable from that whole extraordinary enterprise of discovering and affirming 'Englishness' which is so marked a feature of the period 1880–1914? The *Mermaid* and *English Men of Letters* and many other series may be linked, no matter how loosely, with journals such as *Merry England*, (for the first number of which in 1881 George Saintsbury wrote an essay on 'Young England'), with the Anglo-Saxonry of the 1890s, with Alfred Austin's vision of a nation 'jocund' with lords and contented peasantry, with Kipling's Hobden the Hedger, Cecil Sharp's pursuit of folksong, with Margaret Schlegel's looking out from Howards End and attempting to 'realise England'; and much, much more besides. I would say that it is only when you realise how all-pervading this preoccupation with realising England is that you can understand why Leavis should place his faith in the organic community, of which he makes so much in *For Continuity*.

I disagree sharply with Baldick when he says that the war created a sense of patriotic pride. The truth is rather that as it went on it made such pride increasingly difficult to hold by. More important, the war seemed to create an almost unbridgeable gulf between past and present. The only way to restore or safeguard continuity was by throwing a ladder across to the presumed Englishness of English literature which had been discovered and made into an orthodoxy in the pre-war period: 'The memory of the old order, the old ways of life, must be the chief hint for, the directing incitement towards, a new, if ever there is to be a new. It is the memory of a human normality of naturalness'.

It is in the light of terms such as these—they come from *For Continuity*—that we can understand why Leavis should be so conservative when it comes to establishing his canon of English literature. In a curiously evasive passage Baldick remarks that:

> The First World War has long been recognised as marking a distinct turning-point not only in world history but also in English literature, giving rise to the literary renaissance headed by Joyce, Eliot, and Lawrence. What is less often observed is the fact that the discipline which has arrived at this assessment—English literary criticism—owes its own renaissance largely to the same catastrophe.

But surely the most persuasive version of English literary criticism is Leavis's, and of the three names Baldick cites as key figures in the literary renaissance, Leavis allows only Lawrence unambiguously to pass. The reason is plain enough. Eliot and Joyce are not English, and neither is rooted in place. By contrast, 'Lawrence always lived on the spot where he was. That was his genius.' Leavis spells the matter out beyond any doubt in words that Baldick quotes: 'it was in the past that [Lawrence] was rooted. Indeed, in our time, when the gap in continuity is almost complete, he may be said to represent, concretely in his living person, the essential human tradition'. For Leavis, the great tradition must be a narrow one, because, so his largely mythic reading of history insists, not many writers can be identified in terms of the organic community, and not all of those are alive to their responsibility to speak out for 'human naturalness'.

There is a further point. Baldick is very good at noting the underlying politics of the rise of English studies. What he doesn't do—perhaps he felt it to be beyond his brief—is examine how this had inevitable consequences for the establishing of the canon and the way in which it was taught. As we would expect, these are matters which Raymond Williams takes up. In 'Cambridge English, Past and Present', he notes drily that students were supposed to know '"the poets of our own land", but then not Taliesin or Dafydd ap Gwilym. "Of our own people" but then not the author of *Beowulf*.' Elsewhere syllabuses may vary, the canon may shrink or expand a little; but the major point is that whether you rely on 'close reading' or choose to 'survey the field', start with Chaucer or Shakespeare and end with Tennyson or Brian Patten, English studies are a means of sustaining or betraying ideological positions. This is not to be avoided. The problem has been to get it acknowledged. Baldick quotes an interesting piece by H.G. Robinson, in which Robinson remarks:

> If anything will take the coarseness and vulgarity out of a soul, it must be refined images and elevated sentiments. As a clown will instinctively tread lightly and feel ashamed in a lady's boudoir, so a vulgar mind may, by converse with minds of high culture, be brought to see and deplore the contrast between itself and them, and to make an earnest effort to put off its vulgarity.

That was written in 1860. Over a hundred years later, Robinson's untroubled sense that he knew what high culture was remains alive and well. 'The test of a gentleman', a senior Shakespearian editor once said to me, 'is his ability to enjoy Scott.' It took a long time to get Blake, Dickens and Lawrence into the canon. Clare is still not there. One of the major complaints I have against literary critics of the left is that they simply haven't done enough to revise or to capture the canon, and I think that a reason for this may be their fear of what Tom Paulin has called 'a formal joy'. The formal delights of literature are what the left is inevitably liable to run scared of; the result can be to persuade you that you ought to prefer punk to Pope. Raymond Williams has been and continues to be a great intellectual force, and as the essay 'Notes on English Prose' shows, he can also be a perceptive critic. But not of poetry. It is unfortunately the case that with very few exceptions the best Marxist critics are always much happier dealing with prose than with poetry. Perhaps this is because of the embarrassing matter of form, perhaps because poetry is thought to be too readily identified with 'refined images and elevated sentiments'. But studying the semiology of bus tickets is no substitute for studying Milton's handling of caesura. We ought not to leave the enemy so much.

Notes

1. Raymond Williams, *Writing in Society* (London, 1983).
2. Chris Baldick, *The Social Mission of English Criticism 1848–1932* (Oxford: Oxford University Press 1983).

15
A Fit of Criticism Against Criticism

> It must be borne in mind that there are many men who, without being productive, yet want to say something significant; and thus the most curious things are brought to life.
>
> Goethe

Is there a crisis in English studies? If so, what is it? I begin with these questions because anyone who has kept half an eye on recent publications in the field of literary criticism and theory will know that it has become more or less accepted that a crisis exists and that it is the task of each new book to combat it. This may of course be a classic case of anxiety-making. Identify something as being in bad shape and that gives you a certain magical power to propose remedies. The history of medicine is full of anxiety-makers, and perhaps they are now taking over in English studies. As a matter of fact, I think that this is what has happened, for so many people have been talking about the crisis that they have inevitably helped bring it into existence. 'A state of crisis' is now a powerful allergy, resistant to much soothing medication. Something stronger is therefore called for, and in what follows I hope to go down to the root of the matter, simply because the most effective way of getting rid of the effect is by attacking the cause.

But what is the cause? One way of beginning to answer that question is to look at a debate that was for some time featured in the pages of the *London Review of Books*. It was provoked by the poet Tom Paulin's ferocious review—some would say character assassination—of a collection of essays called *Re-Reading English*.[1] The contributors to the book use a variety of approaches, but they have in common a belief that a crisis in English studies undoubtedly exists. In Paulin's view they also have in common a crass philistinism, an ignorance of literary matters and a readiness, even an eagerness, to destroy what is of most value in the professed subject—that is, literature itself. One might characterise his position as that of an embattled elitist, defending a canon of literary works against barbarians who, like James's Millicent Henning, embody an 'impulse of destruction'. One might characterise his opponents as democratically inspired teachers, determined to unmask the false assumptions of those who claim 'naturally' to know what is of most value in literary studies. The contributors to *Re-Reading English* differ on some matters, and this means that the book as a whole has more variety than Paulin will grant it, but they do undoubtedly share a desire to demystify literature. They all see it in terms of production, as labour and as a marketable commodity; and they also see it and those who comment on it as exposing and/or betraying ideological positions. Literature does not descend like manna to the hungry earth; it is manufactured in time and place. The student of literature ought therefore to be encouraged to dismantle many of the pretensions surrounding the material production of literature. It is not a special category: literature (art) and non-literature are equally cultural artefacts, and the crisis has arisen because at last some reader/writers have drawn attention to this fact; they have whisked away the clouds of protective colouring that have hitherto shrouded 'literature' and given literature a falsely important claim on our attention. From now on students must be encouraged to focus their attention on the circumstances of production, and to use a variety of tools, including such spanners and monkey-wrenches as structuralism and deconstruction, in order to dismantle individual works of *any* kind. Only then will the student justly know him/herself to be in control of cultural formations rather than suffer as their victim, forced to accept whatever teacher recommends.

The tone of these remarks no doubt indicates my disquiet over the enterprise that the Re-Readers propose for themselves and others. And there is certainly a brash, incautious optimism about their wishes. Yet to be fair to them I have to add that much of what they say is no more than common sense and that it needs to be said. Works of art can and often do betray ideological positions and should not be taken as unquestionable achievements. In my own way I have tried to open up nineteenth-century fiction to critical examination and to show that those who uncritically endorse particular texts do so because those texts fit snugly with a particular cultural/political view that (surprise, surprise) happens to be shared by their admirers. There is no doubt that those admirers have on occasions commanded the heights of institutionalised centres for literary studies—schools, colleges, universities, literary journals and, very importantly, examination boards. I am all for storming the heights and taking over command. *But*. What are you going to do when you have seized control? The Re-Readers seem to feel that once they and their views prevail, the crisis will be at an end. I think it will be beginning.

For when they speak of literature, they are plainly a long way from Goethe's remark that 'in reality we learn only from those books we cannot criticise'. More importantly, the Re-Readers are a long way from a powerful tradition of socialist thinking about the nature of art. And it is here that I offer my contribution to the debate, here that I want to begin my attack on some root causes of the crisis. To do so I must first make plain my own position. I am a socialist who finds himself more in sympathy with Paulin than with the contributors to *Re-Reading English*. I am with them when they denounce those unquestioning snobs who somehow take it for granted that they know what art is. But I am bitterly opposed to them when they say that 'art' is no more than a collection of products which certain people in positions of vested interest collude in identifying as 'works of intrinsic value', and for which they claim inherent qualities. The truth, say the Re-Readers, is otherwise. Those 'inherent qualities' are merely a way of mystifying the products in question. It is all a trick to persuade the helpless, passive reader to agree to find in a work what is not actually there. 'Quality' is an expression of ideology.

In his great essay 'An Experiment in Democratic Education', R.H. Tawney wrote:

> If persons whose work is different require, as they do, different kinds of professional instruction, that is no reason why one should be excluded from the common heritage of civilisation of which the other is made free by a university education, and from which ... both, irrespective of their occupations, are equally capable, as human beings, of receiving spiritual sustenance.

Tawney was an impeccable socialist. (He also, by the way, wrote a beautifully lucid and forceful prose, which I am afraid cannot be said

for many of the Re-Readers.) I am on Tawney's side. It is the
common heritage of civilisation that matters, and we ought to be
making certain that everyone has access to it rather than arguing
that it never amounted to much in the first place. If the Devil has all
the best tunes, then take those tunes away from the Devil, instead
of saying that they are of no great worth or that we can have as
much fun with our own tunes, never mind how bad they are.
Shakespeare is a great writer, not because some more or less
snobbish people pay a great deal of money to see the Royal
Shakespeare Company stage productions of his plays which in
their lavish emptiness endorse audience values, but because his
plays speak to us all.

But at this point a problem arises. When I say 'us all' am I not
insisting that my experience is representative, and that I am
therefore in a position to speak for 'us', irrespective of class, gender
and race? Yes and no. Art does speak to us all, but we may hear
different things. It is one of the functions of criticism to cleanse the
doors of perception, to correct faulty hearing as well as faulty sight;
and it is also a function of criticism to put all generalisations to the
test. *Of course* it is true that critics/readers claim to speak for all
people and that sometimes the claim is merely coercive. 'We find in
the following work . . .' doesn't guarantee it's there. And what 'we'
are asked to approve of may well be patterns of behaviour, belief
etc. that happen to be those of the critic. *Of course* it is true that as
Eng. Lit. became institutionalised, taught in schools, colleges and
universities, so it inevitably became a way of endorsing particular
ideologies (usually those of the cultural and political
establishment). But there need be no great critical huffing and
puffing about this perfectly obvious fact. Or rather, since it is or
ought to be obvious, the wise critic will want to guard against
readings of literary texts that invite agreement with ideological
positions that those texts don't support, or which they do support
but in insupportable ways.

I take it for granted that a socialist critic will wish to expose
readings of Shakespeare which dodge the difficult questions or
remain utterly incurious about areas of a play which would
challenge their particularly class-based, thin and dehumanised
account. For example, in a recent Stratford production of *The
Winter's Tale* the clown and shepherd were made into comic
buffoons. The company, director and actors, all knew the audience

would find that not merely funny but *right*, or at least thought they ought to do so. If you have paid ten pounds for your seat, it does give you a certain point of view about these things. But if entrance were free, or much cheaper, and if coachloads of the Union of Agricultural Workers had shown up at Stratford, I am fairly sure that the actors would have been in for a hard time. Rightly, too. For Shakespeare's text makes it clear that the shepherd and clown are *not* buffoons, and that those who treat them dismissively are themselves shown up as brutal.

In his account of *Henry IV Part 2* E.M.W. Tillyard comes to the remarkably unpleasant scene where Hal taunts Francis the Drawer. Francis has behaved extremely well to Hal, and in a few lines Shakespeare establishes the Drawer as a good man. Hal behaves in an excusably nasty way to him, or so one surely thinks. Tillyard, however, will have none of this. We are not to think badly of Hal:

> The Prince wanted to see just how little brain Francis had and put him to the test, and ... in matters of humanity we must not judge Shakespeare by standards of twentieth-century humanitarianism. In an age when men watched the antics of the mad and the suffering of animals for sport we must not look for too much.

As a piece of criticism this is beneath contempt. How on earth can Hal be defended on the grounds that it's all right for him to be nasty to Francis because we are in no danger of sympathising with the Drawer? The point about the scene is precisely that it confuses, troubles and embarrasses its audience's allegiances; it leaves them asking awkward questions about the nature of power and those who use, or abuse, it. And what are we to make of Tillyard's appeal to 'the age'? Can he seriously expect us to believe that a century that produced Stalin and Hitler is somehow better or more humane than Elizabethan England?

But then it turns out that Tillyard not only wants to persuade us that Elizabethan England was a nasty place, he also hopes to make us believe Shakespeare simply accepted that fact, and 'reflected' it in his work. In other words, we are asked to regard the greatest writer in the language as no better than the merest brute of his or any age. The insulting stupidity of this could hardly be improved on, or so one would like to think. Yet the fact is that Tillyard's clumsy ignorance of the meaning and power of great art is echoed

by one after another contributor to *Re-Reading English*. Derek
Longhurst for example says:

> Of course [the culture of Elizabethan England] did not develop in a
> vacuum, and contemporary concepts of order, authority, kingship,
> culture, women, marriage and the family, justice and law, usury,
> religious beliefs, reason, etc., need careful *historical* attention. The
> tendency has been to isolate such concepts as abstractions, but it is
> vital to locate them in the social, political and economic processes of
> the period ... This should not be viewed as merely background to
> 'literary interpretation' but as a primary objective, the material
> context in which the texts were produced.

And when you have done all this, examined all those
concepts—including perhaps bear-baiting—are you still not left
with the question of how well or badly individual authors or texts
work inside such a material context? I do not think that Longhurst
is so very different from Tillyard. Both are essentially reductive.
Shakespeare must be lopped and squeezed until he can be forced
into 'the processes of the period'. It does not seem to occur to
either of them that a writer is great to the extent that he cannot be
neatly fitted into the material context, or to the extent that he
challenges, alters or bursts the framework. We know what that
convenient abstraction 'the Elizabethan mind' thought about
kingship. How does that help us with Shakespeare's presentation of
Hal? Tillyard creates an identikit concept of 'kingship' with which
Shakespeare's character can be perfectly matched. Longhurst
probably thinks Tillyard hopelessly reactionary. Yet his own
approach is equally reactionary, equally devoted to explaining
scenes away rather than responding to their particular power.

As it happens, a slightly subtler approach to questions of context
would produce rather different results. Suppose, for example, you
were to ask what the Francises in an audience of the 1590s would
have made of Hal. Suppose, in other words, you chose not to
emphasise a determining context but a variable one. Would you
not then arrive at the possibility that Shakespeare knew exactly
what he was up to and that he wanted to startle, discompose and
unsettle his audience? And would that not depend on his power, his
greatness *as an artist*, to bring troublingly before an audience issues
that cannot be explained (away?) in terms of material context?

Tillyard of course would not want to accept or even think about that. He dimly senses the scene is unpleasant and so *has* to explain it away. How dare he. And how dare Longhurst echo him.

Shakespeare, I repeat, is for us all. Which is not to say that he is beyond criticism. But it is to say that when Tawney spoke of 'the common heritage of civilisation' he thought of that heritage as comprised of works of real worth, which are great insofar as they resist absorption into the 'material context' which is supposed to explain everything. In this he is part of a great socialist tradition that stretches back from Morris to Shelley. It is a tradition with which I eagerly align myself, and yet which most of my fellow socialists seem equally eager to disavow. By implication, if not by explicit utterance, they are opposed to the very possibility of great art, wish to beat it down and deny the heritage. I want that heritage for us all. I do not accept that it is the inherited glory of the rich, and I think I know what Wordsworth had in mind when he spoke of 'joy in widest commonalty spread'. (Whereas I strongly suspect that the Re-Readers and their allies would be merely embarrassed by his words.)

It may be objected against this that I am merely trying to stand an outworn creed on its legs. The mystique of the great artist ought to be seen as precisely that—a mystique. I do not deny that this can be the case. There will always be pretenders, frauds and emperors with no clothes. But this is not to say that there are no artists of true worth. A few years ago a young history graduate from Sussex was researching the archives of various Chartist groups, and to his puzzlement discovered that among such groups it was common practice to hang on the walls of their meeting places protraits of English poets. What could the Chartists possibly want with such images? The answer is simple and important: those men were unashamedly declaring their allegiance to, their delight in, great art. When John Clare first read Thomson's *The Seasons* he said that it made his heart 'twitter with joy'. I have a deep suspicion that many contemporary literary theorists, particularly those on the left, would not know what he was talking about or would insist that he was deluding himself. How could a semi-literate Northampton-shire peasant take delight in the work of someone who wrote out of an entirely different material context, and whose sub-Miltonics plainly valorised those dominant norms that proposed for themselves the ideological constituents of a ruling cultural hegemony. (You think I unfairly parody this sort of writing? Try reading some of it.) And suppose Clare were to be believed? What he experienced would be of small importance because such joy would be a merely aesthetic delight, a trivial flutter of the pulse.

But Clare was *not* deluding himself, and his experience was of the utmost importance, even though, or perhaps because, it cannot be quantified. For one thing it helped make Clare a poet, and I imagine that not even the most determined of Re-Readers would think that of small importance. For another, it testifies to the enduring power of art to give delight to a 'a few natural hearts'. The phrase is Wordsworth's, and he was being deliberately provocative. In so artificial an age as the end of the eighteenth century, he hints, there are not many of us left. My fear is that at the end of the twentieth century there are fewer still, and one reason is that the Re-Readers and their allies are busy with the task of exposing art's mystificatory basis.

But of course, I will be told, you speak like this because you choose to deny the material context out of which 'art' is produced; you ignore the fact that a work is, and can never be other than, an expression or betrayal of the ideology of the person whose labour it is. What then will my opponents make of the following?

A poem is the very image of life expressed in its eternal truth ... Poetry is ever accompanied with pleasure; all spirits upon which it falls open themselves to receive the wisdom which is mingled with its delight ... [Poetry] lifts the veil from the hidden beauty of the world and makes familiar objects be as if they were not familiar ... The great secret of morals is love, or a going out of our own nature and an identification of ourselves with the beautiful which exists in thought, action, or person, not our own. A man, to be greatly good, must imagine intensely and comprehensively; he must put himself in the place of another and of many others; the pains and pleasures of his species must become his own. The great instrument of moral good is the imagination; and poetry administers to the effect by acting upon the cause. Poetry enlarges the circumference of the imagination by replenishing it with thoughts of ever new delight, which have the power of attracting and assimilating to their own nature all other thoughts and which form new intervals and interstices whose void forever craves fresh food. Poetry strengthens that faculty which is the organ of the moral nature of man in the same manner as exercise strengthens a limb.

I have little doubt that some of my opponents will dismiss these words as idealistic clap-trap. But for others, who recognise that they come from Shelley's *A Defence of Poetry*, I hope that they will cause some uneasy reflections. Like Tawney, Shelley's credentials as a socialist are impeccable, and those of us who are socialists—and most who are not—might surely wish to accept the possibility that Shelley is here stating important truths. When he says that those spirits upon whom poetry falls 'open themselves to receive the wisdom that is mingled with delight', he is surely saying something that is true. If so, is that not something that we would wish for all? And, returning to the scene in *Henry IV* that causes Tillyard so much embarrassment, does not its power lie in Shakespeare's ability to imagine 'intensely and comprehensively' lives which 'we'—that is, those in a certain class, occupying a particular social position—would wish to ignore or fix in a manner that will cause 'us all' no discomfort? And finally, but most importantly, is there not in Shelley's account a blessed simplicity which will explain why great art is great? Think of those many tortured and tortuous 'explanations', mostly from a Marxist slant, which over the last fifty or so years have tried to make sense of the power and authority of great art, or which have tried to deny its power and authority (presumably in the uneasy awareness that it does, after all, seem to possess such qualities); and think by way of illuminating analogy of those constantly more involved and intellectually ravelled attempts to defend untenable theories about the origins of the world, the causes of various diseases, the chemical composition of air or water, the winter ways of sand-martins ... whatever. Why *should* one be asked to pay respectful attention to theories about the nature of art-as-production which have constantly to be updated, revised or abandoned, according to how empiricist Marxisms yield to idealist Marxisms, or depending on whether Lukacs or Althusser, Benjamin or Macherey is currently in favour. What Shelley says is quite sufficient to account for the nature of great art. It certainly makes much better sense than talk about the defining or determining nature of material contexts.

But here another problem swims into focus. Suppose my opponents agree that Shakespeare is uniquely able to rise above the constraints of his ideological determinants, his material context: it does not follow that this can be so for other, later and therefore more hindered writers. For as society develops so, it may be argued, class-formations and ideological determinants become increasingly complex and thus increasingly dominant. Such an argument seems to be lurking below the surface of the contributions to *Re-Reading English*. If this is so, they imply, it is all very well for Shelley to claim that an artist 'must put himself in the place of another and of many others', all very well for Auden to suggest that the novelist should suffer 'all the wrongs of man', or for Camus to argue that the artist's true vocation 'is to open the prisons and to give a voice to the sorrows and joys of all. This is where art justifies itself against its enemies, by proving that it is no man's enemy': it is all very well for these writers to say such things, but in truth it is impossible to believe that their words amount to any more than the old idealist wish for the artist to rise above his material circumstances. The artist cannot do this, he cannot hope to escape the conditions of production of his work, including its ideological determinants. To say of such-and-such a work that it is 'great' is therefore to conspire with a cultural 'world' in which producer and consumer share an ideological framework that allows them to mystify work-as-production in terms of work-as/of-art, of genius, of universal application. The works which it is agreed shall be thought of supreme value are chosen by people in a culturally dominant position, and they force the 'fact' of this value on others who, in their turn, are required to accept such valuation even while doubting it, and who as a result are alienated from the whole idea of culture.

As it happens I have almost complete sympathy with the latter part of this argument; indeed, in essays on 'Elizabeth Gaskell and Brotherhood' and on 'The Idea of the Provincial' I have tried to show how matters of taste inevitably become expressions of class assumptions and how as such they run contrary to any serious investigation of artistic worth.[2] But once again the point is that there *is* such a thing as artistic worth, even if it is by poverty or many other forces depressed. Who are the great writers of the past two hundred or so years? I would say that it makes perfectly good sense to ask that question; and in the very act of answering it you are made to realise that they are great precisely because they cannot be appropriated by a certain class, or that this can be accomplished only at the expense of denying what is truly important about their work. It does not surprise me that Blake, Dickens and Lawrence, for example, have all had a hard time of it as far as the Academies are concerned, because in their very different ways each represents a threat to cultural orthodoxy. As a result they have either to be tamed to fit that orthodoxy or the orthodoxy itself has to be modified by the challenge they represent. How far these and other great writers have in fact been absorbed in a difficult matter to settle, and I cannot begin to cope with it here. But it seems to me undeniable that what makes them great is the fact that they can never be fully subdued to or explained in terms of material context, and that because of this they must be seen as part of the common heritage.

This brings me back to Tawney. It also leads me to remark that the Re-Readers will deny that any such heritage exists, except as a cultural convenience. For them the canon is merely what is agreed on by the ruling hegemony and in ways that do not disturb. Again, I accept that this frequently happens. An examination candidate writing about *Mansfield Park* will probably be wise not to speculate on the source of Sir Thomas Bertram's money. Sir Thomas Bertram is the wayward but improvable embodiment of civilised values, or so we are to believe. The fact that those values depend on the finance of his estates in Antigua is not something we are supposed to enquire into, especially since Antigua was known at the end of the eighteenth century as the most brutal of all the slave islands. And if John Clare had found himself in an examination hall having to write about *The Seasons* he would probably have been well advised to deny his own love of the poem in favour of some sober-sided and essentially meaningless waffle about sub-Miltonics, the traditions of epic and Georgic in the eighteenth century; and so on. Which is not to say that I want anyone to be ignorant of the tradition out of which Thomson's fine poem comes and to which it contributes. Far from it. I want more knowledge, not less. But I also want anyone who encounters literature to be able to do so honestly and not have to fudge matters in order to please some *soi-disant* 'official' view.

And let it not be thought that such views do not exist. They are powerfully present, even if those holding them would deny it. The silent conspiracy is a powerful force in English cultural life. But that should not lead to the conclusion that there is no such thing as art, or that no one piece of art is better than any other. In his ill-written and, yes, philistine contribution to *Re-Reading English*, Antony Easthope claims that for Leavis 'the poet exists *prior* to both experience and language, since if he can take an interest in both, he obviously transcends them, is not made in and of them'. Easthope argues that this is clearly wrong because the poet is in fact determined by both experience and language and that the reader ought to be encouraged to see this and acknowledge its consequences (which essentially means cutting the poet down to size).

I hardly know where to begin with such nonsense. But one point at least must be made: language and experience are not monolithic. We choose, and the quality of our choice is all-important. Choice is a form of imagining. It is precisely by the quality of their choice that we recognise the great artists. They renew language, create answerable styles, give words to experiences. There are conditioning factors—of course there are. In the Preface to his *Revolt of Islam* Shelley was quick to acknowledge that the writers of an age must have certain things in common:

> In this view of things, Ford can no more be called the imitator of Shakespeare than Shakespeare the imitator of Ford. There were perhaps few other points of resemblance between these two men than that which the universal and inevitable influence of their age produced. And this is an influence which neither the meanest scribbler nor the sublimest genius of an era can escape; and which I have not attempted to escape.

But although there are resemblances between Shakespeare and Ford, Shelley has no difficulty in telling them apart, nor in recognising that how they choose to work produces very different kinds of art. 'Choice' is, I accept, a crude way of putting what is a very complicated matter, but it at least rescues the creative act from that belief in helpless inspiration which is only the other side of the coin from the notion of overdetermination favoured by Althusserian Marxism: in both, to adapt a brilliant remark of E.P. Thompson, you do not play the game, the game plays you.

It is a distinction which would be lost on Easthope. According to him: 'literary criticism usurps the name of criticism. Far from being critical, it is unconscious, complicit, passive. Approaching poetry as "presence", it supposes the poem as somehow always already *there*, a product beyond question rather than a production that could have been other'. But this is absurd. For one thing choice—making something that could have been other—is, as I have argued, at the heart of the creative endeavour. For another, there is no such thing as literary criticism, there are literary critics, good and bad. The best are those who maintain a wary, keenly responsive but *critical* attitude to a poem, (not 'poetry'—another of Easthope's meaningless abstractions) and who do indeed see that it could have been other. I would dearly like to think that such critics are the common readers, and it seems to me that all of us who teach literature should wish to aid our students to become such readers. That is not inconsistent with accepting that we may be less intelligent or perceptive than them; and it is certainly not inconsistent with acknowledging that great writers are undoubtedly more intelligent than we are and that we ought to be humble in their presence. 'It took me years', Douglas Brown once remarked to me, 'before I understood that I was far less intelligent than Wordsworth'. I would hope that those words, coming from a man so wise, might have a sobering effect on the Re-Readers, but I doubt that they will. According to Easthope, in the world of literary criticism 'the reader is posed merely as passive consumer, invited into empathy and identification with the Poet'. Nonsense again. To know that a writer is greater than you is not to become a passive consumer. On the contrary, you have to be unusually *active* in order to cope with what he/she offers. But the point is that the experience you gain makes the activity worthwhile. That is why great art has so powerful a claim on our full attention. Great art—any genuine work of art—opens up before us and opens us up before it. That is what Shelley had in mind when he said that art enlarged 'the circumference of the imagination by replenishing it with thoughts of ever new delight'.

I do not suppose that Easthope would understand Shelley's words. And what can he hope to make of Keats's explosion of delight at his discovery of Chapman's Homer? Were there no important questions to be asked of that work? What evidence is there that Keats paid careful *historical* attention to the material context in which it was produced? Poor, passive Keats, luring himself into empathy with the poet. Had he been a student of Easthope's he would have known that 'literary science will discuss the poem as construction, acknowledging it as labour; and in so doing it will pose the reader as active and productive in reading the poem'. Science, of course, does not discuss anything, scientists do.

It is typical of Easthope that at the very moment when he wants to 'pose the reader as active' he gets rid of that reader in favour of an abstraction. Could anything be more horrifyingly mechanistic, more vilely reductive? This *will* be done, that will *not* be done. If Easthope's declamation does not make the reader passive, I do not know what does.

Re-Reading English is long on exhortation on how the reader will be made to read texts. It is very short on sensible application. (Kate Belsey's essay is a particularly honourable exception.) I suspect that this is mostly because the contributors are so busy advising on and arguing about theory that few of them read much of the raw material. 'Students should study criticism and interrogate critical approaches', Derek Longhurst says. Well, yes, but might they not be better employed studying literature? 'Criticism does exist, doesn't it', Randall Jarrell despairingly asked, 'for the sake of the poems, novels and plays it criticises?'

I am afraid not. The Re-Readers want students to spend more and more time reading them and less and less on literature itself. (But then, if literature is labour and has to be acknowledged as construction, it will not sound particularly appetising.) They are by no means alone. For it is the growing trend in American academic criticism to want the same. Geoffrey Hartman, for example, says that 'we have entered an era that can challenge even the priority of literary to literary-critical texts. Longinus is studied as seriously as the sublime texts he comments on; Jacques Derrida on Rousseau almost as interestingly as Rousseau'.[3] Who are 'we'? The answer would appear to be: a number of well-paid academics who no doubt suffer from a guilty feeling that they should be doing more to justify the money they get, but that ... well, teaching is not half so much fun as making yourself sound important by securing large sums of money from a Foundation in order to write a book that justifies your disinclination to teach. All the student has to do is to read what his superiors have written. Superiority is the key word. The vanity of academics is of course nothing new, but the current version is breath-taking in its insolence. Homer was poor; we scholars live at ease. Make me as many Homers as you please. There are editors who make it appear that they are a better author than the writer whose work they edit. Oxford dons are particularly adept at implying that if only they had less taste, were less fastidiously aware of themselves as persons of quality, then they too could descend to the writing of literature. In his useful study, '*Deconstruction*'; *Theory and Practice*, Christopher Norris says that Hartman wants critics to 'come out', and that in making up their minds to do this they should take courage from 'Derrida's deconstructive merging of origin and supplement, or text and commentary. Criticism is now "crossing over" into literature, rejecting its subservient, Arnoldian stance and taking on the freedom of interpretive style with a reckless gusto'.[4] And so Hartmen urges critics to throw off their 'inferiority complex vis-a-vis art'. Criticism is to be the equal of, even superior to any poem, play or novel the critic may alight on.

As far as I can tell, the appeal to the 'superiority' of the critic is in the name of criticism's ludic powers. So, at least, the deconstructivists seem to argue. The Re-Readers would probably baulk at that, yet since they rely so heavily on structuralist, deconstructivist and post-modern approaches, it is difficult to see how they could distance themselves from Derrida or Hartman. And anyway, they would not think it mattered. Criticism is the name of the game: more criticism about more criticism about more criticism.

In his great *Nobel Lecture* of 1980 Czeslaw Milosz points to the hidden link between much contemporary literary theory 'and the growth of the totalitarian state'.[5] For the state can tolerate works which are 'conceived as autonomous systems of reference, enclosed within their own boundaries. Only if we assume that a poet constantly strives to liberate himself from borrowed styles in search of reality is he dangerous. In a room where people unanimously maintain a conspiracy of silence one word of truth sounds like a pistol shot'. The problem is that if you believe literary works to be wholly determined by a material context it follows that not one of them is capable of intervening in the historical moment at which the writer thought it or they were conceived. And 'thought' itself is of course a delusion: according to the new Marxism, nobody can conceive a work of art, it is somehow 'conceived'—how we are not told—by determining factors over which the writer has no control. If he imagines otherwise, it is merely because he clings to that discredited notion of 'choice' which literary science has shown to be a delusion. Easthope wants it both ways, of course. On the one hand a poem could have been other than it is; but against that, the poet is a deluded fool if he thinks he is free to choose. Milosz does not like the silence, and he is right to fear it. Yet what I find truly appalling about the present state of affairs is less the silence of the poet than the noise of the critic (which, to be fair, Milusz also fears). For the noise says above all: 'Art does not matter, or it matters no more than criticism.'

All this will no doubt make it seem that I am utterly opposed to critical theory. I am not. It depends on the theory and on the critic. I accept that we need to create the taste by which true writers are to be enjoyed. *That is what literary critical theory is for.* But when Hartman thinks that his critical writing about Wordsworth is as interesting as Wordsworth, the time has come to call a halt. When Easthope, Longhurst *et al.* think that students should pay more attention to them and by implication less to creative artists, and when they argue that we should not even pretend to enjoy the work of major writers, should not think it uniquely valuable, then the time has come to shout No, in thunder.

It is easy to become depressed by the braying stupidities of those many talentless, vain people who uphold each others' egos at the expense of art. Their books sell in thousands, the work of poets I care about sells in hundreds. But then a saner thought asserts itself. For all their insistence that students read *them*, interrogate *their* procedures—and given their powerful positions in educational establishments they are bound to meet with a good deal of success—the fact remains that, as one great critic wisely and modestly remarked, 'by the common sense of readers uncorrupted with literary prejudices, after all the refinements of subtility and the dogmatism of learning, must finally be decided all claim to poetical honours'. And I reflect that, cough in ink as they may, these critics cannot become a substitute for that common heritage which each generation discovers for itself, to which the best of it adds, and from which it gains wisdom mingled with delight.

Notes

1. Peter Widdowson (ed.), *Re-Reading English* (London: Methuen 1982).
2. Essays of mine that may be relevant can be found in *Tradition and Tolerance in Nineteenth-Century Fiction* (London: Routledge and

Kegan Paul 1966) and *Romantic to Modern Literature* (Brighton: Harvester Press 1982).
3. Geoffrey Hartman, *Deconstruction and Criticism* (London: Routledge and Kegan Paul 1979). Hartman's *The Fate of Reading and Other Essays*, Harold Bloom's *A Map of Misreading*, and Stanley Fish's *Is There a Reader in this Text?* are among the more often cited works of the new criticism. For Derrida see *Writing and Difference* (London: Routledge and Kegan Paul 1977).
4. Christopher Norris's *Deconstruction: Theory and Practice* (London: Methuen 1982), is also in paperback.
5. Czeslaw Milosz, *Nobel Lecture* (London: Faber 1982).